AMERICAN PLAYGROUNDS

SUSAN G. SOLOMON

AMERICAN
PLAYGROUNDS

Revitalizing

Community

Space

UNIVERSITY PRESS OF NEW ENGLAND
Hanover and London

Published by University Press of New England,
One Court Street, Lebanon, NH 03766
www.upne.com
© 2005 by Susan G. Solomon
Printed in the United States of America
5 4 3 2 1

Library of Congress Cataloging-in-Publication Data
Solomon, Susan G.
American playgrounds : revitalizing community space /
Susan Solomon.
    p. cm.
Includes bibliographical references and index.
ISBN-13: 978-1-58465-517-6 (cloth : alk. paper)
ISBN-10: 1-58465-517-8 (cloth : alk. paper)
1. Playgrounds–United States—Planning.
2. Playgrounds—United States–History.   I. Title.
GV425.S65   2005
796'.06'873—dc22   2005011895

If childhood is a journey,

let us see to it that the child

does not travel by night.

—Aldo van Eyck

CONTENTS

Foreword by Martha Throne, ix

Acknowledgments, xi

Introduction, 1

PART I THE PAST

Chapter 1   History: Pre-1960, 7

Chapter 2   History: 1960–1995, 43

PART II THE PRESENT

Chapter 3   Patrons, 95

Chapter 4   Strategies, 126

Chapter 5   Variants, 159

Chapter 6   Remedies, 182

Notes, 213

Selected Bibliography, 243

Index, 247

Just as museums were the commissions of choice for architects at the end of the twentieth century, the coveted assignment of the future could well be the urban playground. In the 1990s, museum projects were noteworthy for a variety of reasons. Museum design offered a rare combination of art and architecture. Enlightened clients, working closely with design professionals, guided the development of new city landmarks and homes worthy of their vast collections of painting and sculpture. The resulting creations were widely publicized in the press, bringing architecture and design into the living rooms of families around the world.

Why shouldn't playground design benefit from the same attention in the twenty-first century? No other type of commission has so much potential or so much at stake. Playgrounds have a special place in our urban fabric, acting not only as places for children to play but also as spaces for public gathering and community expression. Playgrounds also play a special role in our collective memory of childhood, offering lasting memories of thrilling discovery, fanciful role-playing, and daring escapades.

We should value the design of spaces for play as much as we value the children who use those spaces. We need to recognize the substantial contribution carefully crafted urban spaces can make to our children's lives and the lives of our communities. And though children's playgrounds may not change the urban environment on a macro scale, they have the potential to change the world in small, meaningful ways. A well-designed playground offers a chance for a child—and a community—to explore, to imagine, and to take risks.

This important book prepares architects, educators, parents, and policymakers for wholesale renewal in the world of playground design. Following decades of overly intense, even obsessive focus on playground safety—a concern that has too often resulted in dull spaces for children, while providing parents with a false belief that all risk has been eliminated—today, fresh ideas are circulating about spaces for play. Creative new projects are beginning to take shape. In the first chapters of this book, Susan Solomon has grounded us in a historical discussion of playground design over the past one hundred years, creating a solid foundation from which readers can understand and analyze the new trends beginning to take shape in playground design. Solomon has here identified and brought together noteworthy examples from across the country, including projects designed by architects and landscape designers for a wide variety of clients and missions. The most successful projects presented here challenge both the child's imagination and muscles, while contributing positively to the built environment of cities and communities. This monograph is a welcome book for the many people who are interested in urban design, public space, and children's issues. And perhaps this book will also be a harbinger of a more prominent role for the playground in urban design in the next century.

Martha Thorne
Associate Curator, Department of Architecture,
Art Institute of Chicago

ACKNOWLEDGMENTS

This book has emerged from the professional and private strands of my life. As a graduate student in the 1990s, I was drawn to the playground that Louis Kahn and Isamu Noguchi designed in the 1960s. It seemed a natural for further investigation. When I had a chance, also in the 1990s, to sponsor a playground in memory of my parents, Rita and Nathan Goldberg, I learned firsthand about contemporary problems. I sensed that the time had come to combine a view of the past with a guide for anyone undertaking a similar commission in the future.

The outline for this book took shape when I was the curator of an exhibition on the playgrounds of northern California. Marta Gutman, Ning de Coninck-Smith, and Barrie Thorne, who labored hard on the conference that hosted that show in 2002, were eager proponents. Architect Mark Horton was the "patron saint" who designed excellent display panels and selflessly donated his extraordinary skills. These people energized this book project. Ellen Wicklum, editor at University Press of New England, kept this project going when it started to falter and then added her own wise counsel. She has been a dedicated champion of this book, something for which I am profoundly indebted.

The Graham Foundation for the Advanced Study of the Visual Arts honored me with a travel grant for which I am truly appreciative. This generous support, which enabled me to make a lengthy trip to several American cities, shaped my views and conclusions. My research could not have been as extensive without the Graham Foundation's confidence.

Martha Thorne has written a thoughtful foreword. I appreciate her longstanding commitment to this topic. It gives me immense pleasure to have been the recipient of her insights and friendship.

Debra Solomon, Pamela Grossman, Roger Hart, Jane Perry, and Andrew Shanken were good enough to spend hours poring over my manuscript and offering shrewd criticism. I have benefited enormously from their help.

I have been fortunate to have been welcomed by libraries and archives that have given me access to unpublished materials or long-forgotten volumes. The following have eased my task: the Architecture Library, Marquand Library, and the Seely G. Mudd Manuscript Library at Princeton University; the Isamu Noguchi Foundation; the Architectural Archives of the

University of Pennsylvania; and the Hoskins Library at the University of Tennessee.

John Blazejewski again has shown that an excellent copy photographer is an indispensable ally. Jared Polesky lent a great image.

I owe many thanks to colleagues, designers, educators, administrators, physicians, psychologists, and park users who patiently answered my many questions and shared their exceptional ideas: Vito Acconci and Acconci Studio, Aditya Advani, Glen Allen, David Armstrong, Steve Badanes, Victoria Baker, Alton Barron, Cheryl Barton, Stephen Beacham, Wendy Beacham, Jay Beckwith, Charlotte Bialek, Richard Blender, Marvin Bressler, Kathryn Bridges, Elizabeth Brody, Denise Brown, Marisa Angell Brown, David Brownlee, Marian Burleigh-Motley, Bill Buchen, Mary Buchen, Eric Bunge, David Carlson, Yuval Carmel, Nancy Chambers, Willliam D. Chambers, Emily Chiswick-Patterson, Gregory Chow, June Chow, Alice Chun, Mark Cooper, Richard Dattner, Karen Dea, Tim Denny, Jim Diamond, Patty Donald, Brian Drypolcher, Fred Druck, Clare Dudley, Jeffrey Edelstein, Greg Everhart, Kim Faley, Tom Finkelpearl, Martin Flores, M. Paul Friedberg, Jeanne Gang, Lisa Gelfand, Peter Gerharty, Jim Greenman, Lissa Goldberg, Paul Goldstein, Susan Goltsman, Skip Grossman, Richard Haag, Gary Hack, Amy Hau, Susan Henderson, Susan Herrington, Anita Hill, Joanne Hiromura, Kathy Hirsh-Pasek, Mimi Hoang, Renata Holod, Walter Hood, Mark Horton, Rachel Iannacone, Clare Jacobsen, Kathleen James-Chakraborty, Dan Jenkins, Carlos Jimenez, Sonia Johansson, David Karem, Manuela King, Rita Kimball, Mikyoung Kim, Andrew Kozar, Nancy Eklund Later, Linda Lawton, Liane Lefaivre, Kevin Lippert, Lori Little, Bill Litmann, Tom Luckey, Stephen Ludwig, Zella Ludwig, Barbara Lundburg, Sarah McHam, Eva Maddox, Jeff Miller, Mary Miss, Martha Mendelsohn, Robin C. Moore, Mark Morrison, Cynthia Nelson, Michael Nylan, Amy Ogata, Tom Otterness, Michael Painter, Cesar Pelli, Alan Plattus, Robert Punkenhofer, Tom Richman, Leslie Roffman, Jim Ryugo, Stanley Saitowitz, Martha Schwartz, Maria Segal, Margaret Seip, Jane Shoplick, Susan Sidlauskas, Toby Simon, Ken Smith, Lydia Soo, Brett Stiles, Gregory Stock, Bill Stout, Frances Strauven, Rebecca Tracey, Lia Thompson-Clark, Nancy Thorne, Ilya Tovbis, Billie Tsien, Donna Walcavage, Michael Wakeford, Annie Weinmayr, Lee Weintraub, Neil Welliver, Bill Whitaker, Lynn Winnemore, Kate Wood, Carla Yanni, and Janice Yee.

My family continues to sustain me. Each has offered a unique accomplishment that has enriched my efforts and furthered my pride in their support. My husband, Bob Solomon, was the photographer on whom I have depended most. He produced beautiful photos of playgrounds, often driving many miles in order to get exactly what I wanted. Our adult children have been unabashed advocates and terrific collaborators. Jon Solomon has been a trusted advisor who constructed a superb Web site (www.recentamerican playgrounds.com). Debra Solomon has been a brilliant, tireless editor. Happily, Nicole Scheller and Gil Carmel have come into the fold. I heartfeltly thank all of them for their assistance, humor, and love.

Acknowledgments

AMERICAN PLAYGROUNDS

Introduction

Existing American playgrounds are a disaster. The landscape is filled with variations of a model that has few local or regional distinctions. Today's playground normally is defined by a sizable, colorful piece of commercial equipment that links steps, deck, and slides. It is topped by pyramidal roofs, rests on a resilient surface, and is cordoned off from its surroundings by fences and gates. These assemblages have become so commonplace that most citizens will be shocked to learn that these play areas are cultural artifacts that emit a mixed message. Playgrounds no longer function as a hub of community activity and rarely attract a variety of participants over the course of a single day. Use is set and predetermined, leaving scant prospect for improvisation. Often divorced from the site, the playground does not aid in preserving remembrances of the past. Playgrounds used to reflect theories about how children learn; today they are largely unconnected to seasoned beliefs on the subject. The problem is exacerbated by the American public's increasing difficulty with assessing risk on a daily basis. The playground has become so safe that it no longer allows children to take on challenges that will further educational and emotional development.

American innovators, those who have worked on projects for children, feel great frustration with the situation as it exists. They question whether a playground can be a site-specific piece of art. They think that national and local safety guidelines have restricted their ability to craft imaginative areas in which kids can play. Their discontent is fueled by the specter of product-liability and personal-injury litigation. Those who commission playgrounds—which now can include diverse backers such as redevelopment executives, library directors, or heads of social service agencies—share a common concern from the perspective of active consumers. Designers, patrons, and advocates for children agree that the playground often is an exceedingly dull place in which to spend time.

This book highlights the ways in which American architects, landscape architects, and sculptors have confronted and triumphed over present reality. Investigating the playground as an urban building type and an under-valued, continuously mutating public space, this monograph concentrates on playgrounds that enrich children's experiences in the world and help neighbors or even strangers to interact easily. These play areas are never static and continue to ignite spontaneous use from kids. The playground is not heroic, but its impact can be enormous. The playground can effortlessly unite design with history, becoming an arena that cultivates collective memory. This book brings to light the complex stories that have shaped recent, successful sectors for play.

In order to understand how and why settings for play have changed dramatically since the optimistic enthusiasm of the 1950s and 1960s, this study begins with a survey of innovative, post–World War II European playgrounds and the Americans who responded to the initiatives from abroad. The first two chapters of this book are devoted to this historical background and to the reasons for the decline in American playgrounds since the 1970s. The current story, the last four chapters, reveals shifts in patronage and fresh definitions of play. This section of the book also details strategies and remedies that should be useful to anyone who will commission a playground. These projects satisfy three essential criteria: they enhance community life; they support well-executed uncluttered design; and they echo the latest perspectives on play by providing for individual exploration, socialization, negotiation, fantasy, and gentle unexpected consequences.[1] These examples return playgrounds to the realm of aesthetic and developmental consideration from which they have been removed for several decades. They even meet radical standards of successful design where achievement is measured by improvement in human existence.[2] Almost all of these playgrounds, created primarily in the decade between 1995 and 2005, are open on a daily basis and do not charge admission fees. A small number of less-accessible exceptions, including projects by Americans working abroad, are considered because they are so strikingly original and have forged community cohesiveness.

Creating a contemporary playground should be seen as an invigorating act that can alter positively the urban landscape. This book should make clear to administrators, parents, and educators that they have many options when planning for play. They can make significant, consequential choices. Readers are encouraged to think of the playground equipment catalog as one of several resources. They are urged to work with a variety of artists, architects, and landscape architects in order to fashion unique environments. Such solutions often can be achieved for a sum almost identical to an outlay for standardized equipment. Sometimes "off the shelf" pieces from commercial manufacturers can be incorporated into exciting, multidimensional locales, orchestrated by skilled professionals. Older playgrounds do not have to be scrapped but can become the basis of fresh visions.

There is a certain urgency in that playgrounds still retain independence from advertising. At a time when some toll lanes on the Massachusetts Turnpike have a sponsor, playgrounds may be one of the last public areas that do not depend heavily on corporate underwriting. There is no guarantee that that will always be true. The high cost of playground equipment makes playgrounds vulnerable to commercial funding. Catalogs from manufacturers show that a sizable, fully installed piece of play equipment can have a price tag of $75,000 to $100,000. Such considerable expenditures bolster further the imperative for decision makers to reconsider how they spend their funds. Surely there are ways to avoid the hulking, sterile, bizarrely colored monster that dominates most playgrounds today.

If patrons and the general public begin to demand more of playgrounds, there is a fair chance for change. Manufacturers, too, must be willing to consider alternative approaches. Resulting collaborations, which bring clients together with creative experts, have the potential to excite children, engage families, and improve urban life.

PART I
THE PAST

CHAPTER 1

History: Pre-1960

The playground is a relatively new concept with a distinctly urban character. European and American playgrounds for children began to emerge as discrete entities in late-nineteenth-century cities. By the early twentieth century, the American public expected a playground to be composed of metal equipment such as isolated swings and slides. The same components defined playgrounds for decades.

War and devastation were the background for innovative playground accomplishments, starting in the 1940s. After a few Americans had made early studies, Europeans took the lead. Several of them were able to blend playgrounds into their reconstruction plans and to incorporate the ideas of psychologists who were addressing the importance of play for children. Copenhagen and Amsterdam, more than any other cities, supported striking changes in playgrounds. The Scandinavians contributed an abandonment of traditional equipment and an acceptance of risk. The Dutch, by way of the architect Aldo van Eyck, led the way in integrating playgrounds into the urban fabric and in providing compositions of potent artistic abstraction. Both of these heritages, the Scandinavian and the Dutch, found their way into the first American postwar reactions and innovations. These achievements were reflected in pockets of interest that developed on both American coasts. The Museum of Modern Art and the manufacturer Creative Playthings were exceptionally instrumental in promoting the union of playgrounds and cutting-edge sculpture.

THE FIRST AMERICAN PLAYGROUNDS

Freestanding purpose-built American playgrounds, in place by the 1880s, resulted from demands that were often overlapping: crime prevention, character building, and just plain exercise.[1] The role of playgrounds in the integration of immigrants into a common society has been studied only recently. The playground, particularly during the Progressive reform movement of the early 1900s, benefited from the widespread belief that play was child's work. John Dewey's theories, which portrayed children as miniature adults who had to adapt to their environment by actively exploring it, functioned as an important source for this conception.[2] Children not engaged in their own profession were believed to stray into delinquency. A slightly different stance maintained that physical activity, especially muscle control, had a moral dimension that would create better citizens. Other popular theories of the late nineteenth and early twentieth century equated play with expending surplus energy or Darwinian reenactments of evolution. An historian of playgrounds, writing in the second decade of the twentieth century, believed that the significance of the playground rested on the fact that it offered kids a place to go that was supervised and removed from the evils of the neighborhood.[3] As an artificial construct the playground has always had to compete with the street for the attention of children.

Major American cities had playgrounds for young people by 1900. The form of the American playground, chiefly identified with individual neighborhoods and their small parks, was defined by a sand pit and the "gymnasium," an early climbing apparatus. The sandbox was an American version of an idea imported from Germany. The derivation of the metal climbing equipment is not as straightforward, emerging out of the YMCA movement of the mid-nineteenth century. Before World War I, the established American playground consisted of swings, sandbox, and seesaw. Placed on a hard surface and enclosed by high fencing, these components were always associated with extensive programming that included paid play leaders and well-orchestrated activities, such as folk dancing and dramatic presentations. That was the norm for more than forty years (fig. 1.1).

The founding in 1906 of the Playground Association of America (which later became the National Recreation Association and ultimately the National Recreation and Park Association) marked the institutionalization of the play movement and the recognition that the public realm was taking responsibility for the activity of children. Before then, private civic-minded organizations had provided recreation services for young people. The first years of public sponsorship already were marked by concerns about safety. In 1912, New York City removed gymnasiums from all of its parks because these were considered too dangerous.[4] Safety criteria were a justified measure of a playground's acceptability.

EXTRA LIFE...
EXTRA VALUE!

★ ★ ★ In Playground Equipment experienced buyers demand durability, absolute safety, proven performance, long service. It is reasonable that only *highest quality* equipment will give you these vital features.

American APPROVED playground equipment

meets *every one* of your requirements. Modern design...top quality materials ...unexcelled workmanship ... maximum safety ... superior performance ...these are but a few of many plus-features you receive when you install American Approved Equipment.

WRITE TODAY

for complete, fully illustrated catalogs. See why American has led the way for more than 35 years!

AMERICAN
Playground Device Co.
ANDERSON, INDIANA
World's Largest Exclusive Manufacturers of Fine Outdoor Playground, Swimming Pool and Physical Fitness Equipment

Fig. 1.1 Advertisement in *Recreation Magazine*, April 1947. American Playground Device, which produced traditional equipment, began operating in the early twentieth century. The Miller family owned it for many decades. Courtesy of Philip Miller.

AMERICAN VOICES BETWEEN THE WARS

Several Americans, all of whom had strong associations with landscape design, began to reconsider and write about playgrounds in the 1930s. Landscape architects Garrett Eckbo (1910–2000), Daniel Kiley (1912–2004), and James Rose (1910–1991) made clear statements as early as 1939. Writing in the journal *Architectural Record*, they made specific suggestions that directly related to recreation and playgrounds of the time.[5] This influential trio established generous guidelines that paid attention to young children as well as teenagers. They urged the creation of ubiquitous play lots for preschoolers and separate, larger sites for the six- to fifteen-year-old set. They also argued for a finer integration of interior and exterior spaces along with the use of contemporary materials. Their views reflect the ideals of modernism, the new attitude toward architecture and design that had blossomed in France and Germany in the late teens and early 1920s. Undertaking social responsibility and seeking a utopian world, modernism intended to achieve a break with past styles that were committed to historical models. Modernist thinkers advocated the use of problem solving, new materials, and free-flowing space in order to meet the demands of an increasingly mechanized era. Eckbo, Kiley, and Rose applied modernist theory to the landscape and established a framework for serious consideration about recreation.

During this same decade, sculptor Isamu Noguchi (1904–1988) was exploring alternative forms of what a playground might look like. This artist later articulated the connections that tied together communal space, children's play, and the creation of artwork in most cultures.[6] Noguchi gave American modernism a specific and abstract form for play.

Born in the United States and raised in Japan until he was a teenager, Noguchi initiated *Play Mountain* in 1933. This was the first of many projects in which he hoped to mold earth. Noguchi, perhaps reflecting the density of Japan that he had personally experienced, attempted to tilt and excavate land in order to extract many uses from a New York City block.[7] Kids would be able to slide along the gently sloped outer pathway of *Play Mountain* and splash in water that would descend along the side of its vertical mound. There would be another slide for winter sledding.[8] New York Parks Commissioner Robert Moses (1888–1981) rejected *Play Mountain,* an act that did not prevent Noguchi from further experimentation.

Noguchi's continuing interest in designing all components for each assignment, a concept that can be traced to Japanese and modernist traditions, became evident when he began to invent swings and a spiral slide (fig. 1.2).[9] After a commission for these in Hawaii fell through, Noguchi tried to sell the idea to New York. The Parks Department rejected the

Fig. 1.2 Isamu Noguchi, *Spiral Slide* This photo appeared in *Architectural Forum* in 1940. Fay S. Lincoln Collection, Courtesy Historical Collections and Labor Archives, Special Collections Library, The Pennsylvania State University, University Park, Pennsylvania.

equipment as too dangerous. Noguchi, in response, devised another playground in 1941, *Contoured Playground,* which featured an undulating landscape and expanded upon the ideas found in *Play Mountain.* The new design, also devoid of any equipment, revealed rising mounds and peaks. Like its predecessor, it was never constructed. In this case, the problem was World War II, during which Noguchi voluntarily spent a short time trying to organize an art program in a detention camp for Japanese Americans.[10] Parks Commissioner Moses did try to re-ignite interest in the project in 1947, but that attempt did not produce positive results.[11] Meanwhile, Noguchi's play equipment entered the consciousness of American culture in a limited way. His unrealized plans for swings and a spiral slide appeared as a set design for a Rita Hayworth movie, *Down to Earth* (1947). Columbia Pictures, which used these without Noguchi's permission, swiftly acceded to the artist's demands for compensation and credit.[12] This was an

Fig. 1.3 Adventure Playground in the Emdrup section of Copenhagen. From *Creative Playgrounds and Recreation Centers*, Alfred Ledermann and Alfred Trachsel. Copyright © 1959 by Verlag Gerd Hatje. Reproduced with permission of Greenwood Publishing Group, Inc., Westport, CT.

early infringement of intellectual property, a problem that persists even today in playground design.

THE ADVENTURE PLAYGROUND

While Copenhagen was under German occupation, Danish landscape architect C. Th. Sørensen (1893–1979) developed the first Adventure Playground in the Emdrup section of the Danish capital (fig. 1.3). Known commonly as "junk playgrounds," these facilities were the perfect solution for a country at war.[13] Sørensen established an enclosed area, slightly over one acre in size, where a play leader gave children useless fragments of wood, metal, or masonry. The same person dispensed a few building implements such as hammers, saws, and nails. These must have been truly worthless scraps and tools if they could be spared during such a desperate time. The single supervisor, considered a respected professional, was available only for guidance and was key to the success of a playground. Throughout the site, kids chose freely what they wanted to do. The simplicity of the concept is still startling: give children some discarded materials and the equipment with which they can alter them; employ a sensitive adult to stay in the background and come forward only when necessary. Nothing was ever stale; the large structures on the playground were dismantled each autumn so there could be an annual fresh start.

Given all of this latitude, children became the self-directors of everything that they produced. Their camaraderie and uncontrolled creativity became the essence of their play experience. The Adventure Playground, an antidote to political control that affected most other aspects of current existence, offered freedom and the opportunity to be experimental. It is not surprising that the impact of the Adventure Playground was immediate and lasting, extending beyond the war years. Within the first decade of its existence, it had surpassed the popularity of nearby, more-standardized playgrounds. Its positive achievement was generated by the variety of activities in which kids could engage and by the naturalness of cooperation required to bring a project to completion. Children did not need to be instructed or admonished to work together. In this utopian setting, they happily gained those lessons while they had fun.

Adventure Playgrounds, counterintuitively, came to the fore as one of the safest facilities available for children. Their fine record was compelling, especially soothing for adult fears. For children, the appeal was more straightforward. These playgrounds seduced kids by making them believe that they had entered a forbidden zone, gaining access to materials that appeared inappropriate for play, and tools that usually were reserved for adults. It was the illusion of danger that made these playgrounds so enchanting. This last characteristic may have been the most salient advantage and the reason why the playground attracted a wide range of age groups and a relatively huge number of children for a comparatively small lot. This type of facility, inexpensive to inaugurate and maintain, provided endlessly varied activities without concern for vandalism.

Adventure Playgrounds sprung up in Great Britain in the 1950s. Lady Allen of Hurtwood (1897–1976), a trained horticulturist and a founder of the World Organization for Early Childhood Education, was the person largely responsible for introducing the concept to the British Isles, where it had tremendous clout and staying power.[14] By 1970, Lady Allen was able to extend the principle to disabled children in London by creating an Adventure Playground for Handicapped Children. By that time, too, it became apparent that the Adventure Playground embodied the more progressive thoughts of educational theory that had appeared almost twenty years earlier. Psychologist Erik Erikson had written about the sociability of play in his *Childhood and Society* (1950), and Swiss psychologist Jean Piaget had formulated a link between play and cognitive maturity in his *Origins of Intelligence in Children* (1952). Lady Allen's stance, curiously, had less to do with heeding didactic methods and more to do with citizenship. She believed that the Adventure Playground was the place where children would have "to come to terms with the responsibilities of freedom."[15] In this way, she extended the early-twentieth-century interest in the playground as a place where immigrant children could be acculturated.

Lady Allen, a prolific writer and lecturer, still found it hard to convince Americans of the worth of her ideas. Some American cities did indeed use surplus military equipment as playgrounds just after World War II and thereby gave their own patriotic twist to local expendables. The title of a magazine article that reported on one such effort, "Where Shall We Adventure," seems to reflect the European precedent of nontraditional play areas.[16] In other ways, the Adventure Playground was a hard sell in North America. This does not mean that Lady Allen and her ideals were ignored or forgotten. Many designers, beginning with those who embarked on projects in the 1960s and continuing through those working today, have tried to infuse the spirit of Adventure Playgrounds into their own creations. The term "adventure playground" still has potency. At least one American manufacturer, one whose equipment looks identical to all the others, has adopted the name, and a number of twenty-first-century traditional playgrounds carry the same moniker.

ALDO VAN EYCK

Dutch architect Aldo van Eyck (1918–1999) brilliantly used playgrounds to improve daily life in Amsterdam after the war. Van Eyck, recognized even during his lifetime as one of the inspirational reformers of modernism after that approach had begun to lose its social and formal edge by the late 1950s, designed over seven hundred playgrounds for the Amsterdam Public Works Department. Toiling first for the city and then independently between 1947 and 1978, van Eyck elevated small, uncomplicated playgrounds into compelling public spaces. Van Eyck viewed children as integral members of society and incorporated the needs of young people into his broader quest of enriching the way in which city dwellers live. His playgrounds became magnets for community activity. Van Eyck, like all successive pacesetters, was encouraged by local municipal leaders who cared about playgrounds.[17]

Architectural historians Liane Lefaivre and Alexander Tzonis have noted that van Eyck was a humanist whose personal philosophy was rooted in conceptions of community.[18] His goal was to create connections among people. Van Eyck believed that a vast net of playgrounds could be a legitimate form of art that sprang from the specifics of a site and its users. He gave his innovations a respectability that did not pander to children and permitted the playground to become an enduring aspect of the urban life. Van Eyck's own experiences, growing up in Britain where his father worked from 1919 to 1935 and where he attended untraditional non-regimented schools, certainly informed his views of education and play.[19]

Van Eyck's production was staggering for its great numbers, variety, and ability to bring together disparate elements of society. The impact on Amsterdam came quickly. The actual financial cost was slight. Success, which can be measured by the influx of users at a facility, can also be gauged by the number of residents' requests that flooded the public works department (fig. 1.4). Once a playground was established, people would plead for similar installations in their own neighborhoods.[20] The citizenry created demand; nothing was imposed.

Van Eyck applied his vision to any available open space. He later reflected: "The sites thus adapted were for the most part there, waiting (as many similar sites are waiting in every city of the world), forsaken, useless and dead: innumerable formless islands and plots left over by road engineers and demolition workers; often better suited for use by children than for development of ornamental public gardens."[21] In Copenhagen, Sørensen recovered leftover materials; van Eyck did the same thing for forgotten space. Scholar Lefaivre has noted that van Eyck seized on these otherwise inconsequential spaces and transformed them into "place," an area with a legible presence that would have enduring magnetism.[22] She has shown that Van Eyck's approach to playgrounds encapsulated a view of urbanism that not only extolled the meaning of intimately scaled sectors but also offered them as an early critique of postwar autocratic planning. Van Eyck's method differed from modernism in his attention to site specificity and his view that an architect's work could continue to evolve after being built. This particularity and lack of finality are two of the traits that distinguish van Eyck's ideas from those of Robert Moses, the infamous Parks Commissioner of New York City. Moses, who also oversaw the completion of more than seven hundred playgrounds during the years he held his post from 1934 to 1960, intended his work to be unrelated to site, a complete and unalterable product made from stock metal swings and seesaws.[23]

Van Eyck's first playground, located at Bertelmanplein (1947, renovated 1974) contains elements that he would replicate and/or revamp in subsequent schemes (fig. 1.5). Bertelmanplein was a stable, unexciting open spot. Bounded on three sides by housing and adjacent to a key thoroughfare in southwest Amsterdam, Bertelmanplein does not have a dramatic past. This

Fig. 1.4 Sand pit in 1950 at an Amsterdam playground (Frederik Hendrik-
plantsoen, 1950) that Aldo van Eyck had designed. Courtesy of the Municipal
Archives of Amsterdam.

sets it apart from other van Eyck interventions where he would reclaim
derelict spaces, many of which did have complex histories. Van Eyck had to
find a way to make Bertelmanplein into a thriving, ennobled annex to its
surroundings. He began by creating a low curb around the available site,
which was approximately 75 by 100 feet. This was both a way to claim it, indicating that play would fill the spatial void, and to set the playground off
from the street without creating a barrier. Van Eyck used wood benches, of
his own design, to define further the perimeter. These offered parents a

place to sit and chat while overseeing their young ones. Caretakers could observe without interfering, at the same time becoming a human wall to prevent children from straying off the premises. By eschewing fencing, Van Eyck avoided the caged character of contemporary play areas. Whereas Lefaivre has noted that historian Johan Huizinga defined culture in terms of play in his *Homo Ludens* (1944), it should also be noted that van Eyck was able to interpret it literally. He makes concrete some of Huizinga's observations about play being a free, voluntary, unpredictable, and repeatable activity,

Fig. 1.5 Aldo van Eyck's first Amsterdam playground, Bertelmanplein (1947), in 1956. Courtesy of the Municipal Archives of Amsterdam.

Fig. 1.6 Aldo van Eyck's Bertelmanplein playground in 2002. Van Eyck designed the hexagonal climbers in the 1960s. Fencing probably was added when the playground was modified in the 1970s. Author's photograph.

carried out within a demarcated area, and generating a nucleus of users who can thrive outside the play area.[24]

Van Eyck sought other ways to make the playground part of the urban context. He worked diligently, even at this first playground, to use surfacing material that was the same as that of the nearby streets and sidewalks (fig. 1.6). He retained the colors of the adjoining streets, usually the dark red or gray of the paving. Local patterns of stone and brick became the flat plane on which play could occur. This reinforced the connection with the urban framework and allowed the playground to meld, at least optically, with its surroundings. A contemporary landscape architect recently marveled at this "seamless" union.[25]

Bertelmanplein, with simple and spare equipment, was indicative of playgrounds that followed. Van Eyck's compositions were always nonhierarchical, a characteristic that is already apparent. There were subtle interplays among elements, without a single central focal point.[26] Here and in subsequent designs, van Eyck made the sandpit the visual and programmatic heart of the design, not the physical center of the space. These sand areas, always oversized and with innovative walls and borders, became a hallmark of van Eyck's designs. Relying on Platonic geometry, van Eyck called for sandboxes with easily recognizable shapes. The rectangular sand pit at Bertel-manplein, approximately 20 by 30 feet, is immense. The top of its concrete enclosing wall is wide enough to run upon and low enough to be jumped over, thereby providing the sandbox with additional ways to play. The flat surface doubles as a seating platform for parents. When many of today's playground designers note that sand and water still offer some of the best childhood experiences, it's instructive to see that van Eyck understood that axiom. He exploited such opportunities for children because of their play value and because such simple devices enabled him to keep within an aus-tere budget.

Van Eyck's first sandbox is of consequence, too, because it contained "concrete play tables."[27] Children could mold sand on these flat-topped cylin-ders. They could stand and jump among them. Soon, van Eyck saw the pos-sibility of moving these disks out of the sandpit and arranging them close enough together to become "jumping stones." Van Eyck later refashioned these, as well as his first low, tubular-steel climbing arch, which were found in the same sand pit. Photos show that by 1954 he had come up with big-ger, freestanding examples of both (see Fig. 1.8). Once he had begun to de-velop large numbers of playgrounds, van Eyck inserted these climbing and jumping elements into many of his later designs.

A quick glance at some intact and extant van Eyck playgrounds illumi-nate how subtle and varied his work could be. While many of his play-grounds have been sacrificed to escalating real-estate demands or some parental requests for glitzier equipment, the playgrounds that remain do have the internal unity and position in their surroundings that van Eyck sought so fervently. Much of his 1950s equipment has endured because it was timeless, without literal references, and almost indestructible.[28] These pieces now evoke van Eyck's belief that the playground should reflect real-ity, a city in which imaginary and lavishly colored animals do not exist.[29]

Van Eyck's playgrounds in large municipal parks in Amsterdam retain his earlier muted palette of unpainted concrete, unadorned wood, and metal. In Vondel Park, van Eyck anchored a playground (near Amstelveense Weg, 1960) close to the edge of the park, making it accessible to local families without a long trek through the rest of the grounds. It is distinguished by low terracing that carefully separates his climbing dome, designed in the mid-1950s, from the sand area. This creates intimate but not isolated spaces. The playground at Herenmarkt (1956, modified 1974), alongside a canal, shows further the relationship to the city. Jonas Daniel Meyerplein (1955, modified 1971), without any added fencing even today, illustrates how well van Eyck's playgrounds fill an environment (fig. 1.7). Here, where the

Fig. 1.7 Aldo van Eyck's Jonas Daniel Meyerplein playground (1955, modified 1971), Amsterdam. Author's photograph, 2002.

surroundings include the seventeenth-century synagogue, private houses, a canal, and the nearby botanical garden, the playground remains a strong visual presence. The brick surfacing reinforces the continuation of urban conditions.

Much has been written, recently, about creating meaningful spaces that activate memory. Van Eyck, more than half a century ago, aimed for an analogous conclusion projected from his own time. Rather than calling up the past, he labored to reestablish the present. Seeing the obliteration of war, he rewrote future history by giving fresh, dignified meanings to empty spaces. Where these represented areas created by default, such as empty strips in the center of a road, he found ways to imbue them with purpose that belied their haphazard birth. Where the spaces held tragic meaning, such as the empty lots where deported Jews had once had their homes, van Eyck tried to initiate a firm and hopeful sense of beginning.[30] Van Eyck's success in transforming an anonymous space into a vibrant inviting "place" can be seen by comparing before and after photos of his Dijkstraat playground (1954, demolished 1972) to a similar before and after sequence taken in Chicago in the early 1950s (figs. 1.8 and 1.9). Van Eyck used subtle placement of equipment and change in surface materials to guide a user through the activities he provided. In Illinois, where the equipment was placed haphazardly, the renovated lot does not exhibit any of van Eyck's controlled composition, visual demarcation, or varied space. The completed product is just as anonymous as it was before it was improved.

Van Eyck, writing in the 1950s, summarized his position:

> These playing children demonstrate the latent possibilities of urban renewal in general. With the aid of a little concrete, wood and aluminum there have come into existence social centers: places where children and parents meet, true extensions of the doorstep—for it is on the doorstep that the outside and inside worlds, the spheres of collective life and of individual life, intersect. Here at any rate the child has moved to the centre. Since the artist is essentially an ally of the child, the job has been particularly rewarding. . . . It is surely for the artist—whatever his medium—to introduce grace and beauty where they have vanished or gone into hiding.[31]

Fig. 1.8 Dijkstraat playground before (A) and after van Eyck's 1954 intervention (B). This playground, often considered the finest of van Eyck's, was one of many constructed on lots that had been occupied previously by Jewish homes. Courtesy of the Municipal Archives of Amsterdam.

The importance of van Eyck's words goes beyond his attempt to forge community by restoring a sense of neighborhoods to a city where there had been so much personal isolation during the war. He also verbalized how to put art into the service of urban enhancement. Each geometric pattern, each placement of equipment takes on aesthetic and utilitarian meaning in order to create a pleasing, cohesive total environment. Van Eyck exalted play and play spaces by believing they were a legitimate art form. Liane Lefaivre, recognizing that van Eyck was well versed in contemporary art, has deemed the Dijkstraat playground, "one of the first site-specific sculptures of the postwar period."[32] In the United States, Noguchi had hinted at a similar stance but wrote little and was still having difficulty in getting a playground constructed. Van Eyck was the person who married theory and action.

AMERICAN PLAYGROUNDS FOLLOWING WORLD WAR II

Europeans, many of whom experienced the horrors of war, never relinquished their focus on the play of children. People out of harm's way often did not have the same commitment. During World War II, American architects, educators, and clergy indulged themselves in debate concerning the nature of their work after peace had come. Discussion about design of playgrounds did not enter most of their conversations.[33] One reason may be that stress continued to be placed on individual play pieces, not on the playground as a single entity or as a public space. Things changed a bit after the war concluded. When Holmes Perkins was chair of regional planning at Harvard, in the late1940s, he assigned studio problems that involved playgrounds combined with parks or schools.[34] Harvard, in the forefront of teaching modern design in the United States since the late 1930s, was the perfect place to nurture that type of investigation. Eckbo, Kiley, and Rose, who had met at Harvard, had initiated interest in playgrounds among land-

Fig. 1.9 A Chicago lot, before (A) and after restoration (B), early 1950s. From *The American City*, October 1954. Courtesy of Primedia Enterprises.

scape designers in 1939; architects and planners picked up those concerns in the following decade.

When scrutiny of playgrounds began actively in America in the early 1950s, the earliest interest was bifurcated. Engaged individuals tended to be aligned with one of two factions, connected either to the recreation movement or to the art world. Park administrators were naturally in the recreation camp. They stressed programming, with a nascent interest in issues such as safer surfacing to put under the existing equipment.[35] These professionals were devoted to planning events that gave priority to drama, music, and dancing. Their concentration on activities may have prevented them from embracing any changes in playground design. The recreation leader, rather than the equipment (which remained the standard sandbox, slide, swings, and seesaw), was at the heart of their strategy. In 1948, close to fifty thousand people were employed at over sixteen hundred park sites.[36] Along with their commitment to staffing, American administrators were dedicated to a playground that integrated schoolyards and parks in order to maximize efficiency and decrease duplication of equipment. Targeting an age group of five to fifteen, recreation planners hoped to provide opportunities for physical activity. They did not make a distinction between the play equipment and facilities for physical exercise such as wading pools, playing fields, and green areas. They did pay attention to lighting in order to make these recreation sites available in the evenings, thereby increasing use and accessibility.

Playgrounds of the 1950s were microcosms of American life, filled with political and religious associations. Parks underscored physical activity because it was tied to creating good citizens, not a small concern during the McCarthy era. Religion, having an intense postwar revival in America, made a contribution. Many who ran park programs believed that there was an association between spiritual and recreational fulfilment. During a time when Americans were embracing religious observance and attendance, it was common to have clergy talk about recreation combined with the spirit of Christianity or about a Christian notion of play. As the 1950s progressed, there was additional deliberation about how to spend increasing leisure hours and how to raise children properly.[37] Analysis of liability for municipalities and their agencies also surfaced, as did consideration of the handicapped. The latter was spawned largely by concern for permanently injured veterans from World War II and the Korean conflict.

Rumblings in the art world, operating independently of those in the recreation movement, began to emerge during the same decade. A connection between playgrounds and sculpture began to take hold. Not surprisingly,

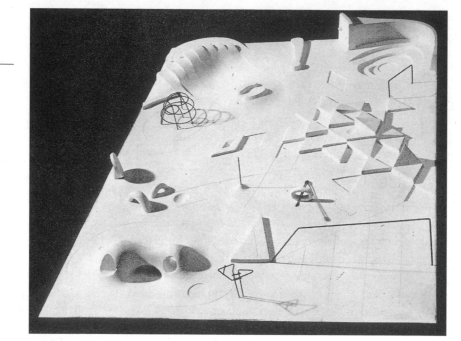

Fig. 1.10 Isamu Noguchi and Julian Whittlesey, model of United Nations playground (1952). Reproduced with the permission of the Noguchi Museum, New York.

a major commission went to Isamu Noguchi. His 1951 plan for a playground at the United Nations, designed with architect Julian Whittlesey (Mayer & Whittlesey) had another sad outcome. Audrey Hess, a granddaughter of Sears Roebuck chairman Julius Rosenwald and the wife of art critic Thomas Hess, initiated the project. She most likely chose Noguchi and persuaded her friends and neighbors to contribute to this privately funded project for children visiting the United Nations and for those living in the neighborhood.[38] Adele Rosenwald Levy, Audrey Hess's aunt, was another patron of this project.

Noguchi and Whittlesey produced a preliminary plaster model (fig. 1.10) that shows how this project expands but also departs from ideas found in Noguchi's 1941 *Contoured Playground*. In the earlier work, Noguchi had poked the surface up to create hills or knobs. Here, the designers accentuated those protrusions to create freeform, largely independent incidents. None of these is physically linked, although a drawing shows that a single surfacing material would have helped to unite the different pieces. This playground is a series of fanciful abstract shapes that depend on customized equipment, with names like "jungle house" and "dodger." In one corner, a climber pushes up from the ground's surface. Slides descend from a side of this mound. An amphitheater with spray pool, in another corner, has the spiral shape of Noguchi's earlier slide without its bold vitality. In yet another corner, an area labeled "grotto" has rounded hills that are indented by circular depressions in their surface. The scheme lacks van Eyck's exquisite clarity.

Parks Commissioner Moses, in his capacity as liaison between New York City and the United Nations, quickly dismissed this design and persuaded the UN to do likewise.[39] Intercession by the Museum of Modern Art, which exhibited the model in its Young People's Gallery in 1952, did not alter Moses's thinking or the UN's decision.[40] The museum showing gave the playground more visibility and offered critics a means to expound on how a playground that was sculpture might affect users. One writer observed that childhood is an occasion for physical activity but also "a time for developing the imagination and an awareness of and sensitivity to beauty."[41] The museum proclaimed that this playground had "possibilities of stimulating the child's sense of space and form through a playground designed as architectural sculpture."[42] Museum educators had grasped the prospect that a playground could boost aesthetic awareness and individual creativity. They also let it be known that this playground would be exclusively for small children; older ones would be kept away by the absence of challenging spaces for them. Noting that "playgrounds, when carefully arranged, require no fencing and seem to run themselves," the museum may have had in mind the spatial organization of van Eyck's sites and the functioning of an Adventure Playground.[43]

Tom Hess, who probably had a hand in the museum's intervention, would not take defeat quietly. The managing editor of *Art News* and husband of the woman who orchestrated the commission, he reacted to Moses's disdain with a stinging editorial.[44] Hess mocked Moses, calling him the "Cheops of toll bridges," and lambasted him for his inability to accept any form of progressive design. According to Hess, this "playground, instead of telling the child what to do (swing here, climb there), becomes a place for endless exploration . . ." He, too, extolled Noguchi for blending art with everyday activity. Both Hess and the museum were, in effect, endorsing abstraction as an apt language for play because it could accommodate varied, imaginative, undirected activity. Two years later, in January 1954, a respected journal cited the thwarted UN project as an example of a new trend, the emergence of "sculptural play forms."[45] The connection between art and play was gaining ground.

THE MUSEUM AND THE MANUFACTURER

After the showing at the museum, the model of the UN playground traveled to the National Recreation Congress and to the Creative Playthings toyshop in New York City.[46] An appearance before the annual meeting of parks administrators might appear to have been the more prestigious venue. It was, surprisingly, the stop at Creative Playthings that would have long-term consequences for the development of playgrounds.

Creative Playthings' current advertising proudly displays a seal that commemorates more than a half century of corporate growth, beginning in 1951. It is, in fact, only the name that is over fifty years old. Sold by the original owners to CBS in the 1960s, Creative Playthings had its loyal customers through the 1980s. Many parents of children born in the late 1960s and early 1970s share fond memories of Creative Playthings' toy designs. Among the favorites were a double wood easel and a dollhouse with a bright blue roof and no exterior walls. Donald Hoffman, who bought the Creative Playthings name in the 1980s and who now produces slides and swings for backyards, felt that it was a brand with a rich history of innovative design.[47] It was that legacy that attracted him to make his purchase.

The original Creative Playthings, started by Frank Caplan and Bernard Barenholtz in 1951, was preceded by a retail toyshop with the same name. Frank Caplan opened the Creative Playthings shop in 1945, and soon added his own products, notably hardwood blocks, to the shelves that had items from other manufacturers.[48] Even in those early years, Caplan sought advice from the Museum of Modern Art and seemingly hoped that its imprimatur would give a certain cachet to his business. In 1946, he announced that a consulting committee would help guide him in selecting products already in the marketplace and in seeking possible designs for the future. In addition to two independent educators, Caplan enlisted a Museum of Modern Art official to represent the "field of fine arts" on his committee.[49] This attachment to the museum, and the publicity that it garnered, paid off by 1949, when architect Marcel Breuer placed Creative Playthings' hollow cubes in the playroom of the demonstration house he built in the museum's garden.[50] Architect Gregory Ain used the toyshop's products for a similar model house on the same site the following year.

Hoping to inspire Americans with the possibility of good design of everyday products and with the notion that toys could enhance the inventiveness of children, Caplan and Barenholtz began to market their joint company in an aggressive way. Art historian Amy Ogata has noted that their commodity was creativity, pitched to middle- and upper-class Americans as a way of combating the conformity of the 1950s while, at the same time, proclaiming

America's uniqueness.[51] In addition to turning out toys, school supplies, and furnishings, Creative Playthings spun off a new division in 1953. This was Play Sculptures, created to produce playground equipment designed by sculptors. It aimed to bring sculptors into the industrial-design process, allowing them to conceive playgrounds. Some American architects, including Anne Tyng and Charles Eames, had set a precedent by designing toys that were kinetic and abstract in the 1940s.[52] These were early, unrefined "proto-playground" pieces. Caplan and Barenholtz capitalized on the concept. They set out to employ sculptors to reach vaster, more public audiences for outdoor settings. Their young company achieved early notoriety by enlisting sculptor Robert Winston to work on playground plans.[53] Winston had displayed his abstract sculpture, which was 30 feet long, at California's Spring Garden Show in 1952 and published it in at least one magazine the following winter (see the right-most small image in figure 1.11).[54]

In early June 1953, Caplan made a pitch to Noguchi. Audrey Hess set up their first meeting.[55] In it unclear how Hess and Caplan would have known each other, but certainly her place in the art world and his associations with the Museum of Modern Art would have made them aware of each other. Caplan made clear to Noguchi that he was interested in securing designs of play sculpture that could be mass produced. He also articulated his hopes for a complete playground that could be planned by "a small panel of key designers" and then marketed to public institutions such as housing authorities, parks departments, and school boards.[56]

During that same month, June 1953, Caplan and his wife took a grueling, multi-city trip to western Europe in order to find new toy resources and to nail down contracts with several sculptors. They made contact with Nino Vitali, who was designing hand-worked wooden figures and animals in Switzerland. It is unclear if Vitali ever did produce a playground design. The Caplans had better luck with a Dane, Egon Møller-Nielsen, who already had pioneered abstract concrete playground pieces in Sweden.[57] Snagging him must have been quite a coup. Møller-Nielsen's work had appeared frequently in art and architecture journals of the early 1950s. He was hailed as the first serious sculptor to intermingle the flowing space of modernism with the fantasy world of children.[58] Møller-Nielsen, not Noguchi, emerged as the artist who was lauded for presenting children with sculpture that was playful and playable. His fame was a byproduct of having actually seen his pieces built and having had children photographed within and on them. The most noticeable example was the cover of the British journal *Architectural Review* in August 1954.

Caplan continued his efforts after the European trip concluded. Toward

**a new
dimension
in playground
planning!**

Creative Playthings, Inc., pioneers in the development of play materials for early childhood education, now offers a *complete playground planning, design and building service* through its newly-formed Play Sculpture Division.

On its staff are leading designers, sculptors, engineers, educators and landscape architects, including such well-known names as Isamu Noguchi, E. Moller-Nielsen (Sweden), Robert Winston, A. Vitali (Switzerland), etc.

The Play Sculpture Division is currently co-sponsoring—together with the *Museum of Modern Art* and *Parents' Magazine*—a nationwide Play Sculpture Competition.

Play Sculpture Division maintains a permanent display and resource center at 5 University Place, New York. You are cordially invited also to visit our exhibit at the forthcoming National Recreation Congress in Philadelphia.

We invite your inspection and inquiry.

Full descriptive literature will be sent you on request.

PLAY SCULPTURES *DIVISION*

CREATIVE PLAYTHINGS, INC., 5 UNIVERSITY PLACE

NEW YORK 3, N. Y. • ORegon 4-7858

Fig. 1.11 Creative Playthings' Play Sculptures advertisement from the September 1953 issue of *Recreation Magazine*. Egon Møller-Nielsen was the sculptor for the piece in the large image (sometimes referred to as the Gothenburg sculpture, 1952) and for the sculptures in the two small photographs at the left. Robert Winston executed the piece in the right-most small image. Courtesy of Donald Hoffman, current CEO of Creative Playthings.

the end of summer 1953, Caplan wrote to Henry Moore and solicited his participation in the playground campaign.[59] Moore accepted, with the caveat that he would be occupied with other projects for at least the coming year. There is no evidence that he ever followed the initial contact with any design.

In September 1953, at a time when *Recreation Magazine* was beginning to include a few articles on unusual playgrounds, Creative Playthings burst on the scene with a dramatic full-page advertisement of abstract play sculptures (fig. 1.11). Most other advertisements in this publication were for sporting-goods equipment. There were a small number of advertisements for playground apparatuses. A few companies dominated those ads by showing children on swings or jungle gyms. Creative Playthings transformed the presentation and the content. Suddenly, their startling, visually bold promotion proclaimed "a new dimension in playground planning!" It backed up that statement with a large photo of a Møller-Nielsen sculpture. Three smaller images, two of which showed Møller-Nielsen's pieces and one of Robert Winston's sculptures, accompanied the large image. The spare text noted that Noguchi, Møller-Nielsen, Winston, and Vitali were already on the Creative Playthings staff. Caplan and Barenholtz must therefore be seen as smart promoters and as patrons of sculptors. Their gift was to see how abstract art, which could accommodate any kind of playful activity, could be of use to a child's development. They did not denigrate the art, they elevated the child. These men were enthusiastic about modern art and wanted to participate in its universal acceptance. It was not by accident that Barenholtz would later hand architect Peter Eisenman his first commission, Barenholtz's private toy museum and addition to his own house, in the late 1960s.[60]

Creative Playthings also used its arresting advertisement to announce that it was co-sponsoring a 1954 "Play Sculpture Competition," in conjunction with *Parents' Magazine* and the Museum of Modern Art. The advertisement provided no additional details; but information was already spreading throughout the country.[61] Winners were promised prize money, participation in an exhibition at the museum, and royalties for their product design. Creative Playthings' Play Sculptures would manufacture the winning pieces.[62] The Museum of Modern Art would retain ownership of those designs.[63] Caplan, who had long massaged his contacts with the Museum of Modern Art, seems to have been rewarded for his diligence.[64]

The competition entry form asked designers to satisfy some requirements, including imaginative play as much as physical activity. The emphasis, interestingly, was not completely on abstraction, since submissions could include versions of representational items such as ships or airplanes.

The organizers asked entrants to use materials that were readily available—including wood, metal, or cement—and to make pieces that could be adaptable to public and private settings.[65] The attention to the private consumer is a bit disconcerting, tending to shift these works from a discussion exclusively about public use. This thought was counterbalanced by an assessment of the competition's urban goals. That was voiced in an unsigned August 1954 article:

> Playgrounds for children are an essential part of modern city planning, and the quality of their play equipment is of vital importance. However, the cement-floored, wire-fenced patches of recreational areas set aside in city parks and schoolyards, and fitted with monotonously identical metal constructions for physical exercise, are cogent proof of how inadequately we have estimated their importance in our communal life.[66]

The implication of this writing should not be minimized. It made clear that the playground had a critical place in defining how urban space is used. The Museum of Modern Art competition had begun to solidify the connection between art and playgrounds; this article added the urban component that van Eyck had endorsed passionately.

The year 1954 was the perfect moment for these things to gel, as evidenced by a section heading for the January 1954 issue of *Architectural Record,* highlighting social and recreational buildings: "Playgrounds Have Discovered Design." The first wave of "boomers," born between 1946 and 1950, were already vertical, active, and school age, or about to begin their education. The threat of polio, a continuing menace during most summers and the frequent cause for closing recreation facilities in prior summers, was beginning to abate. In 1954, Jonas Salk's vaccine had its first large-scale trials, and although there was a glitch with one batch, the mass inoculation of children did take place in 1955. On the art front, the success of abstract expressionist painting was trumpeting America's role as the world leader in pioneering artistic endeavors. Creative Playthings' executives must have been especially delighted by an early report on their first playgrounds that declared that these accessible works would "melt the stiffest resistance to abstract sculpture."[67]

The Museum of Modern Art competition, and the subsequent display of selected playground pieces at the museum during the summer of 1954, generated excitement. There were more than 350 entries. The museum did not take its duties lightly. An assistant curator was the competition director, and Philip Johnson, director of the museum's Department of Architecture and

Fig. 1.12 Virginia Dortch Dorazio, *Fantastic Village* (1954). This won first prize in the "Play Sculpture Competition," sponsored by the Museum of Modern Art, *Parents' Magazine*, and Creative Playthings. From *Arts & Architecture* (August 1954).

Design, was a member of the jury.[68] Their participation helped to wed the play concept to the general art world. The exhibition and winning entries created a frenzy when shown to the public. Children were brought in to demonstrate how the equipment could be used. The press reported how the kids swarmed over and through one of the pieces and loudly expressed approval of others.[69] The exhibition was highly visible during the hot summer months. Some pieces were shown on a Saturday morning TV program.[70] The news media did not waste any time in reporting on the developing mix of art and populism. The *New York Times* carried a large article that announced, "New Play Pieces for Young Shown."[71] This attention must have been thrilling for the competition winners, all of whom were under thirty-six years old.

The significance of the victorious entries is that they developed module elements that could form new contexts for play. The first- and third-prize-winning projects, both of which were produced in full size for the exhibit, were immediate hits. The premier prize went to Virginia Dortch Dorazio, a young painter from Arkansas who was living with her husband in Rome. Her *Fantastic Village* consisted of seven prefabricated, reinforced concrete panels, each with a different, cutout abstract design (fig. 1.12). These could

Fig. 1.13 Sidney Gordin, *Tunnel Maze* (1954). This won third prize in the 1954 competition at MoMA. From Alfred Ledermann and Alfred Trachsel *Creative Playgrounds and Recreation Centers.* Copyright © 1959, 1968 (second edition) by Verlag Gerd Hatje. Reproduced with permission of Greenwood Publishing Group, Inc., Westport, CT.

be arranged into multiple varieties of 5-foot cubes. Reinforcing bars appear to provide ladders and sliding poles for the exterior and a type of monkey bars for the interior. The full-scale houses, accompanied by small models that showed the varied combinations that were possible, were set on sand.[72] Apropos of city life, these hollow blocks were arranged to resemble an urban square that was a self-contained world.

The third prize went to a sculptor, New Yorker Sidney Gordin. He created *Tunnel Maze* of prefabricated, gently sloped concrete segments (fig. 1.13). A rounded opening pierced through the bottom of each. The possibilities of arrangement were again extensive, including the creation of fields of hills or long tunnels. A number of color possibilities added to the variety. The judges gave it rave reviews.[73]

The second-prize winner, unfortunately, did not receive similar accolades. New Jersey industrial designer Robert J. Garguile won the award without achieving the same level of recognition as his co-winners. His *Stalagmite Cave* was a series of spool-shaped vertical forms of varying height. Flat disks anchored each top and bottom. The museum showed only one of the small components, thereby making it less intriguing to visitors.[74] Garguile's design did become better known through the subsequent press coverage of the exhibit in magazines during the ensuing months.

One critic, Aline Saarinen, saw this 1954 exhibition as a watershed. She believed that it had the potential to energize interest in outdoor space where people could gather. She held that the exhibit might be a harbinger of a movement in architecture away from sprawling and undefined spaces and toward smaller, cozier, settings. Van Eyck, of course, had had that same objective. Saarinen also saw a link between this type of display and aesthetic education, suggesting that the real impact of the exhibit was to teach good design. In that way, children might become better adult consumers for urban sculpture, possibly supporters of some future artist's version of Noguchi's UN playground.[75] A similar argument was being made in Britain, using work by Egon Møller-Nielsen as its centerpiece.[76] This powerful hypothesis, about the lasting affect of early exposure to sophisticated art, was made at a time when modern art was considered baffling by many people. A comparable notion, that children can be educated into being enlightened patrons, is one that only recently has begun to be revived and receive serious consideration in the United States.[77]

The Museum of Modern Art exhibition, with its attendant media recognition, gave playgrounds a heightened legitimacy in art circles and in more general spheres. Within two months, *Life* magazine took note that Philadelphia was a leader in playground innovation and highlighted it in a September 1954 issue.[78] The city was one of Play Sculptures' early clients.[79] The leadership in Philadelphia, under Recreation Commissioner Fredric R. Mann and his deputy and successor, Robert W. Crawford, was unusually strong. Both of them were committed to providing playgrounds that would appeal to whole families.[80] Architects regarded their playground patronage as a plum award.[81]

Life had keen praise for a new Philadelphia park, at Eighteenth and Bigler streets. The magazine considered it one of the best American solutions for an intergenerational recreational area, a concept then being promoted by the National Recreation Association.[82] Landscape architect Cornelia Hahn Oberlander, a member of the city Recreation Department's design team, reinterpreted a 3.5-acre site. She combined a play area (one-fourth of the park) with playing fields, bocce courts, and a horseshoe pitch. Oberlander used circular motifs to enclose her spaces for the tot area, giving them a unified cohesion that had not existed in parks with isolated pieces of equipment. She and her cohorts in the city agency did not flinch from spec-

Fig. 1.14 Cornelia Hahn Oberlander, Bigler and Eighteenth Street Park (1954), Philadelphia. Creative Playthings' division, Play Sculptures, produced the climbing arches and the spiral slide (by Egon Møller-Nielsen). This photo appeared in a Creative Playthings catalog of the late 1950s. Courtesy of Donald Hoffman, current CEO of Creative Playthings.

ifying their own works, including climbing nets and a fanciful dragon.[83] For the Bigler Street park, Oberlander added a tiered concrete island that was 30 feet at its widest and 10 feet high. Kids could play and perform there while parents used the same artificial hill for sitting and socializing.

Oberlander also took advantage of the new mass-produced sculpture that Play Sculptures was marketing. A photo shows that an Egon Møller-Nielsen piece, a heavily polished concrete spiral, held a prominent position in the Bigler Street play space (fig. 1.14). This was reputed to be its first installation in America.[84] Climbing arches, shown there and also from the Creative Playthings inventory, reflect work that van Eyck was producing in Amsterdam and hark back to his prototype at the Bertelmanplein playground. Frank Caplan would have seen van Eyck's earlier versions on his trip to Amsterdam in June 1953.[85] He might also have seen van Eyck playgrounds in one of many Dutch photo books published in the 1950s.[86]

On the West Coast, too, landscape architect Robert Royston (who had formed a partnership with Garret Eckbo and Ed Williams in the mid-1940s) wrestled with choices between designing his own equipment or seeking a suitable manufacturer. He designed individualized pieces for a park in one of the flourishing suburban towns, Palo Alto. For his 1954 Mitchell Park, Royston aimed to bring modernism's free-flowing space to the playground (fig. 1.15). In the area for small children, set within a larger 20-acre park for all ages, he devised freeform shapes that evoke the biomorphic sculpture of European artists such as Jean Arp. These shapes are not meant to be works of art in the same manner that Creative Playthings intended, but they derive from sculpture and appear to be another way to elevate the importance of the spaces where children play. This sets them apart from another contemporary development, the themed playground, where equipment was ornamented to resemble fairytale houses or storybook characters. Royston, instead, thrived on abstraction. He composed a loose circular pattern, with empty space driving into and around each freely devised object.

Fig. 1.15 Robert Royston, axonometric plan for Mitchell Park (1954), Palo Alto, California. Courtesy of Royston Hanamoto Alley & Abey.

Fig. 1.16 Adaptation of the *Saddle Slide* that was first produced by Playground Associates in the mid-1950s. The design team at Balsley Associates was able to locate this version of a piece that has been out of production for many years for Balsley Park (Balsley Associates, 2000), New York City. Author's photograph, 2004.

By 1955, the roster of artists who wanted to create playground equipment started to grow. Following the lead of Creative Playthings, landscape architect Robert Nichols formed Playground Associates in order to further the development of abstract sculpture for playgrounds. He worked with sculptor Mitzi Solomon Cunliffe, landscape architect Hideo Sasaki, and two young American architects, Shephard Schreiber and Edward Larabee Barnes, to produce easily reproducible and affordable pieces of equipment. Harvard Graduate School of Design was again the connecting thread: Playground Associates had several successes, including a fiberglass inverted dome. Their best-known piece, designed primarily by Cunliffe and called *Saddle Slide,* was cast stone that was formed in a fiberglass mold (fig.1. 16). The results were elegant. Kids took naturally to the folded curves with ample and varied round holes.[87]

THE TELLING CASE OF JOE BROWN

In 1959, the *New York Times* announced the first English edition of the seminal book *Creative Playgrounds and Recreation Centers,* written by Swiss recreation specialists Alfred Ledermann and Alfred Trachsel. Two photographs accompanied this news item, placed under the heading "Modern Play Equipment Is Designed to Exercise Both Muscles and Minds."[88] Robert Winston, the artist signed by Creative Playthings, had developed one. The other, which shows children bouncing and laughing on some sort of rope arrangement, was the work of Joe Brown (1909–1985). Hailed by the *Saturday Evening Post* as the *"enfant terrible* among playground designers," and revered by many peers in the architecture world, Joe Brown was concurrently shunned by playground manufacturers.[89] He was a paradox who provides further proof of the connection between playgrounds and sculpture in the 1950s.

Brown's own life meshed physical activity and art. A boxing coach at Princeton University and a teacher of sculpture in Princeton's Creative Arts Program, Brown was well known in the 1950s for his heroic, classically inspired sculptures of athletes. He had learned both crafts in the 1930s in his hometown of Philadelphia. There, after completing college, Brown had been a professional boxer for a short time. He also studied with Dr. R. Tait McKenzie, a legendary Philadelphia sculptor of athletes.[90] After his stint with McKenzie, during which he became a studio assistant for his mentor, Brown went to Princeton in 1938 as a boxing coach. He later became a resident fellow in sculpture.

Brown began to think about play, spurred on by discussions on the Princeton campus. In 1950, at the moment when public schools were being built during a time of economic expansion and an increasingly youthful population, Brown critiqued play equipment designed by Princeton's architecture graduate students. The architecture program, directed by Professor Jean Labatut, clearly was having discussions that had surfaced a bit earlier at Harvard. According to reports of the time, Brown was unimpressed with the student work, believing it was not reflective of how people interact and affect each other. Challenged by the students, and somewhat embarrassed that he had no real knowledge of playground design other than his own experiences as a kid, Brown began to come up with his own devices.[91] Architects and landscape architects were quickly aware of his experiments. Robert Nichols, one of the founders of Playground Associates, wrote to him for help when they formed their company that would soon produce the *Saddle Slide*.[92]

Brown was able to have some prototypes up and running for Princeton University's alumni week in the spring of 1955. He believed deeply that play was preparation for adulthood, a popular view since the early part of the twentieth century. Brown wanted his pieces to demonstrate cause and effect as part of normal behavior, with the aim of forming cooperative future citi-

Fig. 1.17 Joe Brown, *Jiggle Ring*. From *Creative Playgrounds and Recreation Centers*, Alfred Ledermann and Alfred Trachsel. Copyright © 1959, 1968 (second edition), by Verlag Gerd Hatje. Reproduced with permission of Greenwood Publishing Group, Inc., Westport, CT.

zens. He dubbed his works "play communities" because he understood they would demonstrate interdependent actions among people who lived and worked together.[93] Kids learned that they could manipulate the environment, especially if two or more worked together without excessive supervision. An early critic of playgrounds that were so safe they were lifeless, Brown maintained that playground accidents resulted more from boredom than from unsafe apparatuses, a dictum that has been repeated by most critics of today's equipment.[94]

Brown's piece, *Jiggle-Ring*, was the one that had been shown in the *New York Times* (fig. 1.17). A low rectangle supporting a net of steel-cored rope, fiberglass joints, and steel posts, it reminded one observer of a boxing ring.[95] A kid maneuvering on any part would affect the balance of others trying to steady themselves on the same piece. Shown in architectural journals during 1954 to 1957, the *Jiggle-Ring* also appeared on the pages of popular magazines, such as *McCall's Magazine* in 1955 and the *Saturday Evening Post* in 1957. The article in the latter was extensive and well illustrated. It claimed that the controversial Brown had produced radical designs that made him "the most hotly debated figure in playground architecture—a sort of Frank Lloyd Wright among the teeterboards."[96] That was a triumphant comparison; the elderly Wright was receiving worldwide attention for the Guggenheim Museum in New York and his Beth Shalom synagogue outside of Philadelphia. Both were then under construction.

Jiggle-Rail was another early prototype, developed by 1954. This comprised six arms of spring steel, each piece 20 feet long and 4 inches wide, emerging from a central core. Brown claimed that jumping on one side would affect the opposing arm, thereby allowing kids to realize the benefits of cooperation or the possibilities for wreaking havoc. At least one of these objects was installed in Philadelphia, where Recreation Commissioner Robert Crawford was fast to hail it. He had ignored parents' initial concerns that it was unsafe, confident that it eventually would be appreciated. That is exactly what happened. Brown noted that the commissioner cited his experiences with *Jiggle-Rail* to show how it was possible to educate "the public by not backing down everytime a criticism is offered."[97]

Whale Yard, still one more of Brown's contrivances, was the most interesting in terms of a freestanding playground (fig. 1.18). Described as a "plastic, life-sized whale in the process of making a U turn," it combined cargo netting, an interior slide, pipe with ropes, and holes through which tiny tots could climb.[98] It had the potential to be a self-contained playground based on diverse types of activity. Children could use different areas simultaneously; a wire enclosure presented a chance for additional activity and a way to spread out actions. The enclosure, furthermore, marked off a space larger than a single piece of equipment and extended use into the landscape. Brown picked up on the postwar infatuation with plastic, a love affair with which most other playground designers did not indulge until the 1970s.[99]

Brown began to work precisely at the same time that the Museum of Modern Art was driving interest in its playground competition and he may have been animated by the stir that event was creating, although he probably declined to enter it.[100] Media attention for Brown mushroomed, anyway. In 1956, he was a guest on an NBC radio series that highlighted leisure. That same year, he took part in the Will Rogers television show. His appearance on Garry Moore's television show, considered a premier gig in 1957, was a success. Included in many pieces of fan mail, some of which were sent directly to Moore, is a typed postcard from a woman in California, who said simply: "Get the Prof. from Princeton back soon."[101]

Sadly, Brown's increasing public recognition began to be frustrated by his inability to mass-produce his products. Demand increased while production stalled. Brown formed a company, licensed one piece to a manu-

Fig. 1.18 Joe Brown, advanced prototype of *Whale Yard* (ca. 1955). From *Creative Playgrounds and Recreation Centers,* Alfred Ledermann and Alfred Trachsel. Copyright © 1959, 1968 (second edition), by Verlag Gerd Hatje. Reproduced with permission of Greenwood Publishing Group, Inc., Westport, CT.

facturer, entered into a manufacturing agreement with another firm, and began a production phase with yet another company. None of these endeavors was successful, usually because the workmanship was shoddy and Brown would not accept the final product. He was able to build several prototypes, but none is known to have gone into full-scale production.

Brown later wrote that all of the established companies had ignored him. One of these must have been Creative Playthings, then located just a few miles from Princeton in Cranbury, New Jersey.[102] Most likely, Creative Playthings with its long-standing alliance with the Museum of Modern Art and with its own outlook as an artistic innovator, would not have been captivated by a sculptor whose cast work depicted detailed athletic bodies in classical poses. Creative Plaything's own agenda had always been to promote abstraction as the language that linked play and progressive sculpture. Deeming Brown's cast pieces as too conservative, Creative Playthings probably would have shunned any connection to him. These actions, no matter how regrettable they may seem now, give further evidence that playgrounds of the 1950s had the potential to be considered high art.

Some landscape architects and architects were able to look beyond Brown's representational art and endorse his contributions to play. Many of them pursued Brown and hoped to purchase playgrounds from him. This only added to his commercial paradox. The list of those who approached him is impressive. Innovative landscape architect Garrett Eckbo, the person who had written about recreation space in the 1930s, took note and made inquiries.[103] So did the offices of Victor Gruen & Associates, then a major developer of shopping centers and the employer of Cesar Pelli.[104] Architect Walter Gropius weighed in too, calling the *Jiggle-Ring* a "lovely contraption."[105]

By 1957, full-size prototypes of Brown's work were in place in Philadelphia, London, Tokyo, and some New Jersey towns. A whale even graced the play area of a drive-in movie theater on Long Island.[106] This put Brown's work at the heart of a then-current debate: whether the burgeoning industry of drive-ins promoted "passion pits" or family-centered recreation areas. None of this was putting Brown any closer to production of his designs. The personal effect on him became unbearable. He became increasingly frustrated and seems to have regretted the whole undertaking.[107] Accepting a cancellation of an order, Brown wrote that he hadn't wanted to be his own producer of equipment, had been abused by both customers and manufacturers, and had had enough of being an unintentional nonprofit corporation.[108] Making matters worse, other companies had appropriated his concepts by the early 1960s. By October 1961, Playground Corporation of America was producing "wiggle walls" and "ring dings." The "wiggle wall" was "a resilient net of aluminum struts which moves as children climb it." Reputed to "develop reflexes by requiring adjustment to actions of others competitively or cooperatively," this newcomer sounds uncannily similar to Brown's invention. While Brown was still finding it difficult to market his designs, an ambitious manufacturer had clearly filled the void.[109] For much of the 1960s, Brown continued to seek licensers while he did some custom pieces and acted as a consultant.

THE END OF THE 1950S

American playgrounds, perhaps aided by their association with sculpture, were highly respected by the end of the 1950s. Compared to a considerable number of European innovators, the American pioneers remained few.[110] A high point for the Americans came when playgrounds represented a facet of life in the United States at the American National Exhibition in Moscow in July 1959. Best known as the venue where Vice-President Richard M. Nixon hotly debated Soviet General Secretary Nikita Khrushchev in front of an American kitchen, the trade exhibition featured Charles and Ray Eames's seven-screen film collage and an up-to-date playground. Creative Playthings' Play Sculptures division had supplied all of the equipment, indicating again that they continued to be the standard for the industry.[111] In an odd conflation of public and private spheres, the institutional playground adjoined the model home where the Cold War kitchen debate had occurred.[112]

The harsh truth was that an extensive and innovative Creative Playgrounds ensemble was rare in the United States. Playgrounds were vaunted for what they could be, not for what they had become. Equipment such as this was not known to most Americans and huge numbers of playgrounds remained blacktopped, uninspiring accumulations of the same equipment that had been around for decades.[113] With hindsight, it is clear, too, that the playground in Moscow may have been equipment only, a somewhat random display of most things from the current Creative Playthings catalog. That company's early desire for an integrated whole had not yet materialized. Within two years, the situation changed. A modernist tenet—well-designed objects for daily life—which had surfaced in the 1950s, would gain ground in the 1960s.

CHAPTER 2

History: 1960–1995

The stirrings of change that marked the 1950s became concentrated enthusiasm for American playgrounds in the 1960s. Influential American playgrounds emerged and garnered recognition in professional design journals. Interest continued and accelerated in the purpose-built playground, which could be an example of abstract art. During the 1960s and early 1970s, the physical form of the playground finally began evolving rapidly. Based on linkage of posts and platforms, a new concept became the model. Manufacturers swiftly exploited it. In the 1970s, there was also a short-lived fascination with self-built playgrounds. Less heralded methods, which included cultivation of natural gardens and acceptance of scrap materials, had the longest resonance.

The situation took a wrong turn in the mid-1970s. Americans, historically conscious of safety, began to misassess risk. They lost the ability to distinguish between real and perceived danger. The American character became defined, at least partially, by risk aversion. Safety guidelines began to take hold and commercial products became dominant. One educator has noted that when safety restrictions increase, there is a corresponding decline in the play value of a site.[1] That was the outcome as a plethora of banal equipment, much of which owed its form to earlier well-crafted pieces, began to swamp the field with repetitions of static designs. Equipment manufacturers ignored the trend, which blossomed after the 1970s, to use computers to generate customized products.[2] It was not long before Americans put so much trust into equipment that they failed to realize that the equipment alone did not constitute a playground.[3]

The union of playgrounds and unique art was one of the first victims of this increased commodification. The consensus among all types of artist

43

was that only large companies could sustain the possibility of legal defense.[4] A dwindling number of architects, landscape architects, and sculptors were willing to undertake unique playgrounds. Most professionals maintained that their imaginative abilities were being compromised and their legal exposure was too great. Communities often have had no choice but to use recent versions of tired equipment that limits creativity and restrains social or educational experiences.

A PARADIGM IN A PARK

A single defining project, begun in 1961, altered successive American thinking about playgrounds. This was Louis I. Kahn and Isamu Noguchi's collaborative project for a playground in New York's Riverside Park, near 103rd street. Planned for a steeply terraced site of more than 8 acres, this playground was to be named in memory of Audrey Hess's aunt Adele Rosenwald Levy (1893–1960).[5] For more than five years, this playground was the center of controversy before the entire project was abandoned. While under consideration, it instigated an imbroglio, becoming a divisive public project that has had few rivals in terms of nastiness and litigiousness within a city district. Neighbors, the Parks Department, and the donors each had conflicting visions of what was needed. The positive aspect of this strident debate was that the project frequently was mentioned in the press and was widely known among architects, sculptors, and art patrons. Although its loss can be lamented, its role as a formative work may have expanded because of the controversies that kept it in the public eye. The timing, too, was ideal. Jane Jacobs, in her legendary 1961 book, *The Death and Life of Great American Cities,* deplored the lifelessness of current playgrounds and parks.

The site was, and remains, a complicated one. There are three distinct levels: one at grade with Riverside Drive; the esplanade (covering the tracks of the New York Central Railroad), approximately 45 feet below Riverside Drive and bordered on one side by the retaining wall that shores up the adjacent high spot; and a third also steeply descending level that comes close to the West Side Highway. Prior to 1960, this section of Riverside Park had been underutilized, considered an unsafe eyesore. During that summer, neighborhood groups had banded together to clean up the park. The city provided a recreation leader and greater police presence.[6] A group of residents, with the aid of city and private agencies, began a free summer day camp that attracted participants of racial and socioeconomic diversity. This park program was the impetus that led some local residents to campaign for further upgrading of their old facility, making it more suitable for year-round and multigenerational use.

Proponents for an improved park contacted Audrey Hess and she willingly got involved. This playground was, at least partially, her attempt to revive the ideas that had underscored Noguchi's proposal for the United Nations.[7] Her resolve for a playground most likely was intensified by the death, in March 1960, of her aunt, for whom she hoped to find a suitable memorial. Hess contacted Noguchi in October 1960 with the news that a group of people on the Upper West Side of Manhattan was interested in innovative playgrounds, and that she was approaching him on their behalf.[8] She assured him that this consortium, the Bloomingdale Conservation Project and its lead agency the United Neighborhood Houses of New York, wanted to engage him and had already shown photos of his work to Parks Commissioner Newbold Morris. Hess reported that Morris, who had just replaced Robert Moses in this position, was enthusiastic and that there would be no hitch in his approving Noguchi's concepts. The sculptor agreed to participate and made a trip to the site in December 1960. This seemed to be a flawless mix of engaged client, able patron, and seasoned artist.

By the following summer, 1961, Hess recognized that the project could be extensive and that there had to be an architect to collaborate with the sculptor. Frank Caplan of Creative Playthings, whom Hess had known since at least 1953 when she introduced him to Noguchi, offered to recommend someone.[9] He also appears to be the individual to whom Hess turned to serve on a memorial committee for Levy. He attended early meetings, labored on the executive committee, and received copies of the important correspondence.[10]

The Museum of Modern Art was, once more, not far removed from the story that unfolded. Caplan could not possibly have avoided the fact that the museum was currently presenting an exhibition on Philadelphia architect Louis I. Kahn (1901–1974). This display was devoted entirely to the building Kahn had just completed, the Alfred Newton Richards Medical Research Building at the University of Pennsylvania.[11] Not surprisingly, Kahn became the architect for Noguchi's playground project by August 1961. The sculptor, perhaps stung that he did not get to choose his own collaborator, would later say that he chose Kahn. Noguchi argued that New York officials, who he believed would never accept his work, might be more sympathetic to proposals that were associated with a distinguished architect.[12] Noguchi did act quickly to try to segregate their responsibilities. He wrote to Kahn that he presumed "my part will be more the form, yours more the structure although it may be difficult to differentiate one from the other."[13]

The choice of Kahn, no matter how decided, was a solid one. In spite of the fact that he had been a practicing architect and teacher for more than thirty years, he only recently had arrived at a mature phase of development and was just beginning to receive key commissions. His architectural objective was to reinterpret modernism, which had grown to become synonymous with vast continuous spaces and often flimsy-looking glass-and-steel structures. Kahn sought to reintroduce solid materials and a hierarchy of finite rooms. For Kahn, these would be the means to achieve buildings that would be responsive to human needs and use. He hoped to instill each project with places for quiet personal contact among users. Some of these goals were, of course, similar to those espoused by van Eyck. Both of these architects knew each other's works, had crossed paths at several points, and appear to have had a cordial relationship. Kahn's articulation of secondary spaces, what he called the "servant" areas that supported the main "served" spaces, has an analogy in van Eyck's refinement of leftover spaces as critical areas in urban planning.[14]

Kahn's experience with play and play spaces, more limited than Noguchi's, was still of consequence. He had designed the Memorial Playground at the Western Home for Children in Philadelphia in 1946. There, he had devised a sensible plan that formed four functionally distinct zones: a partially shaded freeform walkway and seating configuration, in addition to separate sections for swings, hearth and climbing sculpture, and unstructured empty space (fig. 2.1). Each of these areas had a different surface, with the hearth providing an additional barrier between the open space and the climbing piece beyond. Kahn was able to squeeze varied uses out of the small site and dignify it with a sizable, fanciful mural.

Kahn's work for the Trenton Jewish Community Center (TJCC, 1954–1958) in Ewing, New Jersey, offered him many opportunities to design areas for play, but neither the program nor his response elicited a design for a purpose-built playground. TJCC plans, for a large main building and several supporting structures on a suburban site, show that Kahn was intrigued with landscape; it was integral to all of his TJCC designs. A site plan for the campus (unbuilt, 1956) illustrates how Kahn would have manipulated earth to realize a type of amphitheater and auxiliary seating arrangements. Like Noguchi, who had been reconfiguring earth since the 1930s, Kahn more recently had been trying to reshape land.[15] During this same period, both men would have been aware of interesting toys. Kahn, in particular, was familiar with the Tyng Toy, designed by his associate Anne Tyng in the 1940s. Other artists marketed their toys through the 1960s.[16]

Asking Kahn and Noguchi to collaborate was a notable idea. In this case, a playground, especially one that could be considered a work of art, would be an appropriate way to remember Adele Levy. The Kahn-Noguchi playground would reflect Mrs. Levy's twin legacies of support for the arts and aid for dis-

Fig. 2.1 Louis I. Kahn, axonometric plan for Memorial Playground (1946), Western Home for Children, Philadelphia. Courtesy of the Louis I. Kahn Collection, University of Pennsylvania and Pennsylvania Historical and Museum Commission.

advantaged children. Levy had had an outstanding record as an advocate and collector of modern art and as a philanthropist who had a special interest in the rights and concerns of children. She had been devoted to the Citizens' Committee for Children of New York, an advocacy group for indigent children.[17] Her niece Audrey, too, had taken a keen interest in that charity.

Audrey Hess, who previously had embraced the UN playground, did not hesitate to memorialize her aunt with a playground. Just three years earlier, her spouse, Tom Hess, had lambasted the United States pavilion at the Brussels World's Fair. He felt that the American pavilion, chock full of kitchen gadgets and frozen foods, lacked gravitas.[18] With their unflagging support of playgrounds, the Hesses indicated that they did not consider playgrounds to be in the same frivolous category as consumerism or popular culture. The Levy playground would have additional prestige because Mrs. Levy's surviving spouse, Dr. David Levy, was a leader in the field of child psychiatry. He coined the term "sibling rivalry" and is still remembered for work he did in the 1940s on "maternal overprotection."[19]

The preliminary program for the Kahn-Noguchi collaboration called for a multipurpose stage, an informal skating rink, a building for an all-weather nursery school, and a place for teenage sports.[20] Kahn and Noguchi created a clay model in November 1961.[21] Kahn quickly executed drawings. These men took full advantage of the sloping site, placing most of their work on the intermediate level. The natural topography provided all the enclosure that was necessary; the land made it inviting to make a bold gesture without cordoning off the surroundings. It would be impossible to see any of their structures from Riverside Drive. An interior nursery school and a community building were buried into the land. The nursery was connected to an outdoor area dedicated to toddlers, where there would be a sandbox and "sculptured climbing mountain." For older kids, there were "slides sculpted from earth."

Kahn and Noguchi made their initial, formal presentation to city officials in January 1962. Kahn's drawings show that he had conceived a series of ramps, making it easier for parents to reach the site with small fry in tow. The ramps also meant that the school could be under a superstructure, with some sort of clerestory lighting or sun-traps. There were triangular layered steps that were reminiscent of the UN playground and mounds that recalled Noguchi's designs for the *Contoured Playground*.

Parks Commissioner Morris and his staff were appalled. Morris wrote a detailed response to one of the sponsoring neighborhood organizations: "The very imaginative design which your people presented to us is in our opinion entirely too expensive in construction, too large in scale and too dramatic in conception to be suitable for neighborhood use by mothers and small children."[22] He then said that he originally had supported the idea of a play area close to Riverside Drive and easily accessible for nearby moms. He said he could not endorse a playground that had the potential to be "an unjustifiable architectural monument" whose appeal would be to tourists and the "avant-garde" who traveled to the still-new Guggenheim Museum.

None of this criticism, which was an early harbinger of Morris's distaste for the amalgam of play and art, deterred the patrons or the artists. As Kahn and Noguchi refined their ideas, they incorporated such things as a play area on the roof of the nursery building and giant slides that sliced through lofty mounds. They specified concrete as the building material. It was early 1963 before the city approved a matching plan for funding, whereby the city would pay half the costs. A private foundation, begun by friends and family of Levy, would underwrite the remainder. Kahn and Noguchi were hired officially at that point.[23] This is one instance where the cost, then estimated at $1 million, did not prevent implementation, although it may have contributed to resentment by the neighborhood families who began to oppose it.

A faction of nearby residents, believing that green space would be destroyed and replaced by massive concrete structures, formed the Riverside Parks and Playgrounds Committee in January 1963. Their objective was to stop the playground by initiating legal action.[24] Even worse, those who disproved the plans took to picketing the private homes of Mrs. Hess and her aunt, Mrs. Max Ascoli. Their residences, miles away at Beekman Place and Gramercy Park South, respectively, further highlighted the patrons' physical distance from Riverside Park. Mrs. Levy, too, had not lived nearby.

Local residents, who did have a valid gripe that outsiders were orchestrating their facility, had had several opportunities to express concerns and wishes to the designers. It is unclear why the neighborhood became so enraged. Their concerns might have been aesthetic, environmental, political, or even racist. Noguchi, in the late 1960s, proclaimed that there had been fear by middle-class neighbors that there would be an onslaught of users from poorer areas.[25] The earliest opposition may have been to embarrass Mayor Robert Wagner, who was known to have endorsed the project.[26] Wagner had had to overrule his own Parks Commissioner, Morris, in order to keep the plans alive. Morris was proving himself to be staunch follower of his predecessor, Robert Moses, who said he didn't need advice because he knew what worked.[27] Morris not only abhorred the Kahn-Noguchi plans, but also had exhibited contempt for the efforts of two hundred architecture students whose playground designs were on display in New York in February 1964.[28]

The protests and ensuing litigation against the Levy project did not infringe on Kahn and Noguchi's work. They continued to revise and enhance their concept, and their version for early 1964 had a big splash in an architectural journal (fig. 2.2). It was described in the New York Times as "A fanciful wonderland for children to be carved and molded out of a slope in Riverside Park."[29] Within a few days, a New York Times editorial heartily endorsed the proposal.[30] The New York Times was impressed that no new structures could be seen on the landscape. Although the project went through several more design stages before it was abandoned in 1966, these were all modifications of the plan that was published in 1964.

The 1964 design was significant for the ways in which it bound together all aspects of the scheme. It was a single, unified composition of bold geometric shapes based on interrelated and interconnected parts. A wall, of varying height, tied all the elements together and created overall unity. Several broad, low stairways provided ample space for climbing and jumping but, even more importantly, demonstrated that there was no dictated way to enter the site. This amalgamation of events, linked by time and space, was breakthrough for playground development.

A typical Kahn composition of dynamic parts that push and shove themselves in a centrifugal way, the plans contain a series of rooms for indoor play. These are nestled into the ground, pierced by light wells, and covered by grass. The interior and exterior area conformed to Kahn's attention to creating areas for specific human interactions. The many angles seemed perfect for that, as did the way that all of the earth and ramps were intertwined together. Mounds and pyramids, frequently truncated at the top, were dedicated to climbing, exploring, and sliding. There was a shallow pool for water play.

The two designers had merged, but not necessarily balanced, Kahn's interests in monumentality and interdependent but finite spaces with Noguchi's demands for sensory exploration of play. It does appear that Noguchi was correct in complaining in late 1964 that the architecture dominated the whole. Noguchi's complaints were more than egotistical rantings; they carried an important warning. He argued that unless there were something that was an exact alternative to play equipment, then the city would substitute some piece from its stockpile.[31]

Later drawings show that Kahn seems to have allowed more room for Noguchi's ideas (fig. 2.3). There were more varied shapes and many circular holes that punched openings into walls. The geometric purity would have appealed to Kahn and the additional climbing possibilities would have suited Noguchi. This gave the project a less daunting look. Even though the

PROGRESSIVE ARCHITECTURE MARCH 1964

NEWS REPORT

Architecture's Monthly News Digest of Buildings and Projects, Personalities, New Products

Photo: Louis Checkman

Design of neighborhood park by Kahn and Noguchi utilizes natural earth forms to create dramatic landscape for children.

67	PARKLIKE PLAYGROUND FOR MANHATTAN	72	STUDENTS DESIGN SYNAGOGUES AT PRATT
68	ANTA AUDITORIUM MAKES DEBUT	84	WASHINGTON/FINANCIAL NEWS
69	SAN FRANCISCO CATHEDRAL UNVEILED	91	PRODUCTS: PNEUMATIC SYSTEM
70	BOSTON ARCHITECTURAL CENTER WINNER	98	MANUFACTURERS' DATA

Fig. 2.2 "News Report," *Progressive Architecture* (March 1964). This photo shows the status of Kahn and Noguchi's design in early 1964.

Fig. 2.3 Louis I. Kahn, sketch for Adele R. Levy Playground (ca. 1966), New York City. Courtesy of the Louis I. Kahn Collection, University of Pennsylvania and Pennsylvania Historical and Museum Commission.

playground called for construction in hard materials and things such as tunnels and slides were fixed, there is every reason to believe that Kahn sought to embrace variety for children who would play here. He reasoned that "play must be free and uninhibited, spaces to be discovered with shapes not imitative of nature yet unrestrained in their making."[32] Echoing Tom Hess's earlier defense of the UN playground, Kahn was endorsing abstraction as the backbone of creative play. He also may have been alluding to Lady Allen. She made her trip to America in the spring of 1965, giving eighteen speeches in eleven days.[33] It is not known if Kahn met or heard her, but during the time of her visit Kahn did tell landscape architect Karl Linn that Allen was a wonderful woman who had been committed to children.[34] It does appear that Kahn's equation of play and abstracted discovery was derived from her arguments.

The notoriety of the Kahn-Noguchi project continued through 1965 and 1966. The agitators and their lawsuits resulted in more articles in the press. The political machinations gave additional reasons for this project to pop up in the local newspapers. Bids for the playground went out before the November 1965 Election Day that brought in John Lindsay as New York's new mayor. Outgoing mayor Wagner, a close personal friend of Mrs. Levy,[35] arranged to have a public signing of the playground contract on 29 December 1965, just a few days before he left office.[36]

The situation got even trickier after the Lindsay administration came to city hall. During the campaign, Lindsay and Thomas P. F. Hoving, who would become Lindsay's parks commissioner for one year before heading off to lead the Metropolitan Museum of Art, issued a position paper gently suggesting that the playground be placed elsewhere, close to where there were needier beneficiaries.[37] A month and a half after taking office, and while the issue was still in the courts, Lindsay and Hoving declared tepid support for the Levy plan. They were swayed not by the design but by the fact that it was so close to construction.[38] It was April 1966 before a final court decision sided with those against the project and, in effect, ended any hope that the playground could go forward. At that time, at least one supporter of the project blamed Hoving for the project's demise.[39] Mrs. Hess felt some of the culpability should go to the designers, both of whom had been intensely involved with other commitments during the long litigation process.[40]

This crushing end of the project was, of course, a deep sting to both Noguchi and Kahn. For Noguchi, it was further retribution from the city that had already dismissed him several times before. For Kahn, it represented the loss of a major public space. This was a project that had the potential to force its users to discover new activities, things that they had not been able to verbalize but that would emerge from confrontation with the structure. Kahn had campaigned for that type of discovery for over a decade.

THE NEW YORK REBELLION

Noguchi later remarked perceptively: "But the things that do not happen are as valuable as the things that do happen, because the idea is there, and even if you don't do it, somebody else will. And that has happened quite a lot."[41] It was the totality of Kahn and Noguchi's design, evidenced by the intermingling of play with linked spaces and activities, that allowed it to endure in the minds of professionals who had been reading about it during the early 1960s. The heroic geometric forms solidified its image with those who followed. One architect was swift to note that the design would continue to survive in the memory of young architects just receiving commissions.[42] A generation of youthful designers assimilated and refined those concepts even before the Kahn-Noguchi project was concluded officially in October 1966.[43]

In the mid-1960s, New Yorkers Richard Dattner (1937–), an architect, and M. Paul Friedberg (1931–), a landscape architect, worked independently to fashion the total play environments that had been sanctioned by Noguchi and Kahn. Both young artists, Dattner and Friedberg, made New York the locus for some of the most original American playgrounds in the postwar period.[44] Their approach was simple. Both men stressed that playgrounds should comprise linked and integrated pieces and spaces. They wanted to challenge children's creativity by departing from the common urban formula of isolated incidents. Observers at the time were quick to connect Dattner and Friedberg to Noguchi's early work and to the recent Kahn-Noguchi plans.[45] Dattner, who has had a fine career designing public buildings, including schools and the impressive Riverbank State Park (1991) in New York City, has steadfastly acknowledged that the Levy playground was indelibly on his mind.[46] Dattner, motivated by existing conditions, later noted:

> The typical New York playground (which is typical of 99 percent of all the playgrounds in the United States) could not be a more hostile environment for children's play if it had been designed for the express purposed of preventing play. Characteristically, it is an unbroken expanse of concrete or asphalt pavement, punctuated by the forlorn presence of metal swings, a slide, and some seesaws. Not only does this design lack any possibility for real play; the most interesting activities are prohibited anyway by signs saying "NO" in huge letters, followed by a list of all the things children like to do.[47]

Friedberg, who also has gone on to have a thriving private practice, one that has included designs for Battery Park City's World Financial Center in the late 1980s, had a similar view of existing playgrounds in the 1960s—to which he added a sense of urgency. Friedberg claimed that there was a pressing safety issue: If children were not engaged on a playground, then they would be finding more interesting things to do in the street or on some unattended abandoned lot. He was backed up by studies that showed kids already preferred experiential play of sand and water over current equipment.[48]

Besides being designers, both Friedberg and Dattner were authors who were able to get their ideas to press quickly. They spread their thinking through well-considered books that became manifestos. Friedberg did not shy away from calling his 1970 book *Play and Interplay: A Manifesto for New Design in Urban Recreational Development.* In Dattner's remarkable book *Design for Play,* published in 1969, he discusses the social function and philosophy of play as well as developmental psychology. He used this book as a vehicle to delve more deeply into the theoretical changes that were affecting play, an unusual stance for the time. His natural curiosity was stirred by his wife, who was completing a doctoral dissertation in clinical psychology, and by the fact that they were about to become parents for the first time. Dattner noted that play, a child's attempt to construct a perfect world, is accomplished through imagination, spontaneity, and socialization. He acknowledged, too, that the research of Piaget had successfully made the connection between play and learning. By explaining Piaget's theories, Dattner became an interpreter who took Piaget's work to the general public, specifically those who were not necessarily trained educators but were individuals interested in structuring play environments.

It is to Dattner's credit that he tackled two thorny issues. One was cost, where he noted that creative experiences were often equated with elevated expenses. He deflated that argument by noting that popular areas became less expensive on a per capita basis because the use increased steeply.[49] The other was disabilities. Dattner was one of the early American proponents of playgrounds for children with handicaps.

Friedberg, too, was clearly in the camp of psychologist Piaget, whose teachings had been reflected in the adventure playground concept. This is apparent when he wrote that a child "learns by doing, and much of what he learns is through play."[50] For Friedberg, the playground was always part of a larger scheme that would be enticing for all ages, including the elderly. His continuing attention to playgrounds that become intergenerational gathering places, without artificial boundaries to wall off children, shows how his views derived from those of van Eyck.

Friedberg's opportunity to utilize some of his principles had occurred even before he published this diatribe. In 1965, with funding from the Astor Foundation, which hoped to decrease juvenile delinquency, Friedberg designed a playground at the heart of the public Jacob Riis Houses (Pomerance & Breines, 1949) on New York's Lower East Side.[51] This partnership between a public institution and a private funder allowed for an extensive and expensive project, one that cost about a million dollars. Designed and executed within a span of ten months, this was Friedberg's "first total play environment."[52] The organizing principle was a series of broad, terraced spaces along a slightly skewed central spine. The section designated specifically for play was at one end. Other areas included a spray pool, an amphitheater, and an elaborate stepped garden. Friedberg was pleased that he had eliminated fencing, something he referred to as a "cage."

The play area, a broad rectangle, was filled with sand. This activated the ground surface, mingling its play dimension with actions taking place upon it (fig. 2.4). Pyramids, mounds, hefty wood blocks, and a tree house sat directly on this constantly changing floor.[53] Much of the playground was con-

Fig. 2.4 M. Paul Friedberg & Associates, view of playground (ca. 1966) at Jacob Riis Houses, New York City. From *Creative Playgrounds and Recreation Centers,* Alfred Ledermann and Alfred Trachsel. Copyright © 1959, 1968 (second edition) by Verlag Gerd Hatje. Reproduced with permission of Greenwood Publishing Group, Inc., Westport, CT.

structed with granite blocks. By projecting some of the stones out from pyramids or mounds, Friedberg provided easy grasping for youngsters. The stone was a neutral color that had the look and feel of permanence. It was a perfect nod to the ambiance of a city. At the same time, Friedberg was hoping to simulate the endless vistas, movements, topography, and textures that were available to children growing up in a rural setting.[54]

Friedberg jammed the granite and wood solids close together. Some had slides embedded into them. Kids could jump or run from one structure to the other. Metal arches straddled the forms from above. Friedberg claimed that the interdependence of all of these objects achieved complex possibilities that were unlike the use of single parts. He maintained that the new combinations would have unexpected and enriching outcomes, that play would now become multidimensional in both literal and figurative ways. Friedberg, invoking the work of Lady Allen, hoped that linked uses could become an analogy for the boundless possibilities that were inherent in an

Adventure Playground.[55] Lady Allen returned the compliment by including the Riis Houses playground in her 1968 book *Planning for Play.*

The importance of the Riis Houses playground was to show what linked play would look like. It demonstrated that generous funding supported play and a broader public space. Surprisingly, neither Noguchi, Kahn, nor any of their supporters on the tony Upper West Side then pointed to this project on the poorer Lower East Side. Timing may explain the lack of attention; Friedberg's success was beginning just as Kahn and Noguchi's playground was winding down. Friedberg's work certainly proved that hard materials and linked spaces could be hospitable to individuals without overwhelming the entire area. It successfully established a series of smaller, more intimate niches that enhanced what previously had been a vast and open wasteland.

Friedberg's arrangement, combining play and adult spaces, welcomed theatrical and music performances during the evenings.[56] Art historian Marisa Angell Brown has noted that the amphitheater had play value when part of it was used as a wading pool, while the playground coaxed theatricality; participants were also actors who performed for their neighbors and peers.[57] Within a few years, Friedberg was able to report that the amphitheater brought together more than a thousand people at night, a respectable number relative to the eight thousand residents of Riis.[58]

Beginning in 1966, the same year the Riis Houses playground was jubilantly dedicated by Lady Bird Johnson, architect Dattner was exploring some of the same themes for another private foundation.[59] The Estee and Joseph Lauder Foundation wanted to make a significant donation to children. The time seemed right because then–Parks Commissioner Hoving, in a less confrontational setting than the Kahn-Noguchi project, was receptive to new ideas.[60] Dattner, then doing other work for the Lauders, became the architect for this commission. As he recalls today, he was in his late twenties, idealistic, and "on top of the world."[61] With hindsight, one can see that the new leadership of the Parks Department blended with active support from prosperous foundations. This infusion of action and money allowed New York City to become the epicenter of innovative playgrounds in the United States.

The Lauders, intelligent clients familiar with events in Europe, suggested some sort of Adventure Playground.[62] Through their Lauder Foundation, the donors also agreed to endow a fund to cover maintenance. Local parents consented to pay for a play supervisor.[63] Dattner, familiar with Lady Allen's accomplishments, sought a way to give permanent form to the Scandinavian concept. He saw fit to name his playground—the first of five he would eventually design in Central Park—the Adventure Playground. The site for this is close to the 67th Street transverse road and right off of Central Park

Fig. 2.5 Richard Dattner, Adventure Playground in Central Park (1966, renovated 1997), New York City. The view is north toward the amphitheater. Author's
photograph, 2003.

West. Dattner, who here elaborated and expanded the work Friedberg had
initiated at the Riis Houses playground, also sought inspiration in the unity
and complexity of the Kahn-Noguchi plans.[64] With a program to accommodate only play, the cost was approximately one-tenth of that at the Riis buildings. Working on the site of an older playground, Dattner retained its footprint, trees, benches, plumbing, and entrances. The location, on the top of
small rise, is filled with mature trees that make this a cool space in which
kids can play for extended periods. Dattner was careful to maintain an entrance nearest the street, a reflection of one of van Eyck's strategies.

Key to Dattner's plan was his belief, informed by Lady Allen, that kids
benefit from chances to experiment and make mistakes, without the direct
interference of adults.[65] He began by emphasizing the lopsided oval con-
tour of the site by boldly placing a serpentine wall around it. This became a
wonderful enclosure, low enough for exploration and climbing along its flat
top (fig. 2.5). Dattner specified sand for the surfaces within the wall. He designed circular granite mounds, a low treehouse, and a pyramid of cobble-
stones from which a slide descended. All these small, intimate areas were
linked further by interior walls, slides, and tunnels. Dattner balanced these
with a single water channel and amphitheater placed furthest from the street

entrance. He designated that space as an area where children would be able to help themselves to paper and paint. By providing for small project-making and by offering many welcoming spaces in which it can occur, Dattner was setting in motion what was becoming known as the "theory of loose parts."[66] Considered an outgrowth of the Adventure Playground movement, this emphasis on giving children a chance to manipulate and alter wood or paint could be accommodated within Dattner's scheme. He also provided panels that interlocked so that kids could build small structures for climbing and hiding.

Like Friedberg, and like van Eyck, Dattner relied on the textures of his materials to give interest. Color, as in the city buildings around it, was muted and neutral. This play space was meant to be an urban treasure, and that is celebrated in its honest, undecorated materials. Dattner's view of community space was inclusive and related to van Eyck's. As a result, the impact of Dattner's Adventure Playground was considerable. It was a hit locally and even regionally. It remains, even today, impressive to note how many walls and steps are available to parents for observing without being intrusive. It is striking that this playground is often crowded; the adjacent tot lot, modified in the late 1980s with up-to-date equipment, is typically quite empty.

This does not mean that Dattner's playground has been continually cherished by all. Residents of the neighborhood articulated concerns in the 1990s. Some caregivers felt that this playground was inherently unsafe. Their biggest grievance was that they could not see the children when they were in the tunnels or some of the other hidden spaces.[67] There was pressure on the city and the nonprofit Central Park Conservancy, which privately funds most park projects. Some neighbors wanted to tear down all of Dattner's Central Park playgrounds and replace them with standard equipment. That almost happened, until other local residents heard that these playgrounds were threatened. They mounted an active campaign to save them and worked with Dattner to arrive at a compromise. A few of their letters reveal how clearly local parents and kids valued his work. One letter, written by someone who had grown up a half-block away from the 67th Street site, noted that sociability among users was what separated this playground from most other experiences in the city.[68] Another letter writer noted that this playground functioned as an extra room, an extension for her children of her own apartment. The same person revealed that she had chosen the neighborhood because of the playground.[69] For a resident of the Upper East Side (across Central Park), Dattner's similar East 72nd Street Playground (Gift of the Louis & Bessie Adler Fund in 1970), was where her four-year-old son "meets his friends, the 'Batboys,' on Thursdays in their

'Bat Cave' to discuss how to rid Gotham City of Evil" and where he meets another friend once a week "to scale the castle fortress to fight the other knights." Amazingly, this four-year-old also played in the same space as his siblings, seven, eight, and eleven years older than he.[70]

Today's users are no less passionate than those in the past. Dattner's Adventure Playground is still a gathering spot for people in the neighborhood, including the elderly. It has become a source of social networking for foreign nannies. Renowned architect Billie Tsien (Tod Williams Billie Tsien & Associates) underlines the longevity of this playground when she notes that her young adult son has never tired of the Dattner playground near their home; he still brings friends there when he returns to Manhattan.[71]

In the end, the city and the Central Park Conservancy, with Dattner's participation, restored all of his playgrounds.[72] Dattner cemented over some of the holes that had annoyed parents so greatly and replaced the large sand areas with safety surfacing. He lowered the pyramids and added some railings where there previously had been none. This rescue has been a victory, not only for the local neighbors, for whom the play losses would have been severe, but also to a sense of history. Expunging Dattner's playgrounds would have erased a chunk of innovation and investment in community that was unique to this place. Unfortunately, that is what has taken place at the Riis Houses, where Friedberg's playground has been obliterated and high fencing now seals off what previously had been public space.

Dattner and Friedberg took different paths in the way each subsequently developed their accomplishments of the 1960s. South Park, in San Francisco, has old equipment that illustrates their approaches (fig.2.6). Dattner made a short detour into the world of manufacturing, designing colorful fiberglass-reinforced polyester "PlayCubes." These could be arranged inventively. The modular units were fourteen-sided cuboctahedrons with circular openings on the flat sides. A PlayCube needed only a small amount of space in order to provide opportunities for climbing, sliding, and crawling through tunnels. Dattner abandoned his commercial effort when these did not sell well in the United States, although the price tag was moderate. In other countries, it was a different story. PlayCubes were very popular abroad. That posed a different threat. They were successful enough to be copied and replicated easily, making it financially impossible for Dattner to continue with his concept.[73]

Friedberg explored further the possibilities of a modular system of sturdy logs and wood decks. Beginning with work for the United States Department of Housing and Urban Development and with an experimental program in New York, he initiated prefabricated equipment that could be erected

Fig. 2.6 South Park, San Francisco. Dattner's *PlayCubes* (left) and Friedberg's *Timberform* structure (right) illustrate the two paths for playgrounds in the late 1970s. Photograph by Robert S. Solomon, 2003.

or taken down easily.[74] The early pieces tried a variety of materials: tubular steel, cables, logs, precast concrete panels. All elements were bolted together and related to each other both functionally and visually. Each playground had some pieces that could be moved by the children or by parks professionals, thereby connecting the construction process to a simulated Adventure Playground experience. These pieces soon became a new standard, the genesis of what has became known as "post-and-deck" or "post-and-platform" construction. Friedberg, too, began a company to adapt this concept to modular pieces made from sturdy logs. He later sold his successful venture to a larger manufacturer.[75]

Now often constructed in combinations of metal and plastic, the post-and-platform playground has become the paradigm for most of today's equipment. It has been the ubiquitous American success story, far removed from the simplicity and elegance of Friedberg's early wood design. It is distressing to see how a fine concept has been eviscerated. There was no way to foretell how this revolutionary concept would be adapted by large-scale manufacturers and eventually debased. It is equally disheartening that when these same producers attempt to make changes, as several have recently tried by including low climbing walls, they tack the newest additions onto the post-and-platform unit without harmoniously integrating the newer and older units.

THE END OF A GOLDEN AGE?

During the enlightened period for playgrounds, the 1960s, architectural journals were exhibiting a refreshing interest in individual pieces of equipment that were just coming to market. *Architectural Forum* dedicated an entire article to "Design for Children."[76] Noting that kids don't have much to say on the topic of play and that psychologists might have too much to offer, the unnamed author argued for pieces that would stimulate imagination and allow kids to mimic adult behavior. Reproducing painter Neil Welliver's playground surface at Yale University's Married Student Housing (Paul Rudolph, 1962), even the author seems not to have grasped that the artist had found a way to transform a surface into an animated play space (fig. 2.7).[77] Welliver, already a well-regarded artist, had used only road enamel to eschew typical play equipment. The floor painting created areas for games and bike riding. The cost was minimal, the aesthetic experience was intense. The same journal, in another issue, alerted readers to a graduate student who was marketing playground equipment based on the geodesic domes that had been promoted by Buckminster Fuller.[78]

The years 1966 to 1968 appear to have been the high point for playgrounds in America. This was the brief time span when the place of playgrounds in the realm of art, itself being shaken up by environmental earthworks that challenged long-standing concepts of permanence, seemed ensured.[79] Ada Louise Huxtable, architecture critic for the *New York Times,* devoted several articles to recent accomplishments in playground design. Dattner's Adventure Playground, which had opened in 1967 (*Architectural Record* showcased them in 1967), would soon be "the single most famous playground in America."[80] Respected industrial designer Michael Lax created a participatory playground exhibition called "Cutout for Play," that occupied the United States Plywood showroom in New York. Combining playground and furniture designs, Lax expected four of his playground designs to be used in a local park in 1968.[81] A piece of playground equipment, the winner in a competition sponsored by the Corcoran Museum School (with matching funding from the National Endowment for the Arts), graced the cover (November/December 1967) of *Art in America* (fig. 2.8). The Corcoran School, in addition to organizing the competition, agreed to install the winning entry on a local playground. The successful artist was sculptor Colin Greenly. His *Wishbone House* was a solid, abstract, and freestanding climber with interior benches for rest and quiet activities.

Fig. 2.7 Neil Welliver, playground floor painting (ca. 1962) at the Married Student Apartments (Paul Rudolph, 1962), Yale University, New Haven, Connecticut. Courtesy Alexandre Gallery, New York.

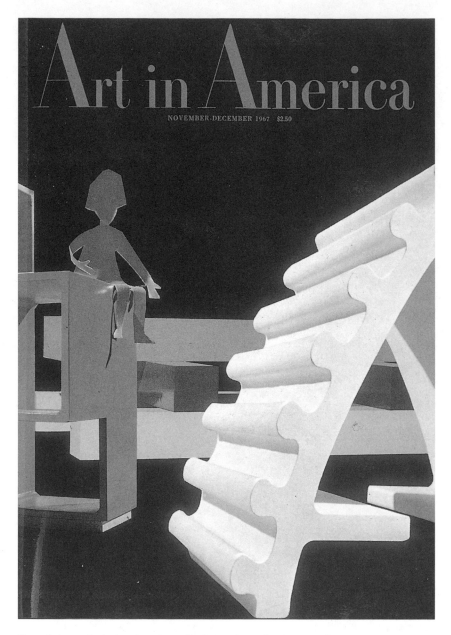

Fig. 2.8 Cover, *Art in America*, November/December 1967. Courtesy of Brant
Publications, Inc. Photograph by Victor Amato.

Author Jay Jacobs, writing the lead article for the *Art in America* cover (November/December 1967), proclaimed a new union, saying that "after generations of neglect, the public playground is suddenly in the midst of a renascence as designers, sculptors, painters and architects strive to create a new world of color, texture and form for toddlers."[82] To prove his point, Jacobs included illustrations of play sculpture by Mark di Suvero, Tony Berlant, Lyman Kipp, and Roger Bolomey. Jacobs also highlighted Pepsi-Cola's sponsorship of a playground composed of industrial equipment and storage containers. Other publications picked up on the joyful mix. The *New York Times* had reported on this last project, giving it a well-illustrated spread in the paper in November 1966. The unidentified newspaper reporter delighted in listing the different ways that mundane materials had been transformed into appropriate play objects. These included the yellow polyethylene cover for a DC-9 engine, converted into a type of sandbox filled with industrial beads rather than sand.[83] Playgrounds were becoming the point where it was not easy to distinguish between high and low art. There was even semantic spillover whereby projects geared primarily for adults, such as British architect Cedric Price's proposed multi-use Fun Palace for London, were tagged with the expression "people's playground" without any sense of condescension.[84]

Jacobs's watershed article cited, too, an example of the Museum of Modern Art's continuing endorsement of playgrounds. This was architect Charles Forberg's Cypress Hills Playground in Brooklyn's tough East New York section. Though complete by May 1967, the playground had been in construction since 1963. The Citizens' Committee for Children, the group with which Mrs. Levy had been so active and to which Audrey Hess continued to dedicate her time, guided the museum's efforts.[85] In 1963, Hess still might have been encouraged by the plans of Kahn and Noguchi. At Cypress Hills, the museum's Junior Council worked with the New York City Housing Authority and the Park Association of New York City to commission three play spaces.[86] There is nothing to indicate that the other two were ever constructed.

The East New York site, an open area surrounded by fifteen seven-story buildings that housed more than fourteen hundred low-income tenants, was perfect for an urban experiment. Forberg believed there was potential to make a difference in how residents perceived their otherwise barren surroundings. His target group was three-to-eight-year-olds; he aimed at providing a space where they could play safely on indestructible materials, without any supervision.[87]

Forberg, who had worked previously for Edward Larabee Barnes but was unfamiliar with his former boss's "saddle slide," placed all of the play elements into a 72-foot-diameter circle.[88] Using no fencing and creating several patterns with asphalt block paving, he accentuated ideas that van Eyck had employed on a smaller scale (fig. 2.9). Forberg tried to offer varied experiences. There was a maze formed by vertical, 7-foot-high cast-concrete slabs. These had variable widths and were not set uniformly apart, making it possible for children to have a continuing sense of discovery. There were also three circular enclosures: one slightly banked for water play; one for a tower and slide; and one for a series of concrete half-cylinders for both climbing and hiding. A centralized spherical lighting fixture illuminated the entire site. This lighting devise accentuated the sculptural aspect of the playground, especially when seen from the nearby apartments.[89] Attention to lighting was a useful addition. In the 1940s, there had been discussion about the need to provide lighting on playgrounds but Forberg seems to have exaggerated the possibilities, making lighting critical to his scheme.[90] The museum believed that this space was an ideal spot for children during the day and a gathering place for adults at night. They were so positive of its success that they retained the concrete fabrication forms in order to replicate them inexpensively on future sites.

Architect Forberg, indicating that nothing was movable, placed himself counter to most contemporary views on how children could affect their en-

Fig. 2.9 Charles Forberg Associates, view of Cypress Hills Playground (1967), Brooklyn, New York. From *Creative Playgrounds and Recreation Centers*, Alfred Ledermann and Alfred Trachsel. Copyright © 1959, 1968 (second edition) by Verlag Gerd Hatje. Reproduced with permission of Greenwood Publishing Group, Inc., Westport, CT.

vironment. He believed that children would be encouraged to move throughout what he hoped would be "rich and varied spaces." He envisioned abstraction as the means through which kids could make their own choices.[91] Forberg was driven by dedicated aesthetic consideration, something he refined in the house he designed for fabric innovator Jack Lenor Larsen in the 1980s (Longhouse Reserve, East Hampton, New York), and a belief that children need to have action and fantasy in their activities. While his solution now appears to have been an unforgiving hardscape, it did attempt to provide architectural significance for both children and adults. Like Friedberg's playground at the Riis House, Forberg's innovation has been replaced by standard equipment.

The 1967 *Art in America* article and the pieces featured in it invoked optimism and faith in individual creativity. Along with the second English edition of Ledermann and Trachsel's book *Creative Playgrounds and Recreation Centers,* which appeared in 1968, the *Art in America* piece appeared to be identifying a vital role for artists as playground designers. Author Jacobs made a strong case for the acceptance of abstraction as an appropriate language for playgrounds by including only one figurative interpretation in his article. This was José de Creeft's *Alice in Wonderland* in Central Park, a literal interpretation of Alice and the best-known characters from the Alice tales (fig. 2.10). Jacobs went out of his way to castigate it, citing it as an example of how it was sometimes a mistake to have a sculptor design a playground. The author made a point of claiming that the statue was slippery, hot in summer, cold in winter, and filled with dangerous "spiky protuberances." All of these complaints seem to be secondary to his conclusion that "the whole lamentable enterprise is at once too literal to stimulate the imagination and too 'unreadable' for a literal piece."[92] Jacobs' remarks signal that he was judging this sculpture on aesthetic merits more than on its utilitarian value for play. Jacobs found *Alice* unacceptable because it was figurative with an emphasis on detailed representation. He could not condone its overt realism. Both the photo that Jacobs included and observation today tell a different story, indicating that this sculpture remains a favorite for small kids and has been since its arrival in Central Park in 1960.[93] In spite of its figurative presence, *Alice* is nondirectional and unauthoritarian. *Alice* shares these characteristics with abstraction, a possible reason for its enduring attraction.

Rather than pointing toward a glorious future, which did not materialize, the writings of the 1960s can now be seen to underscore a peak that would soon decline. On three fronts, the zenith already had passed. Creative Playthings was, sadly, the source of one retreat. Once the pioneer and un-

Fig. 2.10 José de Creeft, *Alice in Wonderland, Margarita Delacorte Memorial* (1959), Central Park, New York City. Given to the city in 1960, this sculpture attracts children because of its easy accessibility, varied textures, and different hiding and climbing spaces. Author's photograph, 2003.

abashed supporter of abstraction, Creative Playthings became more conservative. In 1963, perhaps preparing for the sale of the company, they began to introduce playground equipment that was intentionally "realistic." Their new items, which included a "firehouse" and a "stage coach," were added to a line that still contained prize winners from the 1954 Museum of Modern Art show. To a viewer today, these new additions still might be considered abstracted versions of a firehouse or stage coach. But they were clearly a step back from nonrepresentational concepts. Co-founder Bernard Barenholtz declared that there needed to be " a happy balance between the realistic and the abstract." Claiming that some children warmed to "structured" equipment more than to abstract designs, Barenholtz seemed to admit that the earlier forays had not been a total success.[94]

Also in the 1960s, a small European backlash emerged against the alliance between artists and play. Ledermann and Trachsel, the Swiss authors who wrote the initial definitive book on playgrounds, were expressing some hesitation. They suggested that the Egon Møller-Nielsen sculptural playgrounds might have had more appeal to adult sensitivities than to those of children.[95]

Negative prophetic news was coming quietly out of central New Jersey and Philadelphia, too. Joe Brown was continuing his lecturing, speaking out on a variety of play-related issues. Reiterating things he had said earlier, his tone became more bitter. He bemoaned the fact that playgrounds had become annoyingly safe; he railed against those who feared lawsuits; he lambasted recreation commissions who bought equipment from catalogs without questioning whether better pieces were available from other sources; and he belittled toy manufacturers who were reluctant to introduce anything different from items that had already proved successful.[96] Similar rantings come from progressive educators today.

Strange things had begun to happen to Brown in 1965. At first, there had appeared to be a positive purchase: the Philadelphia Art Commission approved a Brown playground sculpture in January 1965.[97] This was an important event for Brown and for the development of playgrounds. His playground was being considered sculpture, to be paid for by a local Percent for Art clause, one of the first in the country.[98] Some final vindication appeared to be in store for him. Brown's luck failed him the following year, when the city determined that a playground could not be a piece of art. This pronouncement, in 1966, can now be considered a moment when the distinction between playgrounds and art began to take hold, when the gulf between them began to be imprinted on public consciousness—something from which it has been hard to recover.

Change occurred. A few architects and sculptors who produced unique work or adaptations of manufactured examples over the next two decades often were confronted by cries that art and play could not mix, an attitude that widened and signified a growing gulf.[99] The term "designer playground," used first as a neutral term in the 1970s, began to appear in an increasingly derogatory usage. This was further indication that these two terms conjoined were considered an oxymoron.

It is fitting that Columbus, Indiana, the small company town that has been a patron for contemporary architects since the late 1950s, had a playground that differed from most others of the 1970s. By supporting excellent design, the foundation arm of Cummins Engine Company, the largest employer in Columbus, hoped to improve the physical plant and daily lives of local citizens.[100] Cesar Pelli (1926–), who was born in Argentina and had worked for ten years for Eero Saarinen, designed the town's first downtown mall. During this part of Pelli's career (1968–1976), he was working for Gruen Associates. The Gruen firm, in Los Angeles, already had positioned itself as a leader in regional shopping centers and had pioneered the mix of commerce with children's activities. Gruen came into Columbus when the town was searching for a way to revitalize the local shopping district. The Columbus Redevelopment Agency was able to use some federal funding to build what was hoped would become a hub for retail activity.[101]

Columbus's indoor mall (1972) is a place for unexpected rewards. Set within a block of bronze tinted glass, this shopping center differs from common suburban models. This is a building close to a street, brought up to the sidewalk, from which there is direct entrance. Today, run-down and named simply the Commons, it is hard to recognize how imaginative these spaces first had been. The front third of the building, the part of greatest width and double height, is a publicly owned area. A gift from the J. Irwin Miller family, long identified with Cummins's leadership, this section was intended for performances, exhibitions, and public meetings. Pelli was asked to construct a living room for the town, something he accomplished by forming a series of rounded areas for sitting and a meeting place that focused on Jean Tinguely's sculpture *Chaos*.

Pelli located the playground in the public zone. The activity scheme makes clear that Pelli reserved a large space for kids and that he envisioned a playground capable of providing an outdoor extension in good weather (fig. 2.11). Separated by glass and the entrance, the interior and exterior play areas keep a connection to the street. On the interior, there are nearby snack bars and steps on which parents may sit and observe. This sets up a core for families. Complete with carpet-covered mounds that have tunnels and an

Fig. 2.11 Cesar Pelli for Gruen Associates, activity plan (ca. 1972) for the play area of the Commons, Columbus, Indiana. Courtesy of Gruen Associates.

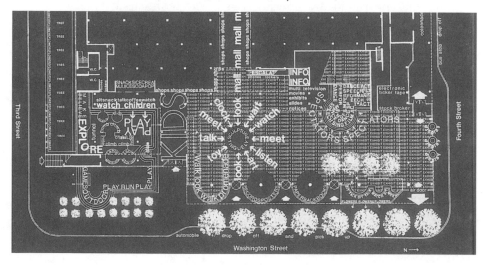

Fig. 2.12 Cesar Pelli for Gruen Associates, playground (1972) at the Commons, Columbus, Indiana. Although the mall is largely vacant, the playground still attracts a large number of families. Author's photograph, 2003.

embedded slide, the playground looks back to some of Kahn and Noguchi's concepts. To these, Pelli added adaptations of ready-made equipment.[102] He included a large vertical climbing apparatus enclosed by a red steel cage, a metal sliding tube, and a bright horizontal fiberglass "playtank."[103] Pelli positioned some equipment along an embankment, thereby assuring that there would be several means of access. Kids still love to run up and down that gentle slope (fig. 2.12).

For three decades, while the mall has gone through various stages of success and decline, the playground has remained a hub of the town. As an area that has combined play with nearby food counters for over thirty years, it may have set a precedent that was taken up later by the fast-food chains with marketing motivations. Not hesitant to use public spaces to attract shoppers, this mall has used the playground to establish an indoor heart during the town's cold Indiana winters. Jammed on any day that school is not in session, the playground provides a large, safe environment where children, including tots and young teens, are comfortable together.

The town of Columbus, through the Irwin Management Company, has supported the play aspects of this venture steadfastly. When it first opened, the playground did attract as many as two lawsuits a week; but the management company has found ways to make the play space safer by making small, sensible adjustments to Pelli's work. They have removed only one piece of equipment. They did add extra bars to the climbing contraption so that bodies could not fall through. Less urgently, the management company has replaced the carpet many times after it has been worn down by active kids. With so few modifications, the integrity of the original playground has been maintained. The management company deserves praise for finding ways to retain the playground without ditching its concept or equipment.

At the time the Columbus facility was being completed, in the mid-1970s, the outlook for playgrounds was changing. There were, for instance, sufficient resources and encouragement for parents who wanted to create their own wood playgrounds.[104] Parallel developments, which were even more widespread, were locally organized and community-built facilities. Parents transformed schoolyards with railroad ties, tires, cable spools, and old doors and boats. Jeremy Joan Hewes's 1975 book *Build Your Own Playground!* showcased Jay Beckwith's designs on the West Coast. Beckwith, who absorbed and expanded many of Friedberg and Dattner's innovations, brought delightful designs of "ramps, tunnels, bridges, ladders" to eager participants.[105] This "do-it-yourself" attitude, prevalent in other aspects of building and home decorating, may have contributed to America's general distrust of professional designers.

ALTERNATIVE APPROACHES

The "do-it-yourself" movement was just one factor affecting other alternative playgrounds that began to appear on the West Coast in the 1970s. In contrast to the early Dattner and Friedberg projects in the East, these were more informal, variable, and less expensive. They added an environmental component to the consideration of play. They also opened the possibility that playgrounds of the future might be constructed without traditional equipment. It is likely that the San Francisco–East Bay modernist architectural tradition, characterized by sensible problem solving using local materials (along with the moderate climate and sympathy to the prevailing counterculture), is what informed creation of two unusual projects in Berkeley: the Environmental Yard and one of America's few enduring Adventure Playgrounds.

The Yard was launched first. Parents and children, working with the architect Robin Moore and educator Herbert Wong, transformed the 1.5-acre asphalt lot at Washington Elementary School into the Environmental Yard. Currently a public school and then a laboratory for the University of California where Moore was teaching, the site is a few blocks west of Berkeley's central business district. Moore and Wong's self-propelled mission was to recapture the ecology that might have inhabited this spot before it had been obliterated by asphalt surface. An even bigger goal, in addition to remedying the constant bickering caused by children not having enough to do on an empty schoolyard, was to prepare the teachers and students for further educational reform. Moore and Wong attempted to stimulate more creative, productive, and cooperative play, thereby achieving a site that could be mined by teachers for curricular initiatives. Inherent in their undertaking was a firm belief that different children learn differently. Their enthrallment with nature as an implement for learning and improvement was a legacy of educational reform found in Germany during the Weimar Republic.[106]

Moore has written that his educational views were similar to the writings of Joseph Chilton Pearce in the 1970s. Pearce had argued for direct sensorimotor experiences that would allow a child to mature intellectually by passing from known occurrences to grappling with unpredictable ones.[107] Pearce's views reflected Lev Vygotsky's early twentieth-century writings. Moore and Wong also were impressed by a healthy but realistic nostalgia for the past. They noted that adults had great childhood memories of "dirt, water, vegetation, and animals, rather than equipment made of invariant synthetic materials."[108]

Local events cannot be ignored. Everyone in Berkeley, and the rest of America, was familiar with the ongoing (and even violent) struggle in the late 1960s between the University of California and local residents. Many who lived near the university wanted to revitalize the land that became known as "People's Park." The Yard was a sublimation of the best attempts to keep People's Park as a community-initiated garden and open space.

Transformation of the Yard began in 1971 and, continuing throughout the decade, presented children with a series of evolving experiences based on nature (fig. 2.13). Local plants and animals flourished. Kids responded positively to the streams, ponds, garden, and waterfall that emerged out of the old school grounds. These lush surroundings guided them into cooperative play and sensory exploration of nature, and served as the basis of an interdisciplinary curriculum. Some of the instruction centered on weather, mapping, or exploring mathematical concepts in the environment. Moore has noted that children learned by making choices, taking chances, making mistakes.[109] This was a powerful learning tool. At the same time, the Yard did not neglect more traditional playground activities. There were tried and true elements, such as a "ballwall," a kickball square, a basketball court, and climbing and jumping equipment, as well as quiet areas for "meeting." Most significantly, the Yard was never locked, making it available to the community at any time.

Fig. 2.13 "Before" (pre-1971) (A) and "after" (post 1971) (B) views of the Environmental Yard at Washington Elementary School, Berkeley, California. After recent seismic retrofitting, the current condition of the school is now closer to this "before" image. Courtesy of Robin C. Moore.

The presence of the Yard remains strong, even though it was altered irreparably in the 1990s when the school was retrofitted with seismic improvements. The current principal, Rita Kimball, is a dynamic leader who arrived after the Yard had been dismantled. She has been so swayed by its objectives that she has sought ways to revitalize its intent. Noting that the Yard might be gone but that she was not going to abandon her hopes for what it meant for education, she has started several programs that have captured its spirit.[110] Using a state nutrition grant, she hired a gardener and a cook. These people, neither of whom has teacher certification, bring intense expertise in their fields into the classroom, where they are supervised by a science teacher. All three adults have worked with the students to nurture a dense, thriving garden. It has become a new focal point of the outdoors, a vibrant hub of activity. The garden has become synonymous with education grounded in the magical intersection of gardening, cooking, and science. This has spawned a novel curriculum that captures the essence of how children learn and, at the same time, pays homage to the Yard that used to exist on the same spot.

While long-time residents of Berkeley lament the loss of the Yard, they do take heart that the city's Adventure Playground has had a more durable existence. Opened in 1979 on 1 acre of land at the municipal marina (Shorebird Park), this facility continues to thrive. A few yards from the bay and with a spectacular view of San Francisco, it has always been an engaging place. This idyllic setting removed the playground from the residential and commercial areas of the city, a situation recently remedied by a footbridge that spans the nearby freeway and offers a pedestrian link between the waterfront and the other sections of town. The footbridge allows older kids, the eight- to twelve-year-olds, some of whom come from the less prosperous areas of Berkeley, to arrive on their bikes.[111]

At the time of its inauguration, this was one of fifteen Adventure Playgrounds in the United States (fig. 2.14).[112] Almost all of the others were on the outskirts of small cities and operated only in the summer. Most of these are gone today. Getting any of these facilities to catch on in America had been a great struggle because of safety concerns. Even before the Berkeley playground was up and running, one author noted that European successes and lack of accidents had not changed the American insurance industry's view that these were unsafe ventures.[113] Another writer noted that "the problem of liability in the event of accidents is the main obstacle . . . in the USA, and this in spite of the fact that almost everywhere [where there is an Adventure Playground] the rate of accidents has proved to be less than in traditional playgrounds."[114] Americans did not heed Lady Allen, the strong advocate of adventure play, who reported in the mid-1970s that no parent in Britain had ever sued an Adventure Playground. That was after more than twenty years of operation.[115] Landscape critic Clare Cooper noted earlier in the 1970s that the "American legal profession has instilled into public officials and citizens such a fear of being sued that this is the first objection brought up when discussing the concept."[116] It did not help that the legal profession began to see its numbers explode, starting with that same decade.[117]

Fig. 2.14 Adventure Playground, Berkeley, California. Author's photograph, 2001.

Berkeley's Adventure Playground has not been an exception when it comes to a sound safety record. Berkeley officials have long maintained that the Adventure Playground gives the illusion of danger while offering a safe space for personal development. Speed of creation is one of many advantages to this type of playground. The Berkeley Adventure site was up and running less than two months after it was approved by the city elders.[118]

Cost was another plus: the price tag was $15,000, of which approximately one-third went for fencing; most of the remaining money was spent on staffing.[119] Even though the materials were donated, the startup costs were actually high for this type of facility. When Huntington Beach, California, opened its Adventure Playground in 1974, the city relied heavily on donations and had to make only a small cash outlay for additional materials for their 3-acre site.

The smooth-working and varied activities of Berkeley's "junk playground" are impressive today. Youngsters, working with minimal supervision, direct their individual and cooperative activity toward fantastic creations and settings. An early advertisement, which proclaimed that the playground would be a place where children could "build, plant, slide & climb," can now be seen to have been accurate.[120] The Adventure Playground attracts kids of a wide range of ages, ethnicities, and socioeconomic backgrounds.[121] This park has been eminently successful in holding the interest of seven- to twelve-year-olds, one of the hardest age groups to animate. Some kids come occasionally; others come on an almost daily basis. There is no admission charge, unless a parent leaves the surrounding area. After more than two decades of activity, there are many freestanding huts, towers, and even a zip-line trolley. It would be easy for kids to use this site as a traditional playground because so much is already constructed. The staff has cleverly avoided that problem. Their solution has been to insist that the children "earn" their tools and paintbrushes. Kids do this by collecting leftover scraps of materials and nails from around the site. For the younger kids, this is fun in its own right. For older children, the fluidity of the day means that no project is every completely finished and it is not possible for them to use "safe" equipment in unintended and hazardous ways.

BIG BUSINESS AND SAFETY

CBS purchased Creative Playthings in 1966. This acquisition signaled the arrival of corporate binge-buying in the lucrative field of educational products for children.[122] By the time the Berkeley Adventure Playground opened, the concept of a playground had changed. This makes the Berkeley experiment even more astounding. The largest playground companies, like today's banks and airlines, began buying the smaller competitors and consolidating their strength. Berkeley's Environmental Yard and Adventure Playground both may have blossomed as a reaction to the plethora of equipment that was showing up in the marketplace. Nationwide, mass-produced items were beginning to fill the advertisement slots of landscape magazines. At least four sizable companies were doing this type of production by the late 1970s. The most popular items were post-and-platform combinations of heavy wood logs. The equipment was sturdy, and the modular arrangements were varied. The same companies sold netting systems that had been imported from Europe. The latter disappeared from the advertisements of American manufacturers by the mid-1980s. There were some advertisements, too, for free-form sculptural playground pieces made of concrete. These, also, began to disappear by the late 1970s. In the early 1980s, wooden post-and-platform structures were augmented with metal modules. Wood pieces of the 1960s had not endured well and began to splinter and crack. Soon plastics, especially polyethylene slides, became a dominant fixture on playgrounds. Metal and plastic products became increasingly standardized.

The 1970s were marked by escalation of insurance costs and obsession about safety. This did not spring out of the blue. Safety considerations, which always had been an undercurrent in playground design, began to dominate how play was allowed to occur. As early as 1965, when Lady Allen made her two-week tour of American playgrounds, she called them "an administrator's heaven and a child's hell." These had been constructed for low cost and easy maintenance. She remarked that Americans "seem to be terrified of risks—they are dogged by fear of insurance claims resulting from accidents in public playgrounds. I've never seen anything like it."[123] And that was 1965!

Urban and suburban governments across the country were complaining, in the 1970s, that their general liability insurance rates were rising dramatically. The insurance companies were quick to blame an upsurge in lawsuits and increasingly generous awards to plaintiffs.[124] The problem certainly was exacerbated by the question of culpability. A 1975 New York State Court of Appeals decision, for example, held the New York City Board of Education responsible for an injury incurred on school property when school was not in session. Some New York City co-op apartments closed down (or even refused to consider) playgrounds in their courtyard spaces in 1980. Their governing boards often feared lawsuits, rising costs for liability insurance, and declining property values if a building were perceived as unsafe or unsavory.[125] Later in the decade, further concerns about liability and rising insurance costs began to have a profound effect on cities. The Chicago Park District, following a $9.6 million injury settlement, removed spiral slides, high monkey bars, and merry-go-rounds from its sites. New York City eliminated its see-saws. Government bodies, once believed to be immune from suits because of the doctrine of sovereign immunity, began to find themselves being held responsible. Dallas and many other cities decided to self-insure after they found that insurance companies demanded exorbitant premiums. For that Texas city, the premium would have been greater than the total of all past claims.[126]

Reports festered, in the 1980s, that municipalities had closed playgrounds when liability insurance became too expensive or was unavailable.[127] The interdependence between the insurance industry and standardized equipment manufacturers is best summed up by the situation in a suburb of St. Louis in 1989. The town of Manchester purchased new equipment because it would be safer and therefore would reduce the cost of the town's liability insurance. There had been two bids besides the winning one, but the "city's insurance advisers"—not anyone who knew anything about play or playgrounds—had disqualified them on safety grounds.[128]

Safety took on another dimension when Americans obsessed about it for its own sake, not solely because of its connection to insurance or liability problems. Fixations flourished, assisted by early computer data of the 1970s. The National Electronic Injury Surveillance System, begun in 1971, set a trajectory that was hard to curtail. America's Consumer Product Safety Act went into effect in 1972. By the summer of 1973, when the Consumer Product Safety Commission (CPSC) had been running for only a month, this agency targeted certain areas that needed guidelines in order to protect consumers.[129] Using data from computers at 119 emergency rooms, the CPSC placed playground equipment high on its attack list. Although it directed its attention first toward residential equipment, the commission soon scrutinized public sites. Their efforts culminated in 1981, when the CPSC published guidelines for public playgrounds (updated several times).[130]

Historian Lizabeth Cohen has argued that the consumer movement, which she believes flourished in the late 1960s and early 1970s, has since been eclipsed by privatization and deregulation.[131] That has not been true when it has come to playgrounds. There has been no decline in consumer advocacy. Consumer stalwarts took on playgrounds with zeal, perhaps because other areas of disapproval had dried up. In the mid-1970s, the National Recreation and Park Association (NRPA) made its own investigation of injuries on playground equipment at public sites. This resulted in a Proposed Safety Standard for Public Playground Equipment, a guideline that came about in 1976. Since 1991, NRPA has sponsored the National Playground Safety Institute, which runs two-day courses and a half-day exam. Institutes are held throughout the country. Successful course graduates become Certified Playground Safety Inspectors who can conduct safety audits; in some states they have the power to suspend any project that involves play. An individual fresh out of a certification program can hold up a project on which a well-trained architect or landscape architect has labored for months.

It is not uncommon for safety inspectors to ax one aspect of a design only to replace it with something that meets their safety requirements yet is potentially even more dangerous than what was specified originally. Playground consultants, a variation of inspector status, represent a vocation that did not exist in the 1950s. Some offer fine services and others feed on the litigiousness of America by specializing in court appearances.

In 1993, the American Society for Testing and Materials (ASTM), an organization that has been in existence since 1898, weighed in with its own standards for public playground equipment; these, too, have had several revisions and updates. Independently, the International Play Equipment Manufacturers Association (IPEMA) has its own set of guidelines. The American Association for Leisure and Recreation has additional booklets and checklists regarding safety.

None of these standards, guidelines, suggestions, or imperatives has ever become federal law, although a few states have started to adopt some of them. Generally, government sanctification has not been needed; restraints have acquired that power merely by existing. Parks commissions or school boards will always choose equipment that purportedly meets the requirements of the testing groups. Their insurance agents and lawyers wouldn't want it any other way. By following guidelines, an individual designer is best protected against future lawsuits and the possibility of liability. Over a decade ago, one reporter noted that government officials followed the CPSC guidelines because they believed the rules "would be cited in any suit over an accident on outdated equipment."[132] The only national rules pertain to the Americans with Disabilities Act (ADA), passed in 1990. This well-intended legislation has spawned its own guidelines in 1991 and a "Final Rule" on playgrounds in 2000. These have contributed an additional layer of requirements that includes ramps and transfer stations.

On first glance, it appears that the guidelines make useful suggestions, including recommendations on distances between pieces of equipment, surfacing, height of equipment, and railings. A closer look shows that they have obliterated any risk and even have tended to eliminate cooperation. The homogenization of playground design, something that makes use of bland and interchangeable equipment, begins to come into focus. The current CPSC guideline for preschoolers, for instance, suggests a list of items to omit that includes the following: freestanding arch climbers (goodby van Eyck), overhead rings, any slide with more than one turn, log rolls, see-saws, and vertical sliding poles. There should be guardrails for anything over 20 inches off the ground and a full barrier for any platform more than 30 inches from the ground surfacing.

Effects of the ADA and the voluntary guidelines can be seen in what is not on today's local playground. The see-saw and the high slide are gone. By the mid-1990s, Chicago was "monkey-bar free" and Seattle had just about unburdened itself from any jungle gyms.[133] Two decades earlier, in the 1970s, New York City decided to ban sandboxes unless a community specifically requested them and agreed to maintain them.[134] Chicago started to remove sandboxes in the 1980s.[135] Sand removal is, perhaps, the most consequential of all remedies. The ratio of pleasure to cost is extremely high for any sand area. Roger Hart, co-director of the Children's Environments Research Group, has said that "sand enables children, at relatively low cost, to create their own environments."[136] Sand allows kids to work together or solo to mold, dig, and sift. They can explore, destroy, or create. They can get dirty!! Educators believe that kids are not getting muddy anymore and that the detergent companies are worried by the trend.[137] The teachers may have spotted something that alarmingly reflects the sterility of how kids are permitted to have fun.

WHAT IS WRONG WITH THE PICTURE?

Concerns about safety, combined with panic about liability and insurance, have created demand for post-and-platform models and all of their derivatives. At least one landscape architect has advised his peers that the use of commercial equipment ensures all safety standards had been satisfied, during a time in which "a designer can potentially be sued for almost anything."[138] These days, an administrator opening a packet of materials from an American playground-equipment manufacturer receives more than a catalog. Reams of material regarding safety accompany each glossy mailing. One of the largest of the companies often includes the Consumer Product Safety Commission's recent handbook. The message is obvious: These manufacturers not only meet but ecstatically and proudly exceed all guidelines. In the past, as art historian Amy Ogata has shown, a company like Creative Playthings tried to sell creativity. Future historians, assessing today's corporate pitch, will have to conclude that the manufacturers of playgrounds were selling unattainable idealism, a totally risk-free world.

So what exactly does this concern yield in terms of play and design? What is the "post-and-platform" experience? Kids can go up or down steps, run across decks, go down slides. Sometimes an additional low climbing apparatus is attached to a deck. That's about it. Small peaked or arched roofs, which usually are supported by high vertical bars, have become a familiar sight on equipment for both the younger and older children. Often, these "posts with roofs" are at the top of slides. Catalogs say that these offer protection from the sun. That's unlikely because kids don't spend much time there. It's more probable that these are a design trick to make the ensemble look taller. Without the roofs, viewers would easily see that most components are close to the ground. The few producers that have tried something different, avoiding the post-and-platform formula, have failed to make a commendable contribution. They have come up with a twirly items and some better designed but equally rigid climbers.

When Americans have attempted to purchase foreign playgrounds, they often find that the hassles are time consuming and costly. European products, often more successful aesthetically and more interesting for play than American examples, are forced to comply with American guidelines when imported. The San Jose Redevelopment Agency is thrilled with its large German net structure, believing that it was worth the aggravation of more than fifty small modifications to make it conform to U.S. standards.[139] Few patrons are willing to go that route.

Accordingly, the American playground is dominated by a "McDonald's model." The playgrounds at McDonald's, and other fast-food outlets, encapsulate the current state of playground design. This corporation, which has purchased equipment for their more than eight thousand indoor and outdoor facilities in the United States, illustrates the most commercial end of product development (fig. 2.15).[140] The company's aggressive marketing is seen in equipment that has taken the post-and-platform model, and then exaggerated it into configurations that appear to be bigger and bolder than anything on a public playground. The tunnels, slides, and decks (now enclosed in bright cubes) have been scaled large and colored outlandishly. This equipment screams out to kids that they should participate. The consequences of these designs go beyond the marketing of fast food and commodification of play. These versions of playgrounds, heightened examples of equipment available in the general marketplace, have become the new standard for America. The post-and-platform paradigm was already the norm; McDonald's has caused consumers to expect similarly shrill examples in their own parks and has set a "standard" that most consumers accept as the only choice available. Tacked on to the side of the restaurant and cordoned off from the parking lot by a menacing fence, this model contributes nothing to a sense that a playground could be connected to the landscape or any natural setting. McDonald's has shown over and over again that today's playground has no real setting. A McDonald's playground contributes nothing to the public sphere: parents eat, kids play, and there is little to make the experience one that is similar for young and old folks. As-

Fig. 2.15 McDonald's playground, Oakland, California. Author's photograph, 2001.

suming the children are safe, adults turn away and concentrate on eating their own french fries.

Kids at McDonald's playgrounds follow the restricted options offered by a post-and-platform ensemble: wait, go up, go across, go down, start all over again. The interactions among young users is limited; there is nothing to do together. The larger the equipment, the longer are the lines to climb up ladders or propel down slides. Opportunities are inadequate for meeting or interacting with peers. Only very small children, those around age three, find the repetition comforting. One art historian has noted that this not only replicates the assembly line actions that cook up the burgers but also trains tiny consumers to follow the McDonald's drill: stand in line, get the goods, consume the product, and get back in line.[141] Kids don't get to make choices, resolve conflicts, or change anything in their environment. To compensate for the curtailed experiences of kids, the manufacturers have incorporated teaching devices into their play equipment. Panels with movable letters offer opportunities to spell. Other panels have numbers for addition and sub-traction exercises. These educational "add-ons" have nothing to do with the ways that kids learn by exploring materials and acting on their own. All of these limitations would be acceptable for a twenty-minute pit stop; the larger problem is that the same equipment and its controlled experiences are repli-cated on playgrounds all over the United States.

Today's playgrounds irritate many of the more thoughtful people who care about how children learn. Several educators have argued that this to-tally safe environment "lacks most of the important elements necessary for meaningful play. These include variety, complexity, challenge, risk, flexibil-ity, and adaptability."[142] Jennie Lindon, who has asked if kids are "Too Safe for Their Own Good?" has noted that children "need opportunities to take acceptable risks in an environment that encourages them to push against the boundaries of their current abilities, to stretch their skills and confi-dence."[143] Furthermore, she maintains that "acceptable levels of risk, with supportive adult behavior, can enable children to learn."[144] Jim Greenman adds to this thesis. He notes that in "a sterile, padded world with insuffi-cient stimulation or challenge, humans either turn themselves off or turn to and on each other for stimulation." Greenman goes on to say that kids tend to withdraw and regress; some become hostile to their peers; others do outrageous acts just to be noticed until "the potential for harm is not re-duced, only the source of harm is redirected."[145] Greenman, who believes that we already live in a "bubble boy" world, further laments the fact that teachers and parents often prefer indoor equipment that is not related to any outdoor exploration or experience with nature.[146] His observation smacks of the barren resources of playgrounds in the early 1950s.[147] It is no wonder that landscape architect Richard Haag believes that "the current state of playground design is a tragic failure."[148]

Since the 1970s, researchers have been arguing that children need to master their surroundings and then push on their accomplishments until they have achieved something they had not attained before.[149] It is sensible to regret the loss of interesting playgrounds, ones that can be aesthetically noteworthy, educationally challenging, and dangerously inspiring. From the viewpoint of modern art, it is sad. From the perspective of education, it represents a setback. Some have argued that if kids can't find a sense of danger on a controlled playground, then they will certainly seek it in really terrifying places.[150] Others maintain that eliminating risk also gives children the impression that adults are human barriers to satisfying kids' curiosity.[151] Barry Blitt's cartoon "Safety First," on a *New Yorker* cover in August 2003, depicts kids maneuvering bumper cars with inflated airbags. It is a funny image that could just as easily be applied to the playground industry. In that context, fanatical concern about safety seems less humorous.

There is even a future loss to consider. Gregory Stock, a professor at UCLA Medical School who has written extensively on the need for risk taking in the world of technology, has noted how critical risk is for children; it is essential if they are to develop into wise adults.[152] They need to make choices and suffer consequences in order to hone skills of judgment. They also need to know the rewards of risk taking in order to become the next generation of inventors. By denying children confrontation with risk, we not only may be stunting their emotional and educational development but also limiting their abilities to pursue challenging careers. The most important lesson is that Americans need challenging playgrounds to ensure that the future will be populated with adults who have been allowed to experiment with their own skills and opportunities.

Yet, some advocacy groups continue to sound alarms by demanding federal standards. Bowing to overzealous consumer advocacy, one congressman proposed additional money to states that would transform CPSC guidelines into law. The Consumer Federation of America and the national office of Public Interest Research Group have joined together several times to survey the safety status of public playgrounds. After investigating 1,037 playgrounds in 36 states, they announced in 2002 that a majority of these place kids in danger. Their primary gripes were "inadequate surfacing" and equipment that was "more than six feet high." There was no indication of whether the surfacing was appropriate but needed to be deepened or whether there were already safety restraints on the pieces that were far from the ground.

Reports continue to assault parents. It is impossible for an adult to ignore a report that claims the number of hospital visits is increasing for playground injuries. The National Program for Playground Safety (NPPS), begun in 1995 at the University of Northern Iowa, has been a particularly irresponsible zealot.[153] This organization inspires fear by claiming that American playgrounds are only safe enough to be rated "C+" in its own grading survey. Using CPSC data to proclaim that a child is injured every 2.5 minutes severely enough on a playground to require emergency-room care, the NPPS tracks playground injuries for individuals up to *fourteen* years of age. It is senseless to base safety decisions on the proclivities of teenagers in today's playgrounds: Teens who are there and injured are using equipment improperly. These statistics fail to recognize that American children, often by age eight or nine, have given up on the playground and either use it inappropriately or seek thrills elsewhere.

The medical profession has reached pragmatic conclusions. A study has shown that, when injuries do occur, they are often the result of poor maintenance of equipment.[154] Design was not a factor. A venerated orthopedic surgeon who has seen many playground injuries has gone even further. He has stated that he never saw a case where the equipment was at fault; injuries occur when kids interact hostilely or act irresponsibly.[155] It turns out that similar analyses, often undertaken by educators, have been available since the mid-1970s and before the stringent guidelines were written. Using data from the 1970s, researchers in 1980 concluded that "playgrounds are not a major safety concern. Accidents, however, do occur and will continue to occur, but most accidents are caused by the operator of the equipment and are not a result of product or design failure."[156] The same report cited surfacing as one area for improvement, a relatively simple request to meet because heavy-duty safety matting had been available since the 1960s. Author and educator Jim Greenman has long maintained that "children are major instruments in their own protection" and that children can do more harm to each other than can any equipment.[157]

One inherent problem is cultural and has to do with Americans' difficulty in assessing risk. It is plausible that the American failure to evaluate risk, guided by the mass media, has resulted in the inability to make a distinction between minor threats and more disastrous ones. Americans find it hard to make a distinction between the chance of a few scratches or stitches and the possibility for mortal injury. Tim Gill, director of the Children's Play Council in Britain, has argued for making a differentiation between the possibility of slight injury, which is acceptable, and the threat of serious injury, which is not.[158] Lack of universal, affordable health care in the United States does raise the stakes of a relatively minor injury for many uninsured families.

Americans have difficulty in distinguishing between immediate threats and distant, less plausible ones. Here are three examples that show how this process is manifest in areas unrelated to play or playgrounds. Researcher David Ropeik has shown that the chances of dying from skin cancer are 1 in 29,500, and the chances of dying of West Nile virus are 1 in 1,000,000; yet during the summer of 2002, 102 newspaper articles about skin malignancies and 2,240 about the mosquito-borne disease were published. His point is that concerns are often misplaced and hysterical, allowing us to ignore real danger and focus on the improbable.[159] On a totally different front, food critic Jeffery Steingarten has observed the difficulty Americans have in evaluating risk when it comes to cheese. Making the case that the risk of infection from raw milk cheese is nonexistent, Steingarten has shown that Americans have tried to ban importation of raw-milk products because they are perceived to be dangerous.[160] The reverse, worry-free extreme is Americans' indulgence in food supplements and vitamin additives. In this case, there are real dangers from a shadowy industry, yet many people again misassess risk and take no precautions. Michael Specter's thoroughly researched and convincing article, "Miracle in a Bottle," has a subtitle that sums up the situation: "Dietary Supplements Are Unregulated, Some are Unsafe—and Americans Can't Get Enough of Them."[161]

It is no wonder that miscalculation of risk has found its way onto the American playground. A sociologist has written about "paranoid parenting," the cultural absorption of fear whereby parents believe they are responsible adults only if they observe their children all the time. Told incessantly to be mindful of lurking dangers and the people who might inhabit the outdooors, these parents often defer trips to public spaces. Going to a playground becomes too exhausting for a parent to contemplate.[162]

Sociology professor Barry Glassner has identified this particularly American phenomenon as a "Culture of Fear," an overdependence on fear that lacks any scientific rigor or underlying philosophy. In his astute book with that same title, Glassner has shown how media and marketers have benefited from campaigns that inflame fear. According to his analysis, profiteers have used erroneous and inflated data about child abduction, school violence, and teen suicide in order to sell newspapers, security devices, private prisons, and medication. Glassner has shown that the public has been manipulated to focus on "misbegotten fears" while ignoring bona fide areas for apprehension and even guilt. He maintains that "by slashing spending on educational, medical, and anti-poverty programs for youths we adults have committed great violence against them. Rather than face up to our collective responsibility we project our violence onto young people themselves, and onto strangers we imagine will attack them."[163] Clearly, the inability to assess risk squarely has contributed to a, perhaps, more serious consequence—our acceptance of fear.

It's not much of a stretch to apply Glassner's critique to the playground world. Avoiding the fact that many kids do not get such things as adequate health care, nutritious meals, or even books at school, advocacy groups have focused on the safety of playgrounds. It is an issue over which they can exercise control and one that meshes with manufacturers' marketing agenda. The playground companies, by emphasizing safety, sell a product that will have to be upgraded continually. There will always be a surfacing material or a slide that will be safer than the previous year's model. Manufacturers implicitly discourage consumers from contacting any individual who could impair the equipment's safety record. The message is clear: Beware of landscape architects, architects, or sculptors because they will adulterate the safety perfection of the manufactured equipment. It is probably not a coincidence that since the 1970s, the American government, feeling that it had to emphasize security over aesthetics and public image, was starting to build its embassies without the artistic vision of well-known architects.[164]

PLAYGROUNDS AND EDUCATIONAL THEORY

Contemporary social theorists argue that all of these safety concerns are a way for parents to retain control of their offspring, the small souls that the adults consider to be helpless.[165] Somewhat similarly, one observer has noted that parents and educators lack faith in children's abilities and resilience.[166] At least one critic has remarked on how today's parents are determined to be the perfect adults with perfect children.[167]

The gulf is now very wide between accepted educational philosophy and the commercial playgrounds in the marketplace.[168] There is a disconnect between variations of classical theory and current practice. This runs counter to the causal relationships that had marked the early and mid-decades of the twentieth century. In the time since Piaget was lauded in the 1960s, other developmental theories have emerged (or become better known) that have broadened an understanding of his findings. Esteemed psychologists working since the mid-twentieth century, such as Jerome Bruner and Brian Sutton-Smith, have built on Piaget's model while adding new perspectives on adaptability and flexibility. Bruner, in particular, has contributed an understanding of how critical narrative is for the way children assess and make sense of their surroundings. In 1976, Bruno Bettelheim published *The Uses*

of Enchantment: The Meaning and Importance of Fairy Tales. This book further advocated for the need of fantasy in children's lives. A look at most of
today's playgrounds, however, shows pitiful few areas where children can
indulge their imagination and support their own storytelling.

One of the most influential theoreticians has been Lev Vygotsky. This
Russian thinker, who died in 1934 but whose work was not widely available
in America until the 1980s, provided theories that are intensely respected
and widely accepted today. Psychologists Kathy Hirsh-Pasek and Roberta
Michnick Golinkoff, whose aptly titled book is *Einstein Never Used Flash Cards:
How Our Children Really Learn—And Why They Need to Play More and Memorize Less,* have stated that "Vygotsky argued that children are at the highest
level of their development when they are at play."[169] Vygotsky valued social
interaction and believed that mixed-age environments were the key to successful learning and play.[170] He explored the notion that children slightly
more advanced than their peers would pull along their cohorts, thereby
forcing unchallenged youngsters to take on activities that they might otherwise avoid. Vygotsky had faith that children would, and should, be sustained
by a continuing sense of accomplishment. Accepting a certain amount of
risk was inherent in his view. American standardized playgrounds restrict
challenge and rarely offer activities where children can master a succession
of skills. There are few ways in which older kids, or even adults, can encourage younger ones.

The practices of the schools in Reggio Emilia have attracted enormous
interest in America. Beginning in the late 1960s, this Italian municipality
has accentuated a process-driven approach. The emphasis is on a curriculum propelled by children's interests and curiosities, creativity in the arts,
and social interactions. The Reggio view was reinforced and expanded in
the 1980s by Howard Gardner's work on multiple intelligences. Gardner
showed how competence can be measured in more than one way, another
theory that would be difficult to accommodate on the "one sizes fits all"
playground. The Reggio objectives, which employ the expressive arts as a
key element, are also hard to accommodate on the typical manufactured
playground.

The most disturbing possibility is that today's ubiquitous equipment *does*
reflect today's education. In this case, it is education driven by ideology and
flawed studies, not by classical theories of how children learn.[171] Independent scholar Gerald W. Bracey takes this one step further. He notes that contemporary practices are not only based on ideology but also are positioning
"public schools for the final knock down" that will replace them with priva-
tized systems and vouchers. No matter what the impetus, American politi-

cians have latched onto the notion that student achievement must always be quantifiable and that teacher efforts have one goal: passing the test. They have endorsed a curriculum driven by scripted lessons and rote learning. Much of today's education has become top-down, rigid, standardized, age-segregated, isolated from meaning, and accepting of only one way to achieve results. Take a look at most American playgrounds, and it is possible to see the physical manifestation of that type of thinking. It's a long way from the National Defense Education Act of 1958. That post-Sputnik infusion of money, which was intended to improve math and science in schools, insisted that there be no federal control of curriculum, administration, or staff. Today's playgrounds are different because our tolerance of government interference is high.

Educator Deborah Meier, a wise voice in the current culture war, takes a dim view of national testing, and advocates for schools that value kids' opinions and allow them to take educational risks. She applauds public schools that grow out of local needs and interests. Meier dismisses fact knowledge and timetables for learning, seeing them as inferior to real mastery, contextual understanding, and less-rigid time constraints. She notes that "most of what life required us to learn happened over time in authentic, natural settings."[172] Meier talks about the importance of intergenerational contact in schools so that children have adult models, not just peer ones. She even writes about "the messy in-betweens required to make schools trustworthy" and viable.[173] Although she applies her expertise to educational policy, she could be describing a van Eyck playground, an Adventure Playground, or the Environmental Yard.

In the 1970s, a growing concern already had surfaced that education was being defined only by book learning. In 1976, the same year that the United Nations proclaimed that 1979 would be the "International Year of the Child," another United Nations conference issued a statement that urged governments to recognize that the "*out of school* life of children is as serious as formal education" and that "play is the child's way of learning about, adapting to, and integrating with his or her environment."[174] Another concern, one that emerged in the 1970s, spotlighted the increasingly passive nature of play. One educator who noted this commented:

> We've developed a weakening [*sic*] Disneyland version of recreation that often involves an admission fee and requires minimum effort, little imagination and ultimately less satisfaction on the child's part. When youngsters had to organize their own games or to devise and improvise their recreation, they gained a lot of strength in the process.[175]

These words, intended as observation and reflection, have become a prophecy. Equipment does not stimulate fantasy or child-initiated actions. Kids and their families are less engaged, because there is no larger context with which to connect. Interchangeable equipment and standardized actions have become both the medium and the message.

The remainder of this book looks for inspiration from the people who are not intimidated by safety guidelines and current educational practices but who are trying to free contemporary playgrounds from all of the current constraints. Educator Theodore Sizer has written that the best schools have an individuality, a particularity that he calls a "sense of place." This goal not only reflects van Eyck's imperative but provides a guide for today's best playgrounds.[176]

PART II
THE PRESENT

CHAPTER 3

Patrons

Playground patronage recently has ignited intense community use of urban space and given a robust focus to neighborhoods and local institutions. In a few instances, the playground has lured visitors to unusual destinations. This is not a revolutionary phenomenon. Parks departments and school boards, the early champions of playgrounds, were joined in the 1950s by museums such as the Museum of Modern Art and private philanthropies such as the Astor Foundation. That mix has expanded during the past twenty years. Now a variety of other institutions, including some that have quasi-governmental roles or are for-profit, have joined the older organizations in commissioning areas for play. The roster of innovators includes conservation funds, social service agencies, and commercial day-care centers that did not even exist several decades ago. As services for children accelerate, including special law centers to handle abuse cases, additional and varied patrons will come forward.

The significance of novice patrons is that they have been willing to think of the playground in unexpected settings. Many of these newer participants see a playground as the heart of their underlying mission. They have begun to reassess their own place within the community and have looked at the playground as a way to signal their continuing commitment to nearby residents. These patrons frequently have mined untapped areas where kids can play and people can gather. Valuing unstructured play, they have inserted playgrounds boldly into spaces that needed to be humanized. These patrons have been willing to hire innovative designers who approached their task broadly and who saw the playground as a key element of urban design. Where projects are not open to the public, the patron has tried to provide models that can be exported for general use. The end results, discussed in

95

the vignettes that follow, show that the concept of a playground is evolving
and that the patrons have had a role in orchestrating change.

Santa Fe Railyard Park and Plaza
Santa Fe, New Mexico, 2004 (preliminary plans)
Sculptor: Mary Miss
Landscape Architect: Ken Smith Landscape Architecture
Architect: Frederic Schwartz

The nonprofit Trust for Public Land (TPL) has been finding ways to conserve land for public use. This organization has grown over the past thirty
years and so has its role as a patron of parks with playgrounds. One park administrator notes that TPL has altered the social dynamics of cities by becoming an advocate for people who previously had not thought of improving their open space.[1] TPL has been especially active in rescuing sites that
had been neglected eyesores. They have begun to do that in a strong fashion in Santa Fe, New Mexico. TPL brought together local citizens (some of
whom had been thinking about the site for more than a decade) to consider
the future of an old, historic railroad yard, then sponsored a national design
competition for the future development of the 13 acres of park land that the
city purchased in 1995. The winning team, composed of landscape architect
Ken Smith, sculptor Mary Miss, and architect Frederic Schwartz, carefully
inserted a play space into their proposal. Miss is shaping its final outcome.
It is impressive that this well-respected artist has taken on a playground, a
challenge that thrills her.

This Santa Fe site is rich in cultural history. The Acequia Madre Canal,
an irrigation channel that Spanish settlers created in the early seventeenth
century, still survives. The Atchison, Topeka and Santa Fe Railroad came in
the 1880s. A large farmers' market, the El Museo Cultural de Santa Fe, a contemporary arts museum, and a teen arts center are nearby. The New Mexico School of the Deaf is across the street from the future park but separated
from it by a busy thoroughfare.

TPL, assisted by the American Institute of Architects' rural and urban
design team, began interviewing the community even before the competition was announced.[2] Residents believed that Santa Fe, with its copious
tourist scene, needed a more private zone for the people who live and work
there. Representatives of Santa Fe firmly requested a place where families
could spend unprogrammed time together, a type of outdoor family room.
The community made it clear that they did not want playing fields but would

be interested in some sort of playground if it could be shared by several generations. Their collective desire for a sense of place was similar to inclinations that propelled van Eyck in postwar Amsterdam. The winning team elaborated on this commitment by taking the natural and industrial infrastructures as underlying themes.

Sculptor Mary Miss's place on the design team assures a lively, appropriate play outcome. Miss is sensitive to the landscape and brings an innate playfulness to her work. Having grown up in rural Colorado, she has a deep affection for this arid environment. An artist who likes both to confront and to observe how people, especially children, react to her pieces, Miss is fascinated by play. She has long maintained that her own sculpture, in pieces such as the South Cove of Battery Park City (New York City, 1988), links high art, vernacular expression, and potential for children's exploration. Miss is also drawn to objects found in everyday life or configured in ways in which they had not been intended. She asks young people and adults to explore these, be surprised by them, and perhaps even experience a sense of danger.

For the Santa Fe competition, Miss kept the play areas as abstractions— several shallow circles. Her initial concept was evocative of the Indian ruins she explored as a child. During the subsequent planning stages, and especially after spending additional weeks presenting ideas and soliciting views of the community, Miss and the rest of the winning team have been refining and expanding the concept (fig. 3.1). They started with natural land forms and water, then combined those resources with agricultural concrete piping that is used to convey water. They have inserted circular arrangements into the land, placing these between an arroyo and a circular ramada. Miss's early drawings show how she worked with the circles, filling at least one with the concrete pipes that reflect human intervention on the land. She placed the pipes in an irregular pattern. These could become a water feature, where kids could use hand pumps to activate the flow. Or, the 48-inch diameter pipes could be tunnels for children to explore. They might even become play towers. Old cottonwood tree limbs, near the edge of the circle, might offer climbing opportunities. For a nearby slope, Miss provided connected activities that further emphasize the control of water, a necessary part of life in this part of America. The play form is a metal trough, which could provide a succession of areas where children can manipulate water through a rock tub, a sand basin, and a sequence of gates.

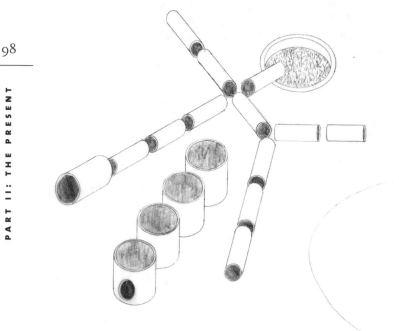

Fig. 3.1 Mary Miss, early pencil sketch (2004) for playground of Santa Fe Rail-yard Park, Santa Fe, New Mexico. Miss, a sculptor, won the park competition with Ken Smith, Landscape Architect, and Frederic Schwartz, Architect. Courtesy of Mary Miss.

Rosie the Riveter Memorial Playground
Richmond, California, Phase 1: 2000; Phase 2: 2005
Landscape Architect: The Office of Cheryl Barton
Visual Artist: Susan Schwartzenberg

It is rare when an artist is given an opportunity to create a piece of sculpture, accommodate the concerns of neighbors, and build a suitable playground in order to mark a historic site. Cheryl Barton, the landscape architect in San Francisco who designed the setting for her city's PacBell ballpark, performed these tasks for the Rosie the Riveter Memorial. She then had the thrill of seeing this locally conceived and funded project become the centerpiece of a new national park.[3] Within a few days of the Rosie dedication, in the fall of 2000, President Clinton signed legislation that created the World War II Home Front National Historical Park. The Rosie memorial will be incorporated into a grander scheme that encompasses thirteen nearby sites related to the World War II defense industry.

The Richmond Redevelopment Agency was the sponsoring agency for the first phase of design. The National Park Service, due to recent federal designation of this site, will supervise the next stage. This switch represents a change in patronage for playgrounds. Redevelopment agencies have been particularly active as funders of unique playgrounds during the past decade, whereas the park service has not usually assumed the same task. In this case, a playground will have a vital role in accentuating the part that children played in the Rosie the Riveter story.

The site is the location of one of the former Kaiser Shipyards, the place where over seven hundred Liberty and Victory ships were constructed during World War II. The city of Richmond, east of San Francisco, wanted to recall a moment when this economically struggling city was a boomtown at the forefront of the wartime defense effort. It was during those years, when approximately a quarter of the workers were women pulled into service by the labor shortage, that the image of an archetypal welder, Rosie the Riveter, began to emerge. A popular song, with the same title, spread the word.

In 1998, the city of Richmond and the Richmond Redevelopment Agency sponsored a regional competition. Spurred on by Councilwoman Donna Powers, who had long hoped to commemorate the role of women in the war economy, the competition organizers sought a way to honor the people and activities that had disappeared from this spot. The designated city land contained a nondescript park, a scruffy playground, and access to the local marina. This site is bounded on three sides by gated townhouses and low-rise apartments where the owners and tenants were not enthusiastic about a public memorial and less than thrilled with the prospect of children congregating nearby. Barton and photographer Susan Schwartzenberg won the competition with an entry that confronted the problem of recalling something that was no longer visible: both the physical plant of the prior shipyard and the presence of the workers who diligently worked there. They sought to invoke history without discounting the fact that the same story had elements of racism, sexism, and deprivation.

Barton organized the site as a long promenade. Naming this the Keel Walk, she designed a 441-foot-long path to replicate the exact length of a Liberty Ship. This new walkway traverses the land and directs visitors from the parking lot to the water. Barton provided a number of incidents along the way that interpret the site and have allowed former workers to make contributions to the understanding of anyone visiting this area. A timeline and personal statements have been etched onto the path. To supplement

Fig. 3.2 The Office of Cheryl Barton, plan for playground (2003) at Rosie the Riveter Memorial, Richmond, California. Courtesy of the Office of Cheryl Barton.

the remembrances, Barton designed a stainless-steel sculpture that evokes an unfinished hull. She and Schwartzenberg worked together on the sculpture's porcelain-enamel panels, which display photos of workers and writings about their experiences. This combination of art and archival material informs the entire memorial with a sense of a vibrant past. The neighbors have been pleased with the results and have endorsed the project.

The second phase, on which Barton subsequently worked, includes the old playground. Barton and Schwartzenberg believed that it would have been inexcusable to remove the playground, because children were active participants in the Rosie the Riveter story. Families, often headed by women traveling with their children, came to the Kaiser plants from considerable distances. The newcomers had to endure difficult living and working conditions. On a brighter side, once they had migrated to Richmond, they did find a lively city that operated twenty-four hours a day and offered round-the-clock childcare and extensive recreational facilities. Barton decided that the playground had to be maintained but, in order to placate the neighbors, at a slightly different location.

Barton settled on a heavily shaded, slightly bowl-shaped piece of land, just off the main memorial pathway. It is close to an area that attracts many users because of numerous barbeque grills. She retained and upgraded these. Barton's choice of equipment, in this case, was critical. This was not an easy job for Barton, an artist who generally abhors the imposition of equipment on land. She has been able to work without it in the past; but this was a different case. For a relatively compact area, she felt that the right equipment would provide the greatest opportunities for play. By selecting abstracted stainless-steel pieces, she was able to replicate the materials of the nearby simulated hull and the actual fabrication of ships (fig. 3.2). This was a deft feat to make sure that the playground is metaphorically tied to the memorial in form and spirit. Barton chose a stainless climbing dome to be the focal point of the composition, the piece of equipment around which the landscape swirls. It is the hub where a resilient surfacing material meets a harder paving of decomposed granite. The latter, chosen as an alternative to concrete, supports plantings. A swath of flowering trees was placed on it and provides even more shade for the playground. Protection from the sun is welcomed by those watching their children and by visitors to the memorial seeking a covered haven from the bright sunlight. The playground has the potential to be a locus of action and contemplation.

Play Circle—Rooftop at Yerba Buena Gardens
San Francisco, California, 1998
Landscape Architect: M. Paul Friedberg & Partners

For three decades, the San Francisco Redevelopment Agency (SFRA) fought lawsuits that would have forestalled creation of new cultural facilities in the area now called SOMA (south of Market). The SFRA was faulted largely for potential loss of inexpensive housing and resident hotels. Subsequent compromises made it possible for many elderly residents to remain in the neighborhood and, at the same time, for the redevelopment agency to create an 87 acre cultural-recreational-commercial center called Yerba Buena Gardens. In an effort to meet needs of neighbors and to attract tourists, the SFRA has vigorously provided facilities for kids. Moscone Convention Center, the largest unit of the Yerba Buena group, is topped by a playground on its roof. This is an important nod to modernist use of the roof to enhance health and recreation. Architect Le Corbusier had successfully placed one of the most famous examples, a preschool and playground, on the roof of his Unite d'Habitation apartments in Marseille in the early 1950s.

The Moscone roof, known by the inclusive name "Rooftop at Yerba Buena Gardens," has additional amenities that are appealing to a wide age range. An adjacent bowling alley, indoor skating rink, and museum for teens complete this child-oriented section of the complex. Adele Naude Santos and Associates was the architect for the buildings.[4]

The playground, named Play Circle, assists the populations that live in this dominantly commercial heart of the city. Designed by M. Paul Friedberg, the same landscape architect who spearheaded the post-and-platform revolution in the 1960s and 1970s, Play Circle addresses the needs of several constituencies. It is the play space for the nonprofit 10,000-square-foot childcare center that is close by but discreetly hidden from view. Other small children reside in the affordable-rate housing that was carved out of nearby luxury rentals or condominiums. Additionally, numerous nonresident children who spend the day with grandparents come often to the play site. These older folks, who live in one of seven nearby apartment buildings for seniors, need a space to which they can bring youngsters. The elderly like the fact that the play area is removed from street traffic and flanked by buildings, thereby making it a difficult spot from which tots can wander. The lack of fencing, and easy accessibility from other parts of the rooftop, recall van Eyck's approach.

Unlike his earlier schemes with tightly packed activities, Friedberg's design is a two-story playground that spreads out over its 2-acre site. The central hub is the circle, defined by sloping walls (fig. 3.3). Friedberg put a resilient rubber material, a standard component on many playground floors, on the ground and extended it up the sides of the angled surfaces. The resulting rubberized walls are intriguing to youngsters who are just starting to walk. Toddlers, who try to climb it, show delight. The rim of the circle loosely links all of the more easily recognizable play areas, such as customized slides with a vertical tower and lower slides that have accompanying steps. All are built into the same circular embankment. These, in turn, are connected by the edge of the circle to the sand area, which is particularly elaborate, with ramps, concrete cylinders, and walls that can be used by parents for seating or by children for playing. The reflection of Dutch architect van Eyck's earlier work seems clear in the way adults and children can use the concrete rims.

Play Circle has a few elements that reflect Friedberg's earlier successes in making play more complex. There is simultaneous activity on several levels. A water trough, where children can control the flow, links an amphitheater with the area that contains the slides and sand pit. A series of gentle inclines and short bridges, overhead, reinforce the notion of two levels for play. In order to increase possibilities for exploration, the railings are topped by pipes that function as sound tubes.

Fig. 3.3 M. Paul Friedberg & Partners, Play Circle (1998) on the roof of the Moscone Convention Center, San Francisco. Photograph by Robert S. Solomon, 2001.

The playground has become an intergenerational space where the population changes hour by hour, a legacy of one of Friedberg's initial goals in the 1960s. Elderly Asian men and women stake out their favorite piece of land, especially along the Play Circle, where they practice Tai Chi each morning. Young professionals who have brought their children with them to conventions in San Francisco often take a respite from meetings at the Moscone Convention Center in order to find some playtime with their kids before lunch. Preschoolers come in the late morning and early afternoon, followed by older children who come after school has been dismissed. Parents and children take the short walk from Chinatown in order to use this site. Families who used to live in SOMA but have relocated to the suburbs bring their children back to this playground when they make daytrips into the city. Teens come via public transportation in the evenings and weekends. They like to hang out on the embedded slides and also take advantage of the bowling or ice skating. The nearby Sony Metreon, a movieplex and shopping mall, is another attraction that brings older kids into the area.

Maintained by a private management company, the playground has the luxury of a generous budget for excellent upkeep. It is removed from one of the biggest headaches that face those trying to erect new playgrounds or even revamp old ones. In this case, the SFRA contributes about 20 percent of the upkeep costs; surrounding facilities contribute the rest. This partnership has been conscientious about maintenance while, at the same time, committed to keeping the playground free of admission charges and available to anyone who comes there.

SOCIAL SERVICE AGENCIES: AMERICANS WORKING AT HOME

Tenderloin Childcare Center
San Francisco, California, 2002
Architect: Gelfand Partners Architecture
Landscape Architect: Susan Herrington

Homeless Prenatal Project
San Francisco, California, Currently in design
Architect: Gelfand Partners Architecture

SOS Village Community Center
Chicago, Illinois, 2005
Architect: Studio Gang Architects

Complicated social problems have generated some remarkable design solutions in two San Francisco neighborhoods that are a distance from Yerba Buena Gardens. Equally daunting problems and a good solution are coming out of Chicago. In all three locations, social service agencies have become patrons of playgrounds because play is essential to their respective missions.

Professionals who work with a homeless population have long realized that the most successful remedies come about by addressing a broad spectrum of needs that includes educational, legal, financial, and medical components. Compass Community Services (known until 1995 as Travelers Aid San Francisco) and the Homeless Prenatal Project offer their individual clients a similar range of services. Both of these organizations have hired Lisa Gelfand, a founder of the architecture firm Gelfand Partners in San Francisco. In addition, landscape architect Susan Herrington, who works and teaches in Vancouver, British Columbia, has provided her expertise for the Compass project.

Gelfand has a long record of working on public housing and trying to coax intimate and comfortable spaces out of minuscule budgets. Herring-

ton's work, which is both practical and theoretical, is no less compelling.[5]
She has argued consistently for playgrounds that use natural materials in
place of purchased equipment. In urban settings, she has worked untiringly
to find ways to respect the land, keeping equipment to a minimum. For the
Laurel Hill Nursery School, in an upscale San Francisco neighborhood, Gelfand and Herrington worked together on a school addition and improved
playground (1998). There, Herrington exploited the steep terrain by inserting decks, ramps, and bridges among abundant sand, trees, and steps on
different parts of the slope.

Compass Community Services hired Gelfand to transform an older structure into its Tenderloin Childcare Center (TLC). Formerly housed in the
basement of a YMCA, TLC provides a preschool and full-day childcare for
homeless and formerly homeless children.[6] Kids get three meals a day. Play
therapy is available. TLC also offers parents a wide range of options, including on-site vocational counseling, drug treatment, and apartment placement. The center puts great emphasis on parenting and coping skills so
that abuse is mitigated during time of crisis.

TLC needed a building in which to grant all of these services and double
its school enrollment to seventy-two. The organization chose a building that
had been a boxing gym and then a film-storage warehouse. Protected by
local historic preservation ordinance, any changes to the exterior had to be
approved by local officials.

TLC specifically requested an extensive on-site play area for their new facility. When still located at the YMCA, TLC teachers had to walk their students to a nearby park. They expended a great deal of energy just marching
kids down city streets and then checking for needles and broken glass in the
city's parks. Gelfand found an ideal situation by setting aside the roof for all
play-related activities at the new building. She and Herrington created a
quiet oasis of 3,000 square feet.

A playground on the roof was an expense that added to the budget but
one that seemed justified for the daily lives of these children. Using the roof
for the playground site meant that there were expenses for waterproofing it
and providing an extra elevator stop so that the space is compliant with the
American with Disabilities Act (ADA). The client felt that all of these costs
were consistent with providing a sanctuary for play. Gelfand was pleased to
extend the modernist passion of employing a roof for recreational needs. In
urban areas, the roof has historically been a prime site for play. Even before
the advent of modernism, the old Waldorf Astoria Hotel in New York (site
of the present Empire State Building) had a rooftop playground in 1909; so
did many settlement houses in the early twentieth century.

Fig. 3.4 Susan Herrington (landscape architect) and Lisa Gelfand (architect), rooftop playground at Tenderloin Childcare Center (2002), San Francisco. View toward grass patch, stone floor, and sandbox. Photograph by Susan Herrington. Courtesy of Gelfand Partners Architects.

In one of the busiest areas of the city, Gelfand and Herrington aimed for an environment that would best capture the intimacy and tranquility of a private backyard. A large canopy, which extends the amount of time that can be spent outside during the rainy season, shelters an impromptu stage and storytelling area. An oculus provides additional light and a view of the sky (fig. 3.4). The designers, aware that these pupils have no access to the natural world, tried to bring it into their everyday routine. They provided a sandbox with a retractable wooden cover and a broad patch of grass. Stone pavers, on the ground near the sandbox, add the texture of a park setting. This rough surface offers variety from the rubber paving that covers the rest of the roof. Gelfand and Herrington would have loved to have used rocks but knew that they would never be approved by the local building officials. Herrington and the teachers felt that small outdoor toys would increase the playfulness and sense of home they were trying to convey. This loose-parts approach has worked well. Within the confines of a limited space, Gelfand and Herrington have offered a solution that allows for the graduated challenges that Lev Vygotsky preferred.

An open deck, with a single piece of commercial equipment, adjoins the quieter zone. The equipment, which guarantees a space for intense motor activity, is a functional necessity that Herrington rightfully has placed in a secondary position to the larger and more varied nearby spaces. She also has positioned the equipment on the part of the roof that is noisiest and closest to the street.

Gelfand has sought the same balance between institutional and home-like areas in her designs for a first-floor courtyard for the Homeless Prenatal Project (HPP). San Francisco nurse practioner Martha Ryan founded HPP after she returned from many years of work in an Ethiopian refugee camp. Having seen how women helped each other in African villages, Ryan felt that she had experienced a community model that could be adapted to the needs of pregnant American women who were in crisis situations. The program she started, and which has been working out of offices on several floors of a commercial building, provides immediate and long-term services. Within these cramped spaces, Ryan has been successful in her advocacy. She has received several commendations, including the 2002 San Francisco Foundation Community Leadership award.

HPP hired Gelfand to design a new headquarters, one that would consolidate all services in a self-contained building, in San Francisco's Mission District. After Gelfand presented her first designs in 2002, HPP began to rethink the notion of new construction. The dot-com excesses of the 1990s were disintegrating and affecting the commercial real estate market. Previously difficult to secure, buildings were becoming readily available and less expensive. HPP came to the conclusion that it might be better served by buying an old warehouse and having Gelfand design spaces for them within a preexisting facility. Taking advantage of what appeared to be a new opportunity, HPP and Gelfand looked all over downtown San Francisco for one year. They never found a suitable building and have recommitted themselves to erecting a home on their Mission neighborhood site. While many older structures could have been adapted to most of HPP's programmatic needs, none of the buildings could accommodate a playground comfortably. HPP's final decision to build their own facility, rather than renovate an older site, was determined by the need for an ample courtyard play space.

HPP saw the playground as one of its essential aids to its clients. Part of a drop-in childcare center, the playground is key to the efficient and humane way that HPP delivers its services. By caring for children as soon as they arrive, HPP frees a single mother to take advantage of her immediate needs, such as finding housing or removing an abusive partner from her home. Walk-in childcare also prevents a child from just sitting and waiting while counseling takes place for adults.

Although the new building is currently on hold, Gelfand is now working out the details of what form the playground should take (fig. 3.5). She and the client are committed to placing it in an open, sheltered space that will be visible to anyone coming into the building. Again, Gelfand is aiming for a setting that will resemble a backyard more than an institution. There will be sand, land forms, a variety of plants, and perhaps a change of levels for variety. There may be a place for plentiful art supplies. Gelfand hopes to create a space where children will know from their first glance that this is not a regimented school, just a spot for fun and exploration.

The program in Chicago is equally inspiring. The patron is SOS Children's Villages Illinois, part of an international child-welfare organization that has been active for over fifty years. Better known throughout the globe than in the United States, SOS Children's Villages International unites siblings and provides permanent foster parents and stable homelike settings for kids. SOS operates more than four hundred villages in the world; only three are in the United States. The third one, and the only one in an urban setting, opened on Chicago's South Side in 2004.

A key part of the SOS concept is that the "village" should become a part of the existing community around it. In Chicago, the village consists of sixteen single-family homes. Twenty-four affordable housing units are interspersed with the village houses on a 7.5-acre site. The SOS directors had sought, and found, a site that would be just a few blocks from a Chicago Park District field house. The city facility offers sports and excellent recreational programming. Its presence meant that SOS Chicago did not have to fund or maintain a similar site. It also offered an additional venue for SOS kids to mix with the surrounding neighbors.

The SOS board made a point of hiring Chicago architects and contractors. Jeanne Gang of Studio Gang is designing the community center, which will include a childcare facility. Having successfully completed the Chinese

Fig. 3.5 Lisa Gelfand, model of interior playground of Prenatal Homeless Project (2002), San Francisco. Courtesy of
Gelfand Partners Architects.

American Service League Community Center (and won the 2004 International Design Competition for the Ford/Callumet Environmental Center),
Gang was known to the SOS board, which sought her out for this project.
Her objective has been to create a building that is responsive to the varied
and intense SOS schedule. She was determined to create something that
was not just a large box. To this end, she has reinterpreted the local brick
building tradition that is found throughout the surrounding neighborhood
and is seen in the façades of the new SOS houses. She has sought a way to
recognize that brick, today, is a cladding and a rain screen that is tied back
to the wall. She has tried to express this new nonstructural condition by re-

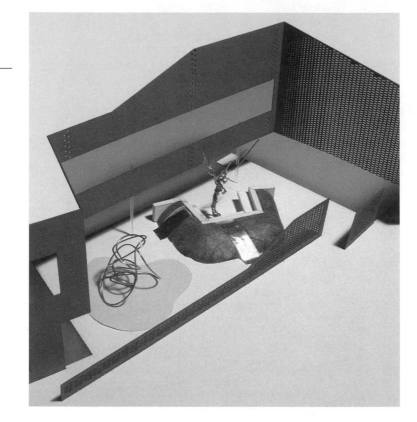

Fig. 3.6 Studio Gang Architects, early model (2004) of play area and elevation
of brick wall, community center for SOS Children's Village, Chicago. Courtesy of
Studio Gang Architects.

moving every other brick on the wall so that brick becomes a type of fabric
that can be seen through.

Adjacent to the childcare center, Gang has designed a 1,000-square-foot
children's play court (fig. 3.6). She has used a variation of the brick rain
screen, a marker of the main community building, for one side of her design. It will give the playground a distinctive background and sense of further depth. She has organized the rest of the playground into two spaces.
One part of this court will have a piece of equipment on a recycled rubber
matting. The other section, forming a C around an existing shade tree, will
be more interesting. It will be a berm, sloping away from the tree. This is
largely for the youngest day-care students, those from newborn to age three.
The berm will be the zone for tactile exploration, the real extension of the

possibilities posed by the nearby wall. The side closest to the tree will have wood benches for adults and take full advantage of the sheltering tree.

SOCIAL SERVICE AGENCIES: AMERICANS WORKING ABROAD

Klein Bottle Playground (Art for the World)
Various sites throughout the world, 2000
Architect: Acconci Studio

Kitagata Garden City
Gifu Prefecture, Japan, 2000
Landscape Architect: Martha Schwartz Inc.

Social service agencies abroad have begun to emerge as patrons of both playgrounds and American artists. Two outstanding projects are Acconci Studio's *Klein Bottle Playground,* done for the Art for the World program, and Martha Schwartz's interior park for a housing project, Kitagata Garden City, in Kitagata, Japan. In both cases, the client believed that play served a restorative role in the lives of young children.[7]

Performance artist/photographer/sculptor Vito Acconci formed Acconci Studio in the late 1980s in order to concentrate on architecture and industrial design. Under Acconci's direction, talented young architects man the studio. The thread that runs between Acconci's earlier and more recent careers is the desire to explore human responses in unusual or unpredictable circumstances. He is intrigued by how people relate to each other.[8] It is this interaction, coupled with surprise and unpredictability, that has informed much of Acconci Studio's recent achievements.

Acconci is no stranger either to aiding progressive social causes or to the design of playgrounds. One of Acconci Studio's first commissions is among the few aesthetically interesting playgrounds of the 1980s, *Land of Boats* (1987–1991) for St. Aubin Park in Detroit (fig. 3.7). It was part of the reconstruction of a boat basin. Defining a space along one side of the administration building, Acconci Studio created a shallow pit with a shape that has been likened to the outline of a sail boat.[9] It is ringed by broad low steps that are good for sitting. The pit and the surrounding plaza contain simplified concrete versions of small sailboats. Some are partly submerged into an imaginary river represented by the pit and parts of others hover along the concrete. These rest at steep angles so that the masts plunge into the ground or pierce the empty surrounding space. The visible parts of the boat

Fig. 3.7 Acconci Studio, *Land of Boats* (1987–1991), Detroit. Courtesy of Acconci Studio.

"sail" into the air. It's an upside-down world where kids are free to climb on the underside of boats or swing from their simulated masts. Acconci notes that this customized playground is exciting to explore, relates to the surrounding sailing context, and gives an illusion of being menacing.[10]

One of Acconci Studio's recent playgrounds has been for Art for the World, a Geneva-based nonprofit agency that uses contemporary art for humanitarian purposes.[11] As part of its mandate to promote international communication, Art for the World has been circulating an exhibition "Playgrounds & Toys for Refugee Children." This show of models and proposals has been traveling since 2000, with the understanding that some of the projects would be constructed at each venue. Artists from sixteen countries responded to a poignant need, with Acconci Studio being one of only three American firms to participate. Some artists devised easily transportable full-size playgrounds; others decided it would be important for refugee children to own a personal game or pillow.

Acconci Studio's piece for Art for the World, entitled *Klein Bottle,* is a self-contained sphere that is an elegant, purposeful, and easily reproducible playground.[12] Playing on the German word for small and the name of respected nineteenth-century German mathematician and inventor Felix Klein, the Studio designed a large transparent sphere that will allow children to climb and explore (fig. 3.8). Klein's adaptation of a Moebius strip is the model whereby this interior always feeds back into itself and the interior and exterior merge. Children, as many as twenty-five or thirty at one time, will be able to romp, slide, and step within a confined but visually expanding space determined by the three or four necks of the structure. Because the surface is perforated, kids will have extensive opportunities to climb on the exterior. It will be possible for children to access the interior from the ground, by pulling themselves up into the sphere, or from other openings on the exterior surface. Play will be unpredictable, varied, and not predetermined.

The sphere, approximately 12 feet in diameter, will be constructed of molded polycarbonate. Its advantages are a clear skin and modest price. The first *Klein Bottle* will cost approximately $200,000 for the prototype, with successive replicas tallying much less. Art for the World has committed itself to building Acconci Studio's concept, most likely in Mexico or Taiwan. Acconci, who would be ecstatic if *Klein Bottle* could be portable, recognizes that that probably will not be possible but remains pleased that it should be easily replicable. In this specific commission, social imperative takes precedence over site development.

Whereas Acconci designed a work that could be erected in any open space, Martha Schwartz responded to a site-specific commission: the courtyard of a housing project in Kitagata, Gifu Prefecture, Japan. The congested

Fig. 3.8 Acconci Studio, *Klein Bottle Playground* (2002). Courtesy of Acconci Studio.

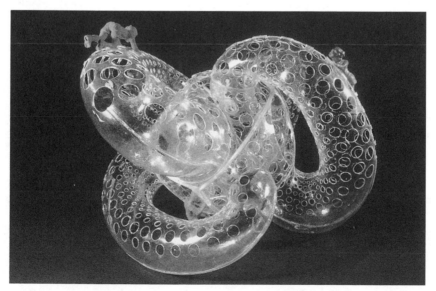

Fig. 3.9 Martha Schwartz, central courtyard at Kitagata Garden City apartments (2000) in Gifu Prefecture, Japan. The Four-Season Garden can be seen at right. Courtesy of Martha Schwartz, Inc.

complex provides 450 housing units for people who can be described as poor even though they have full-time jobs. Japanese architect Arata Isozaki chose four women, two from Japan and two from the West, to redesign an older, rather grim, public housing complex that was seismically unsafe. Isozaki chose architects Akiko Takahashi, Kazuyo Sejima, Christine Hawley, and Elizabeth Diller. He also selected Boston-based Schwartz, a landscape architect who has long advocated reclaiming unused spaces and who does not shirk from using lively colors and unusual industrial materials. She was asked to complement the other designers' work with a central courtyard that would provide a strong unifying element for the otherwise disparate plans (fig. 3.9).

Schwartz's success comes of blending a keen sense of drama and color with pragmatic ways in which the community can use the grounds. The final results evoke the history of the surroundings and bring forth the type of play that appeals to tots, teens, and older residents. Following directives from the local inhabitants, she put spaces for the youngest and oldest users close to each other. The intent was to find harmonies of interest and concerns. This was not an easy task where the population is a mix of young, old, single, and married. Schwartz had to develop a common universality within the specifics of the site.

Schwartz blended Eastern and Western garden traditions. She tamed the long, oblong space by reflecting the nearby landscape. Acknowledging that this is a rural agricultural region dependent on rice, Schwartz took a cue from vernacular methods. She noticed that important local areas are mounded up while the rest of the land is flooded and sunken for rice growing. A mound, therefore, became the organizing element in her design. By establishing a plinth for human activity, Schwartz was able to create a flat plane on which to develop individual outdoor rooms. She saw that these rooms could be spots for play, socializing, and entertainment. These are all critical needs because there are no other open spaces in this housing block. Schwartz invented lively spaces, including a Willow Court, an Iris Canal, a Stone Garden, a sand pit, and a Sports Court. There is a Four-Season Garden, composed of small roofless rooms that are defined by colored Plexiglas walls. Here, the green summer garden provides hooks for hammocks; the yellow spring garden has an S-shaped seat that is perfect for climbing. Children have gravitated to these tiny spaces, attracted to their bright colors and intimate enclosures.[13]

Sensing a connection to their land and finding a variety of intimate areas in which to congregate, residents of the buildings have flocked to the outdoor spaces. The Iris Canal, shaped like a boat, has become a favorite where young kids splash. The twelve- to fifteen-year-old set has been fascinated by the pink granite Stone Garden where computerized water jets soak those who cavort there. Schwartz planned the Willow Court especially for teens, as what Schwartz refers to as a "romantic garden for lovers." Schwartz suggests that the garden will provide privacy and escape for teenagers who need to get out from under the constant supervision of parents. That part of the plan has not yet been tested because the willows have not reached their full height.

Schwartz considered lighting an important factor in her overall plan, and it has been particularly useful as a way of drawing adults to these spaces in the evening. The lighting, too, gives the space a sense of being inhabited and welcoming even when it is fairly empty. This, too, augments play opportunities for teens. Schwartz has successfully reinvigorated lighting as a key component for public assembly, an idea that architect Forberg applied to the Cypress Hills playground in the 1960s.

Rohnert Park—Cotati Regional Library
Rohnert Park, California, 2003
Landscape Architect: Royston Hanamoto Alley & Abey

Libraries have changed spectacularly with the advent of electronic informa-tion. Once a quiet place for study, the public library frequently has become a community hub of a downtown. It is no longer unusual for libraries to sponsor lectures, house cafes, sell book bags, and rent videos. It is not sur-prising to find that today's libraries often take control of their surrounding open space. There are a few precedents. During the Progressive reform era, prior to World War I, it was common for the public library to set up a branch in a small park.[14] In 1935, the main New York Public Library and the New York Parks Department extended book services into adjacent Bryant Park when they set up an outdoor reading room and lending service.[15] Today, li-braries have become partners in the creation of public spaces that speak to their educational mission but also allow children to be active, albeit with a literary bent.

The landscape architecture firm Royston Hanamoto Alley & Abey (RHAA)—descended from the firm Robert Royston, Garrett Eckbo, and Ed Williams originated in 1945—has designed a series of spaces for the civic structures of Rohnert Park, California. The landscape project unites the library (a branch of the Sonoma County library system), the public-safety building, and the future city hall.[16] Using a central plaza as an integrating element, Aditya Advani (the RHAA partner in charge of this project) has permitted the presence of the library to give meaning to this entire area. He has incorporated references to language, written text, and reading into the outdoor space. The gardens have given character to previously undefined sprawl and to the bland public-safety building. The new library (Noll & Tam architects, 2003) and adjoining "reading grove" have provided a strong image for a community that is simultaneously agricultural, suburban, and academic.

The original program did not call for spaces for children. These evolved as the outdoor designs developed. Advani has infused the open areas with references to Lewis Carroll's *Alice in Wonderland* books and to the common-ality of language. A literary conceit, this theme acknowledges that the gar-den is as much for play as it is for reading. It is intended to draw children into the landscape, from the nearby parking lot and from the adjacent li-brary children's room. The sculpture *Alice in Wonderland* in Central Park, a

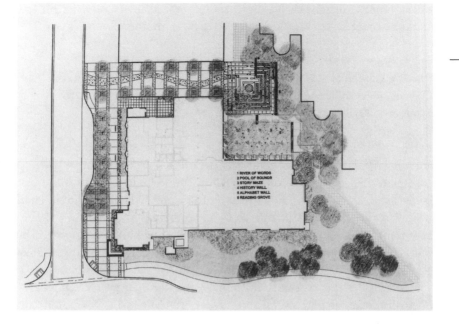

Fig. 3.10 Aditya Advani, plan of Rohnert Park Library (2003), Rohnert Park, California. The library footprint is the central, open element; the future city hall will be in the space at the top. Courtesy of Royston Hanamoto Alley & Abey.

perennial and continuing favorite for climbing and hiding, shows that the *Alice* stories still have wide appeal (see fig. 2.10).

The central plaza, at the heart of the Rohnert scheme, alludes to Alice without an actual model of her. A rectangular maze dominates the space (fig. 3.10). Constructed of turf and tile bands, the maze provides a means of sensory exploration in addition to space for running and jumping. Etched illustrations from the *Alice* stories appear on the face of the tiles. A small, shallow reflecting pool with pebbles lies at the center. This Pool of Sounds contains letters that spell out the basic enunciations that are needed to create speech, and adds further exploratory water play. The play value is enhanced by a history wall that is both a screen through the maze and a tunnel with an arch carved into it. Covered with tiles created by Martha Crawford that depict the development of speech, this wall forces visitors to pass through it in order to complete the maze. This offers further playfulness and mimics the rabbit hole through which Alice plummeted. This abstraction engages children with its variety of activities. In contrast, one of the nearby paths, called "Poet's Alley," is a bit more representational. It is lined with low stacks of concrete books. All are intended for climbing.

Reading Garden at P.S. 19
Queens, New York, 2003
Landscape Architect: Ken Smith Landscape Architecture

Ken Smith is a man of multiple talents, as seen in his work as the landscape architect for both Santa Fe Railyard Park and Plaza and the runner-up scheme (called THINK) for the new World Trade Center. Smith is the first landscape architect to be hired by the Robin Hood Foundation (founded in 1988) for their Library Initiative to fight poverty in New York City. Robin Hood enhances education by providing exciting venues for reading. The foundation has hired talented, progressive architects to reconstruct public-school libraries and has persuaded these professionals to work *pro bono*. It was natural for this patron to think of extending their largesse to nearby open spaces and to employ the inventive Smith. The result, a Reading Garden, is not specifically a playground. It is included here because Smith's solutions offer several instructive and inexpensive paradigms.[17] With minor adjustments, these could easily be adapted for play.

Smith's site, Public School 19, is in the Corona section of Queens. From statistics alone, the school seems a disheartening environment. This is the largest elementary school in New York City, with more than 2,100 students. Local income is low enough for the majority of the students to be eligible for federal subsidized meals. About half of the children, many of whom come from homes where English is not spoken, do not read at grade level. The reality, however, is that such numbers do not accurately reflect the liveliness of this facility. There is no feeling of despair. Principal Cathy Zarbis has partitioned the school into separate, intense learning communities. These focus on such topics as book publishing, science and technology, and communications and performing arts. Students have become enthusiastic learners.

When Robin Hood hired Ken Smith, Tsao & McKown Architects already had redesigned the second-floor library and it had reopened. Taking advantage of the fact that the massive school sits in the middle of a vast asphalt lot, Smith chose to leave one half of that lot as it is. It will continue to support sports, particularly basketball, and all recess activities. Smith chose to transform the other half of the schoolyard into an outdoor space that could be seen from the new library. In the process, he has created an addition to the neighborhood that has made the local residents proud. The schoolyard

Fig. 3.11 Ken Smith, scrim and graphic (2003) at P.S. 19, Queens, New York.
Author's photograph, 2003.

remains pristine, whereas in the past, the principal said that it had been the "toilet for neighborhood dogs."

Smith thought first about the school fencing, something that could not be removed and that exists at all schools and most playgrounds. Rather than fighting its existence, Smith decided to emphasize it. He added a visual enhancement: He designed a silk-screened scrim curtain of clouds. Easily fastened onto the preexisting fence, the ethereal clouds and deep blue ground appear to float over two sides of the previously dreary enclosure. This enlivens the interior of the schoolyard. It contributes even more to the exterior, where it is visible from busy Queens Boulevard, a street that is usually quite dark because the elevated subway blocks the sun (fig. 3.11).

Smith then organized the interior space as continuous horizontal and vertical surfaces, enlivened by bright colored circles that are simply painted. Working with graphic designers Pentagram, Smith applied these circles to the ground as well as to the sides of temporary trailers. The entire space has become vibrant and appealing. Smith contributed further visual and practical excitement by designing T-shaped turquoise seats. Although these were never completed, Smith wanted children to sit on these to read and to shift them around to create instant climbing structures. One of the important lessons to be learned here is that these would not have cost thousands of dollars. Their price would have been approximately $100 each, indicating that "equipment" like this could supply an entire schoolyard for less than $5,000.

Smith's achievement for the seating did not come from finding a low-cost or shoddy manufacturer; instead, he faced the problem imaginatively. Smith devised these seats by noticing the wonderful color, size, and weight of water connectors for city sewers. He saw that these, when capped at each opening, could be versatile and sturdy. Smith believed that these seats would have taken on special meaning in the morning, after the children had had breakfast and before classes started, when they could have gathered in this space to sit and read.

The Reading Garden has one final, impressive component: a series of gardens that Smith designated along its edge. These include a wildflower section, a butterfly and bird area, and a border garden. Working with the Queens Botanical Garden, Smith created a site where children can learn about plants. It is the focus of a curriculum being developed around these varied environments. This could easily become an updated Environmental Yard.

Bright Horizons Family Solutions, Cummins Child Development Center
Columbus, Indiana, 2002
Architect: Carlos Jimenez Studio

The concept of a freestanding and purpose-built preschool or day-care center, as opposed to ad hoc quarters in a church basement or community center, is a product of the late twentieth century. Even newer is the notion that some of these, all-day childcare facilities in particular, might be operated by a for-profit corporation. Bright Horizons Family Solutions (BHFS) is a publicly traded company, which is now a major provider of day care in the United States. Many BHFS clients are large corporations that want to establish day-care facilities but are happy to leave the staffing and management to the professionals. Educators generally have positive things to say about this corporation, and quite a few believe that it is an organization that has learned to blend profitability with the ability to look beyond the bottom line to gauge its own success.

Author Jim Greenman, senior vice-president at BHFS, is a colleague of Robin Moore. Together they run a summer workshop for designers. Greenman, who has written several books about childcare facilities and is a proponent of handing challenging play to kids, is concerned with good design in his individual sites. He is also smart enough to give great latitude to the facilities that BHFS runs. For centers that want to take advantage of Greenman's philosophy and expertise, he is a strong advocate of outdoor, experiential play. He cares deeply about offering more than physical activity in the playgrounds BHFS provides.[18]

BHFS benefited from the expertise of Houston architect Carlos Jimenez for the Cummins Child Development Center in Columbus, Indiana. Adding yet another distinguished building to the architecturally rich mix of Columbus, Jimenez has created a childcare center for children (six weeks old through kindergarten) that is primarily for employees of Cummins Engine. Jimenez, an associate professor at Rice University, is an architect who has been lauded for his sensitive approach to local building traditions.

Jimenez had an unusually large site on which to place his Indiana day-care building. Located outside the downtown and close to one of several Cummins facilities, this land is alongside an active road. A small river, the divider between the school grounds and the busy street, became a natural boundary—but one that had to be out of reach to the children unless they were properly supervised. This necessitated a series of gates and fences on the road side that also sends a message to passersby that this is a well-protected area.

The *parti* of Jimenez's building exhibits several characteristics that augment the usefulness and variety of the designated outdoor play arenas. Jimenez has used his architecture to shape the exterior spaces, making them very commodious for a range of activities. In the early 1960s, architect Joseph Esherick used architecture in a similar manner to mold outside spaces for play. Esherick assigned equal amounts of space for indoor classrooms and outdoor play yards at the Harold E. Jones Child Study Center, a preschool facility on the Berkeley campus of the University of California (fig. 3.12). Given the moderate climate, Esherick allowed for a flowing space to unite the interiors and exteriors. He defined the two outdoor spaces further by placing covered pergolas along the perimeter of the long sides. For the two play spaces, he devised a sandbox for one yard and a sand-and-water zone for the other. This gave kids as much freedom as possible. Esherick's goal, inspired by the curriculum of the school, was to maximize child-directed experimentation.[19]

Jimenez had to think differently about how to shape space for the cold winters of America's Midwest. His footprint of the building is an "L" with the addition of a slightly curved wing that connects the two arms. This produces an internal courtyard, an irregular wedge, which became the playground for the youngest children. Jimenez divided this space further by dedicating approximately one-third to the needs of parents who are free to visit anytime during school hours. This is a space for nursing, storytelling, and quiet play that supports interaction between a parent and his or her child. Jimenez used a fence to separate the public part of the playground

Fig. 3.12 Joseph Esherick, Harold E. Jones Child Study Center (1962), Berkeley, California. Author's photograph, 2001.

from this more private zone. He designed a storage shed, which opens from either side, to straddle the fence. This is functional and clever means of making a fence look more appealing (fig. 3.13). The remaining space, the public part of this courtyard, is geared to physical actions. Jimenez provided clear paths, bursting out from a central oval. Children use these to help guide their small tricycles.

For older children, Jimenez reserved a section at the rear that faces the heavily trafficked road. The director of the Cummins center, Victoria Baker, is particularly happy that students can wave at the cars and that drivers can respond. This is not contradictory to security precautions, just a way to acknowledge safely that these kids belong in the community and to enable them to feel the excitement of people driving off to work and returning home. In this "exterior" playground, Jimenez provided additional thoughtful details. Another simple shed, again with openings on either side, helps to organize the space; it gives a sense of permanence to the spare areas it straddles. Most of the off-the-shelf equipment is simple, conceived as a series of small incidents. The surfaces tie all of the play elements together. In addition to meandering paths for bike riding, the surfaces are composed of either sand or wood chips. In the case of sand, which is raked by students and faculty, this extends the area for play. There is also an exterior bathroom, nestled into the rear wall of this school. This is a particularly useful detail. It has only one door, the one that goes to the playground. Preschoolers can go to the bathroom by themselves and gain a sense of maturity. Teachers do not have to bring all the students inside when one has to use the toilet.

This building has an extraordinary internal security system that may have ramifications for playground use. Teachers do not have to be guardians of gates; they are free to interact with students, unencumbered by the threat of a child wandering off. The role of the teacher is key, a position that is highlighted by the fact that they have not been given any additional seating on the playground. This is a space meant for activism in education.

The Little School
San Francisco, California, 1998
Architect: Mark Horton / Architecture

The Little School is more typical of how most preschools are structured. Founded by executive director Leslie Roffman in 1984, it is a private non-

Fig. 3.13 Carlos Jimenez Studio, Cummins Child Development Center (2001), Columbus, Indiana. View of inner courtyard showing section for parents and the toolshed that straddles the large and small play areas. Author's photograph, 2003.

profit facility for two- to six-year-olds. It is unique in other ways. It emphasizes a play-centered, multi-sensory curriculum that accommodates "typically and atypically developing children." Teachers stress peer-to-peer and
student-to-teacher relationships.

Mark Horton was both architect and parent for this renovation. He devised
a sophisticated solution for this preschool, housed in the former gymnasium
of a church. His accomplishment may provide some guidance for other patrons struggling to incorporate play into an urban space, especially where
there may be more room for activity on the interior than the exterior.[20]

Like so many projects in San Francisco, the Little School was forced to
move when its former home was deemed seismically unfit. Horton worked
with a parent committee for six months before they found a suitable space.
The Little School liked this particular property because they could purchase
the redundant church and gym, quickly reselling the church for conversion
to housing. After the purchase, the parent committee and the school director asked Horton to design their new home. They had only three requirements. There had to be three classrooms; construction had to be completed
on time; all expenses had to be within the budget. He met all three demands.

Horton made no attempt to alter the existing space. Instead, he inserted
a freestanding, serpentine structure into the old rectangular box (fig. 3.14).
Kids and parents have lovingly named it "The Wall." Horton provided an appropriate light touch by painting the original ceiling a sky-blue color and by
hanging light fixtures from it that appear to be floating clouds. The new
wall, with its stark white walls and varied deep openings, is reminiscent of
Le Corbusier's Chapel of Notre Dame du Haut (1950–1954) at Ronchamp,
France.

Horton's curving wall is an abstract background that is both an entrance
to interior classrooms and a backdrop to play. By providing projecting tables,
chairs, cavernous entryways, ladders, and ledges, Horton ensured that the
wall would become the defining element of the school and a magnet for
imaginative play. In effect, the wall has blurred the boundary between "interior" and "front door." The old notion of schoolyard has taken on a more
subtle, innovative, and welcoming form as an inside/outside space where
children are dropped off, picked up, and allowed to scamper with each
other. There is an outdoor playground in the rear yard, one that is filled with
many natural areas of water and trees for exploration and which someday
will be upgraded to an even more exciting facility. In the meantime, the outdoors augment the indoors rather than the other way around.

Parents of Little Schoolers were not thinking excessively about being a
safe haven from outside intruders, although this type of solution seems to

Fig. 3.14 Mark Horton, The Little School (1996), San Francisco, California.
Courtesy of Mark Horton/Architecture.

be one that could be adapted to that type of concern. Another school in an especially harsh climate might also learn from this example. There are two additional lessons here for playgrounds. First, the site and shape of a playground can be more versatile and unexpected than most people would imagine. Second, even small fry can accept interesting architecture and so can their parents and teachers. As Horton retells it, the school did not ask for "architecture." They had no inclination to excellent or high-powered design. When they did get something that exceeded the norm, the teachers of this school were quick to grasp its beauty and incorporate it into the curriculum. They realized that architecture matters and that lives can be positively impacted by good design. Even though this school relies heavily on a play-driven curriculum, the students studied "spaces" in an informal way during one summer session. Students and teachers visited places such as a redwood grove, nearby Grace Cathedral, and Temple Emanuel, where they learned about natural and constructed places. These activities have brought to fruition some of the goals of blending play and art that had been espoused in the 1950s and are making a comeback today.

CHAPTER 4

Strategies

Faced with varied patrons and the resultant expansion of places where children play, designers have had to come up with strategies that will allow them to respond to escalating demand. Recent increases in the birth rate and the need to replace decaying equipment have fueled the pressure. A growing number of parents and educators are seeing that children quickly tire of off-the-shelf equipment and are seeking alternatives. The designer's role has become more difficult because of their "competition": amusement parks and other commercial centers that have emphasized theme- and character-driven play. The manufacturers have picked up on this with more literal adaptations of castles, pirate boats, and spaceships. In the short term, these flashy interpretations can be very appealing to children.

Contemporary architects, landscape architects, and sculptors largely have followed one of three strategies to confront these developments. Pursuing one track, they create site-specific playgrounds that abandon, or at least limit, equipment in favor of manipulating the earth, assembling plants and rocks, or incorporating natural materials, water, and even found objects into varied settings. This type of design reflects a kinship with Robin Moore's prescription for natural learning. It also evokes Noguchi's 1940s designs for shaping earth and using it as an active component in his projects. Noguchi's *Playscapes,* his only playground executed in the United States (completed in Atlanta in 1976, restored 1996), is not as successful as the memory of the unbuilt playgrounds he designed years earlier. The Atlanta equipment is dressed in colorful and inventive shapes that hide the fact that this playground does not depart from the "swing/sandbox/see-saw" precedents of the early 1950s. Noguchi's more significant contribution remains his careful development of the site (fig. 4.1). He set off *Playscapes* by creat-

Fig. 4.1 Isamu Noguchi, *Playscapes* (1976, restored 1996), Piedmont Park, Atlanta, Georgia. Author's photograph, 2000.

ing an entryway of low concrete walls. This series of planes defines the play-ground without isolating it and offers chances for kids to romp that rival those of the nearby equipment.

A second approach is more common. Designers recognize the inevita-bility of using manufactured equipment in order to meet client demand and to address their own liability concerns. They have responded by inte-grating commercial pieces into an interesting and challenging site. This strategy involves relegating the purchased equipment to a peripheral part of a composition. The equipment is no longer the focus of attention; it becomes one of several recreation alternatives that are part of a well-orchestrated whole. These are not equipment-generated solutions so much as spaces that include equipment as one of a several options. The end product tends to break down racial, class, gender, and generational barriers because there are so many ways in which the site can be utilized.

Preservation is the third alternative. Dynamic playgrounds from the 1950s, 1960s, and even 1970s are frequently in need of upgrading and restoration. Americans with Disabilities Act (ADA) compliance and safety guidelines account for a flurry of activity. Neighborhoods often refurbish playgrounds in order to make them more useful and inviting. Designers with a strong commitment to history have been able to reinterpret these, giving them a heightened vitality.

Infant Garden, University of California
Davis, California, 1994
Landscape Architect: Susan Herrington

Landscape architect Susan Herrington has long questioned why play has been relegated to taking place on manufactured equipment when the availability and malleability of earth seems so obvious. Herrington, prior to her work with Lisa Gelfand on the projects in San Francisco, redesigned an Infant Garden for the Child and Family Study Center at University of California at Davis in 1994. At the time, Herrington was on the faculty there and her son was one of ten toddlers attending the facility.[1]

The director of the Davis center—someone who was tired of an unrelated grouping of permanent objects, dead grass, and a single tree—asked Herrington to work with the staff to improve their 4,000-square-foot site. Herrington used trees, water, and sculpted terrain to provide an exploratory garden for infants. She recognized that liability issues, which would have swarmed around customized equipment, rarely have attached themselves to moving the land.

Herrington placed an 18-inch-high grassy earthen ring at the heart of her composition. Its center is depressed, so that it can be filled with sand, and it is capped with a wide concrete curb that is colored. This rim became a balancing beam (fig. 4.2). Herrington wanted the earth to embrace the children. She gave focus to where children start their daily activities and offered parents a place to wait when picking up their children after school. Serendipitously, she found that this same form calls to mind nearby Native American burial grounds and thereby provides an unexpected contextual meaning.

Herrington, keeping equipment to a minimum, called for a low slide and a short tunnel. Both of these are "embedded" in earth and descend into the sand area. Herrington called for a triangular fabric canopy to shelter the earthen ring. This movable form gives children a chance to listen and watch how the winds affect the cloth above them. Herrington dedicated nearby areas to other sensory joys. A pine-tree circle encourages smelling, feeling, and a sense of a private space; a plant maze affords areas for touching, tasting, and hiding; and a misting field activates powers of observation. Slightly older children, able to maneuver tyke bikes, become familiar with varied

Fig. 4.2 Susan Herrington, Infant Garden at the Infant Care Center (1994), University of California at Davis. Courtesy of Susan Herrington.

textures and sounds when they drive their vehicles over paths made of differently varied materials, such as slate, brick, and cobblestone.

One measure of this garden's success is the fact that Herrington and architect Lisa Gelfand were asked to design a larger, more comprehensive childcare center for the same campus. Their plan was never executed but it remains instructive. The landscape is flat, a slice of the local agricultural zone. Gelfand and Herrington suggested cordoning off the childcare center with bamboo trees. They also proposed an allée of trees to delineate the site further. For the play area, Herrington worked on a series of earth mounds. She devised graduated hills: one on which babies could roll; one for kids who crawl; and another for toddlers who could use it like a foxhole. She provided a "wild area" where kids could explore grasses. Gelfand thought, too, of how her architecture could aid in defining these areas. For both architect and landscape architect, collaboration at the initial stages enabled each to think seriously about how their disciplines intersect.[2]

George and Judy Marcus Garden of Enchantment
New M. H. de Young Museum
San Francisco, California, 2005
Landscape Architect: Hood Design

Mystery and atmosphere are two of the feelings that Walter Hood is trying to convey in the garden for children at San Francisco's New M. H. de Young Museum. He is succeeding without any traditional equipment. A professor of Landscape Architecture at the University of California at Berkeley, Hood is the landscape architect for this museum in Golden Gate Park. He is working with Swiss architects Herzog & de Meuron, who are designing a building to replace old earthquake-damaged structures that could not be seismically retrofitted.

Incorporating play into the total scheme should be a friendly nod to the bustling Richmond and Sunset neighborhoods that are north and south of the park and for whom the park's more than 1,000 acres provide close-at-hand recreational activities. This exterior garden will not charge admission, thereby enticing young visitors to return frequently. Located at the eastern edge of the museum's new tripartite building, the children's zone will adjoin Herzog & de Meuron's copper-sheathed education tower and sit atop an underground parking garage.

Hood's participation and design suggest a new alliance between museums and those who advocate for giving varied experiences to kids. Inserting a play area into a museum space has become fairly commonplace but rarely in the way that it is being done here. Art museums have not sponsored playgrounds for a long time. Children's museums and science museums, which often have stepped forward and commissioned highly original pieces, typically have had to yield to a fiscal imperative. Their unique playgrounds tend to remain part of the museum space for which there is an admission charge. These exist outside of the public sphere where they would be available for local families on a frequent, informal basis. The new De Young museum is altering these negative signals by providing a viable, exciting, and freely accessible model.

Harry Parker, director of the de Young, encouraged Hood to consider a children's garden for this site. Parker asked Hood to design an area for children that could be both an outdoor teaching space and a holding compound for school classes waiting to access the museum's classrooms. During the course of construction, George and Judy Marcus came forward to support a children's area, thereby allowing more varied facilities than Hood had planned originally. He was delighted to go back to the drawing board and rethink his first proposal. Hood's response, a 1-acre area called the Children's Garden of Enchantment, reflects his beliefs that children are best served by allowing them to engage in spatial and creative experiences (fig. 4.3). He believes that these, rather than stationary play objects, support kids' activities. This does not preclude Hood's making sure that the view from the education tower to the garden will be filled with visual interest.

Hood thinks in terms of abstraction and emotion—uncommon goals in work for children. He does not pander to kids but maintains a sophisticated stance, believing that they can absorb and benefit from historical, even geological, landscapes by adapting their play to what is presented to them.[3] He is also a keen observer, a dedicated advocate of a "ground up" approach that responds to how kids interact.

Fig. 4.3 Walter Hood, George and Judy Marcus Garden of Enchantment (early study, 2003) for New de Young Museum, Golden Gate Park, San Francisco. Courtesy of Hood Design.

For the new garden, Hood has relocated and adapted a fountain, the Pool of Enchantment, that had stood at the main entrance to the old complex. It provides a shallow area for splashing and tactile adventure. The original rocks and animal sculptures of the old fountain were tagged and numbered, then re- reinstalled when the building was complete. Hood has reused two cast-concrete sphinxes, the work of California sculptor George Putnam, which are other beloved markers from the oldest section of the de Young. These flank the entry to Hood's garden and open up to a fantasy world that evokes ancient Egypt and more generalized dense landscapes of paradise. They also hint at Hood's two-level menagerie, filled with more Putnam sculpture, which awaits kids inside.

Hood's medium for exploration was colored rocks, huge boulders, expanses of grass, tropical plants, and huge redwood trees. He chose to preserve palm trees, first brought into this area for San Francisco's 1894 Midwinter Exposition, which took place in this park.[4] He has used sand to simulate the dunes that had preceded the development of the park in the 1870s. Hood added boulders and planes of undulating hills for the scampering children on field trips. An Enchanted Walk is a boardwalk that leads to a redwood grove, and a "Rolling Dune Fog Bog" and ambient music contribute to the sense that this is a world removed from common experience. Green pavers add more texture to the ground and recall the tapestries that can be found within the museum's collections. Low walls create places for seating and climbing in this varied landscape. Hood provides the atmosphere and the implements; the rest is up to children to use these inventively.

McEnery Children's Park
San Jose, California, 2001
Landscape Architect: The Office of Cheryl Barton

The Guadalupe River, with its tendency to flood, was a huge headache for San Jose. The Army Corps of Engineers, tackling this as a flood-control project, offered the possibility of relief. Fortuitously, the city and its redevelopment agency recognized that flood control and revitalization of the city center could be blended together. Local officials made a commitment in the 1980s to use the realigned river as the heart of a 3-mile-long, 150-acre river park. They envisioned a river that would be bordered by parks, gardens, and museums.[5] They saw it as a major catalyst to improving a decaying downtown by bringing families into the area for a variety of activities, many of which would be free.[6] This was an exceptional strategy, a departure from the more common insertion of retail space into a blighted district. The emphasis on cultural and recreational facilities seems to be a new twist to the Percent for Art programs. These local ordinances, including the one that sank Joe Brown's playground in Philadelphia, began in the late 1950s, became popular in the 1970s, and have attempted since then to lure visitors to urban sites by the inclusion of art work.[7] San Jose's long-term planning, combined with the subsequent boom of Silicon Valley for which San Jose is the physical center, has created a successful outcome. It brings to fruition an idea stressed in 1946 by Harold L. Ickes, the former Secretary of the Interior, who had called for more responsible use of rivers as recreational venues in urban areas.[8]

San Francisco landscape architect Cheryl Barton, the co-winner of the Rosie the Riveter competition, designed one of the parks that abut the river.[9] This is McEnery Children's Park, where Barton has embraced play and planning. She devised something that stimulates kids more than equipment and establishes a corridor that leads visitors from the commercial district to the river. This same space is hospitable to workers from the adjacent computer giant, Adobe Systems, who use it as a lunchtime retreat; and it provides an evening gathering spot for the people who live a few blocks away in an area of Victorian homes that are being revived. Barton has managed to pay homage simultaneously to the natural and economic history of this area, once a major agricultural zone. She has created a quiet retreat in spite of the fact that the park is close to a freeway and on the flight path to San Jose airport. Her strategy involved only minimal equipment. At the city's behest, Barton has supplied a large net climber, available to many children at once, and some spring toys. Barton cleverly chose the latter to look like airplanes, so that young children can mimic the noise and action of the planes that frequently glide above.

Barton, who is interested in the freedom of experiential play, also believes that children will become better stewards of their environment if they have an understanding of its history and fragility. She began by designing a meandering water feature that is the underlying spine of the park (fig. 4.4). This guides visitors in a diagonal manner from a small entrance plaza, close to the downtown, toward the evolving river walk. Natural grasses line the side closest to the street, creating a buffer that prevents children from dashing into automobile traffic. To further engage young visitors, Barton has embedded a counting path and a measuring path into the pavement; these intersect with the path of water. Kids can use these to devise new versions of the old standby, hopscotch.

Because children will not be able to swim in the diverted Guadalupe River,

Fig. 4.4 Cheryl Barton, McEnery Children's Park (2001), San Jose, California. View of diversion channel, with one of Nobuho Nagasawa's dragonfly sculptures in the foreground. Author's photograph, 2003.

Barton has made the water area both evocative and playful. It is a shallow diversion channel, a visible metaphor for the irrigation channels of nearby Santa Clara farm communities. Here the channel is narrow enough to be jumped over, and its shallow water, lined with appealing aqua-colored stones, is suitable for wading. The low concrete wall gives kids a place to sit while they splash. Triple filtering even makes this water suitable for drinking.

Going toward the river, a sandbar appears further along. This will become the primary play space if the artificial river has to be shut down during a drought. Vertical basalt pillars mark the sand sector. These rocks direct visitors to the next area and the largest element of the park, a computer-activated mist fountain comprised of many more of the same stone pillars. This section encourages water play as well as different forms of hide-and-seek. Here, too, there is a contextual message that celebrates the river's mysterious source in the Santa Cruz mountains. By skillfully blending sensory and motor challenges and offering them to wide range of users, Barton has given a physical dimension to Vygotsky's theories.

By dramatically lighting these basalt columns, Barton succeeded in creating an urban park that is active in the early evening. Picnic tables and rows of chairs have become social hubs after dark. This availability ensures that different populations arrive at various times during the day. Diverse constituencies will become more evident as additional housing is added to downtown San Jose. Students at an alternative high school, opened recently across from the park, have already begun to use this site as an extension of their own campus. The newest arrivals are young members of the McEnery family, descendants of the father of a mayor for whom the park is named. Having decided to adopt the park in an informal manner, they frequently come by to collect trash and talk to whoever is there.

Children's PlayGarden at Rusk Institute of Rehabilitation Medicine
New York City, 1998
Landscape Architect: Johansson & Walcavage

It is ironic that one of the most successful community playgrounds, a facility that combines a natural garden with a critique of the ADA, sits behind a high wooden fence. The Children's PlayGarden at Rusk Rehabilitation Hospital (part of New York University Medical Center) serves one of America's premier rehabilitation hospitals, where approximately one-quarter of the patients are children. The wooden enclosure is the only unwelcoming barrier. Nothing else at this facility, designed by Sonja Johansson and Donna

Fig. 4.5 Johansson & Walcavage, Rusk Children's PlayGarden (1998) at NYU
Medical Center, New York City. Author's photograph, 2002.

Walcavage, speaks to exclusivity. It is a place where patients undergoing
physical and occupational therapy are able to interact with kids from the
neighborhood. Anyone can come in, at almost anytime (fig. 4.5).

Rusk horticultural therapist Nancy Chambers, the person largely responsible for development of the Rusk PlayGarden, inaugurated the design phase
by deciding not to restore the old playground.[10] Richard Dattner had designed
that thirty-year-old facility, one of the first expressly for disabled children.
The resulting empty space was a 5,500-square-foot lot with an awkward narrow and deep configuration. The site, adjacent to both the hospital's Enid A.
Haupt Glass Garden for adult horticultural therapy and the main entrance
to the Rusk Institute, seemed promising. Chambers, who began with only
grant money to pay a designer and later had to raise $500,000 for construc-
tion, had several criteria: a safe and clearly delineated perimeter; nature integrated into all aspects of the facility; a strong topographic element that would
depart from the flatness of the old playground; accommodations for both active and passive play, as well as private and group spaces. Other members of
the hospital community, including teachers, aides, physical therapists, and occupational therapists, encouraged her to emphasize different aspects of play
by using sand, hills, water, and slides in addition to natural plant materials.

Johansson & Walcavage met Chambers' requirements by organizing spaces along two meandering paths that diverge from the entrance. Everything is wheelchair accessible. One path is relatively flat and then comes to a low slat bridge. The other follows a higher and more twisting route. A sandpit and low rising hill dominate the space between the two walkways. Rocks, providing additional textures for the users to explore, outline the sand area. Small kids love to roll down the hill. In addition, more than thirty different perennials and over ten different kinds of bog plants grow on both sides of the paths. Kids can operate water spouts, which are easily accessible, with their hands. At the far end, where the paths merge, children drive their bikes or wheelchairs beneath a weeping willow tree, calling it the "car wash." The message is clear: Even kids in wheelchairs have choices and, consequently, control over their environment. Whereas designers of the 1950s and 1960s alluded to a need to simulate nature in the city, this design is focused on the smells, textures, and sounds of actual foliage. The Environmental Yard in Berkeley was a strong generator of this recent interpretation.

Nature is supplemented by low pieces of equipment. Kids can choose from a glider, a hammock, a swing, or two slides. There are several mechanical features, such as a wall of levers and pulleys, that address rehabilitation needs but are equally appealing for kids without any disability. A playhouse without side walls, particularly easy to navigate in a wheelchair, is similarly available to all participants.

The PlayGarden has given a new spin to the ADA. The impulse of the legislation regarding playgrounds, to make public facilities at least partially accessible, was well meaning but the results have been flawed.[11] Horticultural therapist Chambers notes that urban playgrounds have evolved in a peculiar way. City sites tend to be small lots, where there is often money and space for a single large piece of manufactured equipment. All kids compete for places on the commercial piece and the non-disabled users, particularly rowdy boys, commandeer the structure.[12] Young people in wheelchairs frequently are intimidated and tend to stay away even though there are usually inviting ramps and other means of access. It may be that the primary benefit of the ADA—and not a result that should be discounted lightly—is that parents with infants in strollers or carriages now can wheel the smaller tots into closer proximity to the older siblings. Parents or caregivers can interact with both age groups at the same time. Even more appropriately, ramps have made it possible for frail, elderly grandparents to share a play experience with their young grandchildren.

Chambers, Johansson, and Walcavage have challenged the ADA successfully by building a playground that is totally accessible to disabled kids and equally available to those who have no physical limitations. Rather than adhere just to ADA guidelines, they have developed universal design. Chambers extended this gesture further by reaching out to people in the neighborhood and to other social service agencies. Neighbors call it "their park" and, during the summer, arrive dressed in bathing suits to take full advantage of the water features. The New York Public Library sponsors a weekly program of stories and songs for the Rusk patients and anyone else who wants to join in. The PlayGarden provides space for local children to have birthday parties for modest cost. An annual free Community Festival, which draws over one thousand people, also has bound this facility to its neighbors. One of the highlights is an extensive petting zoo brought in for the occasion and provided by a social service agency that provides opportunities for troubled youth. Rusk has a partnership with the National Institute of People with Disabilities (NIPD). Augmenting the Rusk gardening staff, the NIPD young adults come twice a week and acquire some of their first experiences with job-skill training by helping out in the play garden.

The playground's role as a center of community was tested on September 12, 2001. The director decided to open the PlayGarden, although most of New York and much of America was in shock following the attacks on the World Trade Center and the Pentagon. Less than three miles from Ground Zero, Rusk quickly filled with local families. Parents quietly shared their concerns and grief while their children, liberated from apartments and twenty-four-hour news broadcasts, had a chance to frolic in a warm, nurturing, and diverse environment.

THE PLAYGROUNDS AT BATTERY PARK CITY, NEW YORK CITY

Teardrop Park
Landscape Architect: Michael Van Valkenburgh Associates, 2004

Nelson A Rockefeller Park Playground
Landscape Architect: Johansson & Walcavage, 1993

The Real World
Sculptor: Tom Otterness, 1993

Teardrop Park, designed by landscape architect Michael Van Valkenburgh as a playground without equipment, is a place for sensory delights. It complements two nearby and earlier places for play. These are the Nelson A. Rockefeller Park Playground, designed by Johansson & Walcavage, which provides for motor activity, and Tom Otterness's bronze sculpture, *The Real World,* which presents an intellectual challenge. Comprising many separate parts, Otterness's piece is often called a playground. With the arrival of Teardrop Park, these three locales will provide for sensual, physical, and cerebral opportunities for play. All are located in the northern section of Battery Park City, the commercial and residential community that was built adjacent to the World Trade Center and on land recovered from excavation for the Twin Towers.[13]

Urban planners Carr, Lynch, Hack and Sandell (CLHS), of Cambridge, Massachusetts, designed the overall plan for this part of Battery Park. Gary Hack, formerly of CLHS and presently dean of the School of Design at the University of Pennsylvania, has noted that his firm had to meet the varied, extensive, sometimes contradictory demands of local residents.[14] Their requests included athletic fields, play areas for young children, spaces for older citizens, and tennis courts. The design team quickly realized that the demands would fill more than twice the designated site, approximately 8 acres. CLHS approached this long rectangle, oriented north-south along the Hudson River, as a penetrable entity. They first configured a meandering inner path that traversed the site. Their goal was to alternate green spaces on one side and hard surfaces on the other. This immediately created three distinct areas, providing a site for Johansson & Walcavage at the south end and Otterness at the north. Between these was an area for sports, such as basketball.[15]

For the playground, Donna Walcavage was interested in aiding parents who seek new ways to interact with their children. She believes their search has little to do with security fears of children being snatched by abductors; and she does not think that overzealous parents want to control play and ensure a heightened educational experience for their tots. Rather, she believes that the parents, who have intense professional lives, are seeking ways to connect with their children in a shared moment on the playground. She has tried to be as accommodating as possible to this situation.

Using wooden components, Johansson & Walcavage created a series of intimate "rooms" along a central interior spine. Following the neutral colors that Richard Dattner used in the 1960s for his Central Park playgrounds, they eschewed bright colors for their wooden structure. To provide even more play space, the designers added a second story over most of the area. There are bridges, nets, slides, and lookouts at this upper level. Perhaps unconsciously, the designers replicated in miniature the central spine and flanking multi-level low buildings that were the earliest plan (1969, Harrison and Abramowitz, Philip Johnson; Conklin and Rosant) for Battery Park City.[16]

The inwardly focused spine gives this playground a sense of cohesion. A

Fig. 4.6 Johansson & Walcavage, Nelson A. Rockefeller Park Playground
(1992,) Battery Park City, New York. View from the *Dodo* toward the central
spine. Author's photograph, 2004.

bike carousel anchors one end and a water feature in the shape of a dodo bird gurgles lightly at the other terminus (fig. 4.6). Tom Otterness sculpted this bird, a congregating point for infants and toddlers. Little ones adore the gently bubbling water and adorable bronze bird. Otterness says that this dodo's stomach is the most polished work of any of his pieces. The choice of Otterness, a recognized contemporary sculptor whose larger piece is nearby, is very telling. It is a nice touch in a park dedicated to art patron Nelson Rockefeller.

The Battery Park City Conservancy manages the site and a lavish maintenance budget adds to the appeal of the well-tended grounds. The playground has become a magnet for people from Battery Park apartments as well as from the surrounding neighborhoods of Tribeca, Chinatown, and Wall Street. Users come from other areas, too. A silly event in July 2001 highlights how people will travel to use this facility. A three-year-old from a distant neighborhood received a $50 summons for urinating on a tree. This incident created an international brouhaha. The American press and their foreign counterparts, including at least one London tabloid, loved the story. The contrast between the "crime" and the "punishment" was huge. Eventually the case was dismissed, which allowed the New York Daily News to proclaim: "Boy in Park Pee May Walk Free."[17] The press coverage overlooked how much really had been said about the role that successful playgrounds have in attracting visitors from other parts of town, and possibly in creating new communities based not on living in the same geographic zone but instead on participating daily in common activities at a single spot.

Tom Otterness's sculpture The Real World is another magnet (fig. 4.7). Composed of small pieces that are placed throughout the site—a more reflective area that looks outward to the Hudson River—this multi-component sculpture frequently is visited by camps that come to the park for a day trip and eat their lunch here. Even the tables are pedestals for some of Otterness's creations. Although Otterness's Dodo on the playground is lovable and benign, the tone shifts in The Real World. The artist took it upon himself to design something where children could interact with serious ideas. He cloaked these in appealing comical creatures whose actions have much to say about greed, sex, and violence. Otterness hopes that his work will ignite intellectual investigation by the kids who visit. Parents, many of whom might at first be shocked to see their kids playing on bronze sculptures that may illustrate avarice or sexual acts, are encouraged to use the playground to broach these topics in an informal, spontaneous way with their offspring.

The most recent accomplishment in this area, Michael Van Valkenburgh's Teardrop Park, is slightly removed from the other two sites. It is just east of

Fig. 4.7 Tom Otterness, *The Real World* (1992), Battery Park City,
New York. Photograph by Robert S. Solomon, 2003.

CLHS's original park plan. Roughly 2 acres of tranquil space, it is both a
bridge and a refuge.[18] It physically joins the activities of Rockefeller Park
with new athletic fields. At the same time, it provides a calming atmosphere
that relies completely on nature for varied experiences. Teardrop Park sits
in a courtyard created by four apartment buildings. One of these was the
first environmentally sustainable, "green building," in the area. It seems a
fitting backdrop for a natural park.

With appropriate homage to nineteenth-century Central Park, where
Frederick Law Olmsted greatly enlarged upon and exaggerated the natural
forms that were there, Van Valkenburgh has created a landscape that brings
a "supercharged" reality to what previously had been landfill. There is a varied topography of valleys and hills, a marsh, a sand cove. These are joined
by august accretions of rocks and boulders. Van Valkenburgh called for 2,700
tons of stone, imported from the Hudson Valley. His tour de force is a stone
wall, more than 150 feet long and up to 27 feet high (fig. 4.8). This cuts
through the site, helping to separate a more active area from a more passive
one; a very short tunnel pierces the wall, allowing passage from one side to
another. The wall becomes animated by expressing water, "oozing moisture
in summer and accumulating ice in winter."[19] Ten hidden spouts trigger the
flow process.

Robin Moore, who moved from Berkeley in the 1980s and presently directs the Natural Learning Initiative at North Carolina State University, was an advisor to the project. His hand certainly is seen in the way that the landscape allows for varied play with natural materials. In addition, MacArthur Award–winning artist Ann Hamilton has created three stone pieces. These are not meant to encourage climbing, but older kids are able to use them for that if they wish. Care has also been taken to provide a great amount of seating for all ages, and lighting at night helps to draw adults to Teardrop Park. The $17-million price tag comes as a jolt, almost three times more staggering in real money than the $1-million cost of the Riis Houses playground in the 1960s.[20]

Moylan School
Hartford, Connecticut, 1998
Landscape Architect: Mikyoung Kim Design

Landscape architect Mikyoung Kim wanted to build a school play yard without equipment. She was reacting to what she has described as commercial equipment "becoming the focal point of three-dimensional design for play-

Fig. 4.8 Michael Van Valkenburgh, Teardrop Park (under construction, 2003), New York. View is of the huge stone wall that cuts through the park. Photograph by Robert S. Solomon, 2003.

grounds."[21] Having agreed at the end of the design phase to include a single commercial piece to augment her elegant manmade landscape, she now feels that this was a justified inclusion and is pleased with the final results.

Hartford's Moylan School, the site of Kim's work, shares several characteristics with New York's P.S. 19, where Ken Smith designed the Reading Garden. Both are proof that reports about school performance, poverty, and well-being are often misleading and that the situation is incredibly more complex, occasionally even more hopeful than outsiders would assume.[22] There is no denying that Hartford is one of the most downtrodden urban areas in America.[23] The city is home to almost 30 percent of the Connecticut schools that are on the U.S. Department of Education's roster of low-achieving facilities. Moylan School falls within that designation, and the objective facts support that. The school, with six hundred elementary-school students and nine special-education classes, qualifies for federal subsidies. Many of the families are transient, moving frequently within the city. Test scores have been low.

The impression the school gives to visitors is much more substantial. Some of the statistics can be explained. This is a facility that has become a haven for immigrants, many of whom are starting out in this country without any jobs. Moylan students, overwhelmingly, do not come from homes where English is spoken, and this has had a negative impact on testing results. At the same time, the school supports an innovative dual-language program, English and Spanish, that is giving it a good reputation as an enriching environment. Owing to the success of this endeavor, Moylan eventually may qualify as a magnet school. Connecticut's school profiles, last reported in 2000/2001, show that Moylan teachers took fewer sick days than their colleagues in other parts of their city or state. This is clearly not an indifferent staff that loathes coming to work.

As an environment and work space, Moylan is very pleasing and welcoming. The school has a wonderful physical plant, all of which is new or renovated. The original brick block, constructed in the 1920s, was updated to a courtyard scheme in the 1990s. Hartford architect Tai Soo Kim designed the 98,000-square-foot addition. He shifted the main entrance of the school to a side street, placing it along one of the extended walls, where it now provides a covered entryway to the school and a direct axis into the large courtyard. The school principal at the time of planning, Donald Carso, had long hoped for such an open interior space. Carso's main concern was safety, having had four students hit by cars during the prior years that he had been a principal.

Mikyoung Kim, Tai Soo Kim's daughter and a landscape architect who

Fig. 4.9 Mikyoung Kim, courtyard of Moylan School (1998), Hartford, Connecticut. Overview of the courtyard. Photograph by Robert S. Solomon, 2003.

teaches at Rhode Island School of Design, designed the courtyard and its
playground (fig. 4.9). She created a serpentine wall composed of concrete
block. This is the dominant organizing feature for this expansive space. There
is very little color in the wall, except for an occasional red block. Principal
Carso at first fought the wall, thinking it was too dangerous. The younger
Kim and Carso arrived at a compromise that was satisfying to both: she
agreed to put a V-shaped cap atop the wall to discourage walking and climbing; he agreed to let the wall remain.

The wall has two sections. This creates a quiet zone closer to the old
school and a more active area near the single purchased climbing structure.
The quieter section of the wall embraces terraced seating. There is a shallow amphitheater for school performances and awards ceremonies. The
more active section, where the wall peaks at a height of five and a half feet,
is punctuated by varied openings. Some are large enough to be walked or
crawled through. A secondary attached wall springs from the primary divider, creating interior spaces for hiding and talking . This is the area where
Kim thought children could be their most creative. It also provides a slightly
hidden space that can be explored by children in wheelchairs. Low benches
on both sides of the wall encourage clusters of students to come together.

Thus even the active zone imparts a sense of serenity to the whole courtyard by forming pockets for quiet interaction.

The wall is also a backdrop, a marker of quotidian rhythms. The school daily provides a federally funded breakfast and lunch; and after each meal, children gravitate to the wall to hang out before classes. When teachers begin the day, they come into the courtyard and marshal each class together at various parts of the wall. Then, together, they enter the building to begin studies. Parents arriving to retrieve their children in the afternoon also gravitate to the wall for quiet reflection or gathering for small discussions. Many of them are of Hispanic descent and recognize that their children's playground is another form of the town plaza they would have known during their own youth.

Although landscape architect Kim talks about the wall as a metaphor for seeing and being seen, its use has been more prosaic and more encouraging. The right scale for kids, it is neither too high and intimidating, nor too low and not taken seriously. With its breadth and sweeping but not excessive curves, it is imposing and stately. The wall sets a tone, a presence that conveys a message of respect. The inference is that Moylan students are worthy of something that is unique, quite beautiful, and allows them to make choices in how they use it. It enhances both their play and their sense of well being.

Lafayette Square
Oakland, California, Late 1990s
Landscape Architect: Hood Design

Walter Hood has written extensively about "hybrid spaces," areas that create new opportunities for users by recombining forms and functions. One of his successful designs is Lafayette Square in downtown Oakland, California. Hood reconceptualized this area in the late 1990s. He approached this site as a multilayered enterprise that can be inviting to people of different ages, backgrounds, and interests. The Oakland Redevelopment Agency funded this project with the help of an Oakland City bond issue, a grant from the National Park service, and city and state open-space funds.[24]

As in so much of what he does, Hood's strategy was to find the basic elements that have existed historically and socially, and then to magnify and intensify them for contemporary use. Hood's most useful preparation for this and other projects began when he observed and recorded, in daily eloquent journal entries, the activities in his own Oakland neighborhood. He

Fig. 4.10 Walter Hood, Lafayette Square (late 1990s), Oakland, California. This distant view of the hillock shows how it is used spontaneously by children. Photograph courtesy of Hood Design.

began in 1991 and published the resulting drawings and remarks in his book, *Urban Diaries* (Washington, D.C.: Spacemaker Press, 1997). His task at Lafayette Square was aided when the city "made a bold decision not to design the homeless and unemployed regulars out of the park."[25]

Recalling the park's significance as one of the city's original nineteenth-century public spaces, Hood reintroduced old patterns of vegetation and reinterpreted the park's historic ironwork and benches (fig. 4.10). He did not feel bound to preserving the original 1.5-acre Beaux-Arts plan. Hood dismantled the old central space and its accompanying diagonal paths in order to create more compartmentalized areas, ones that reflect current use, not classical concepts of symmetry and order. In an area of the city that houses the old, the poor, and the upwardly mobile, and where there is a mix of black, white, and Asian cultures, Hood hoped to foster a communal piazza. He purposely abandoned gates and enclosures, essentially to let the many old men who come here daily know they would not be forced out. Arguing that this should be a place where "the suits and the homeless" could mix, Hood made sure that the perimeter of this park holds many of the things that would draw in people, including rest rooms, benches, tables, and barbecue grills.

Hood placed a small piece of commercial play equipment in one corner of the site, close to the sidewalk. This is the first time that a structure dedicated to kids has existed in this park. Hood used the equipment to announce that children, too, are welcome and that they might find more areas within the park to enjoy. The equipment's single color, red, implies good luck for the children of nearby Asian communities. Without an axis to guide them, children frequently gravitate to the nearby hillock after they have finished on the play equipment. This hillock, where an old observatory once stood, has become a broad, de facto playground. Children use it for individual exploration, especially biking. Spontaneous team sports, such as touch football, unfold there. Not restricted to a single play space, children have been free to create their own games or interact with adults. Parents seem particularly comfortable with the arrangement. Hood's design makes it easy for them to keep an eye on their children while they find their way through picturesque plantings.

In spite of the fact that plans for nearby office towers were abandoned due to an economic downturn, the mix of people in the park remains diverse. The old men, who have congregated there for decades, still arrive daily. Nonprofit organizations serve meals here during the Thanksgiving and Christmas seasons. Some new investment and building, albeit on a smaller scale than what was first planned, is starting to trickle into the area. This eventually will direct more office workers into the park at lunch time. Hood included an open pavilion in his plan and it already attracts individuals who often sit there, bring their lunch, and listen to music. This open-air structure also can be used for improvised dramatic presentations.

Fellger Park
Chicago, 2003
Architect: Wilkinson Blender Architecture

Fellger Park, in Chicago's evolving Roscoe Village neighborhood, illustrates how local parents and professionals can tease a good plan out of a bland one. In this case, an independent group of neighbors came together to form Friends of Fellger Park. Having the fund-raising skills to bring about a transformation, something for which local advocates have to bear part of the cost, the friends group approached the Chicago Park District (CPD). When CPD presented a revitalization scheme for this aging site, they were challenged by the architectural firm of Wilkinson Blender Architecture (WBA), whose two principals, Michael Wilkinson and Richard Blender, live and work nearby.

WBA objected to the CPD's proposal: a symmetrical layout, isolated equipment, and thick plantings placed uniformly all along the site's perimeter. Offering to work *pro bono,* WBA made an important contribution to what a small city park could look like with a site-specific approach. Echoing van Eyck, they opted for a ground-up approach.[26]

Fellger Park starts with a premise quite distinct from that of Hood's Lafayette Square. Hood had to strive for inclusion, breaking any physical barriers that would become obstacles for people to enter. WBA's task for one of Chicago's busiest street corners, Belmont and Damen Avenues, was different. The designers, led by Blender, had to serve two populations whose needs were not necessarily mutually exclusive: the elderly population that has remained in this historically working-class area and the many young families, with small children, who have arrived recently. The latter group needed some buffers to sights and sounds of traffic, something that would not be rejected by the older residents. The park, opened in 2003, has been successful in retaining that mix of children and the elderly.

Blender began by thinking about the programmatic needs of a neighborhood park, approximately 225 by 125 feet, and how those could be incorporated serendipitously into this confined area. He came up with a deep but variable green buffer along the street to mitigate noise; different play zones for active and imaginative play; expanding and compressing paths for tricycles and pedestrians; an informal performance pavilion for concerts and social activities. Blender wanted to make sure that the items that would appeal to youngest tots, including some commercial equipment, would be the furthest from the street. Then he established a grid of lighting posts. His goal was not to segment the park into distinct functional units but to layer the various needs in order to produce a complex multi-use facility. He wanted to retain the original park entrances, provide adequate seating for parents and older folks, and conserve existing trees so that there was a sense of place in addition to desirable shade for notoriously hot summers. Blender wanted to create a functional and romantic spot, a place that would offer a variety of experiences to a range of users (fig. 4.11).

A small open pavilion became a valued addition to the plan. Located closest to the intersection of the two busy streets, it supplies a space for evening activity. It gives a focus to the park for events that could be musical and/or theatrical and for improvised teen gatherings. The lawn in front remains open for play and sitting. The pavilion is a modernist, bold interpretation of the ubiquitous gazebos that have become sentimental markers on the American landscape. Blender devised a unique structure that could have been built at lower cost than the purchase of a standard-issue gazebo. He called

Fig. 4.11 Richard Blender, Fellger Park (2002), Chicago. Early plan for music pavilion. Courtesy of Wilkinson Blender Architecture.

for a concrete plinth and a simple metal roof clad in sheet metal and supported by a series of thin steel columns. Grouped tightly together and placed at varying angles, these columns were intended to parallel another forest, in this case a simulated industrial one. The CPD, however, insisted on a roof that could be purchased from a catalog. The resulting substitute design has three sail shades, another worthwhile solution for the design problem and one that seems not to compromise the architects' intentions. Even before the music stage was completed, families packed suppers and filled Fellger Park on summer nights during free concerts for kids.

Underhill Playground in Kissena Corridor Park
Queens, New York, 1999
Landscape Architect: New York City Parks
and Recreation Department
Sculptors: Bill and Mary Buchen

Planners of playgrounds can adore or despise teenagers. It is necessary to harness their enthusiasm, provide for their privacy, and segregate them from younger users. Katherine Bridges, senior designer in the New York City Parks and Recreation Department, has had great success by teaming up with artists Bill and Mary Buchen. Bridges' strategy is to use commercial equipment within a narrative context and then to augment the standard equipment with unique designs. She frequently has chosen art work, such as Buchen pieces, to supplement the off-the-shelf equipment and to give distinction to it.[27]

A husband-and-wife collaboration that has been exploring sound phenomena for more than thirty years, the Buchens trained as musicians (Bill remains an able tabla performer) and have created sculpture that is playful and interactive. They began to use the term "sonic architecture"—now the name of their design company—to explain how their work defines these interrelated connections of acoustics, space, and time (fig. 4.12). Often fabricated in bronze or aluminum, Buchen pieces are frequently abstractions of drums and other instruments. They have the benefit of being almost maintenance-free.

Bridges organized the renovation of this 1950s Queens site by establishing a two-phase project. Working with storyteller Laura Simms, she recovered a fairytale that became the underlying concept. Bridges chose the Russian story of Wasalissa the Beautiful. It is, not unlike Cinderella, a tale of the wrongs that were inflicted on a young woman and about her ability to overcome them. The heroine Wasalissa was helped by birds and a doll that been given to her by her dying mother. After several tasks and hardships, Wasalisa was rescued by the king, who married her. There was rejoicing in the kingdom and both king and queen ruled benignly, with special care for animals. Bridges has translated this tale into the location, shape, and color of the playground equipment she selected. Accompanied by storyboards that retell the epic, the playground takes on its own role as part of the narrative. It is enhanced by a custom fence, designed by sculptor Arlene Slavin, that is adorned with steel cutouts of the animals that are key to the story.

Bridges used the Buchens' musical sculpture in an adjoining rectangular space. She chose pieces that resemble drums but could also be tables and chairs. Bridges also selected a parabolic disc. All of these enabled Bridges to carry over the Wasalisa theme, because the tale concludes with endless music and jubilation, the same type of revelry that can be reproduced on the Buchens' work. Providing a chance for musical expression, seating, and a distance from toddlers, this area has tremendous draw for teens. They have commandeered it as their refuge, a place where they can gather. Bridges shrewdly used the surface below the Buchens' work to define further this teen zone. Thinking about the sound waves that emanate from musical instruments, Bridges created a design to reflect sonic movement. She specified pavers to surround each of the instruments. Composed of 18-inch squares,

Fig. 4.12 New York City Parks and Recreation Department, renovation of
Underhill Park (1999), Queens, New York, with the work of Bill and Mary
Buchen of Sonic Architecture. Author's photograph, 2003.

the pavers have red, white, green, and black marble chips imbedded in them to form concentric circles. Bridges also called for pavers with randomly placed marble, employing these in the intervening "empty" squares. All of these surfaces make clear that this part of the park is related to but different from the playground equipment.

Brigadoon Park
San Jose, California, 2002 restoration
Landscape Architect: Catalyst

The city of San Jose has just completed a dramatic preservation and renewal scheme. Landscape architect Tom Richman has said confidently that restoring an old playground is an affirmative gesture: It retrieves playground design from the venue of litigators by making adjustments to what already has had an effect on daily life. Renovating the old has potential to find new use for equipment that usually has material presence and a long local history. Sometimes these are unique pieces. It is not hard to locate worthwhile parks and equipment from previous decades. It is sometimes trickier to get communities to agree to restore them. Parents often feel that reinvigorating an old site is denying their children the shiny equipment that is visible throughout neighboring towns.

Richman's firm, Catalyst, restored Brigadoon Park in San Jose (fig.4.13). It remains a young person's dream and maintains a special hold on teens. A 20-foot-high concrete embankment, complete with three separate twisting embedded slides, sets this park apart from most others.[28] The city of San Jose appreciated their exceptional slide, an industrial wonder unlike the tire playgrounds that were made by parents and PTAs during the same decade of the 1970s. The city, having raised money to update its playgrounds, hired Richman to save this special feature and to integrate it into a larger play zone that would appeal to small kids. Flanked by a high school and an elementary school, Brigadoon Park had to be fascinating to users from both sides of the age spectrum.

Richman directed much of his energy toward site modification by improving hillside admittance to the embankment slides. He complied with all ADA guidelines. Now, two low-grade paths allow access to the top of the slides. Like so many other wheelchair-accessible facilities, this improvement provides a way for wheelchair users to accompany physically unimpaired individuals to the launching zone. It is unclear how someone in a wheelchair would actually transfer to the slide or disembark.

Believing that the old slides resembled either waterfalls or a volcano, because of their sharp descent to the ground, Richman gave the community a choice of which image they preferred. After several meetings, they chose water as the core theme. Richman, who first thought that the slides should be painted blue in keeping with the nautical motif, later rescinded that decision and kept the slides free of coloring. Though color accents appear around it, the raw imposing concrete itself has not been compromised. The results are impressive: the three chutes empty into a circular "river" of blue cushioning material, which effectively separates tot and youth zones in the area at the bottom.

Within the city of San Jose, in an area dominated by single-family homes and apartment complexes, this park has become a new meeting ground for the local Asian and Hispanic populations. A huge achievement of this park slide has been to offer interesting areas for teens, many of whom gather there after school. The thrill of riding the slides has drawn young people from a diverse socioeconomic and racial mix. The slides are known throughout the city. They offer great, free entertainment. Due to the precipitous drop, parents stay close to small children and tend to interact casually with each

Fig. 4.13 Tom Richman, restoration of embankment slides at Brigadoon Park (2002), San Jose, California. View from the top of the concrete slide, designed by Michael Painter in 1970. Author's photograph, 2003.

Fig. 4.14 New York City Department of Parks and Recreation, renovation of Superblock Midblock Park (Landscape Architect M. Paul Friedberg & Partners in collaboration with architect I. M. Pei and Partners, late 1960s) into St. Mark's Children's Playground, 2003. Photograph by Robert S. Solomon, 2003.

other. Brigadoon Park is also a facility that parents can use at the same time that their children do.

St. Mark's Children's Playground
Brooklyn, New York, 2003 restoration
Landscape Architect: New York Parks
and Recreation Department

The New York City Parks and Recreation Department also has reinterpreted and brought up to date a more modest park, one that embodied play and generalized use on a small plot. Frequently referred to as the "midblock," or "street park," it was supposed to alter the streetscape near a housing project in Bedford Stuyvesant. I. M. Pei designed the high-rises in the1960s. Pei and landscape architect Paul Friedberg worked together to create the small park on St. Marks Avenue (fig. 4.14). They were able to carve out a narrow and long site (approximately 75 by 200 feet) on a tree-lined street flanked by low-rise residential buildings. By halting traffic at both ends and narrowing the street, the designers created a new island that became a midblock oasis. They placed it near, but not within, the massive apartment towers so that it would have its own identity and easy access. The Astor Foundation originally funded this experiment.

Within this freshly claimed site, Friedberg inserted a sunken plaza, divided into three separate rooms. The entry was down low steps, on one side of the middle section. This middle area functioned as a setting for passive gatherings. The flanking spaces had very specific, active uses: one was for modular climbing equipment; the other contained a large fountain. The overall impression was of an addition to an urban site, where the hard surfaces of the city had been reused. The park attempted to hand legitimate public space to people who previously had had only their stoops or apartment entries for gathering together.

The New York City Parks Department, which did not have original jurisdiction over this park, recently has secured the right to restore and maintain it. The Parks Department, looking at what had become a ruined and abandoned site, thought first about creating tranquil greenspace. The local block association fought hard to make sure that the play aspects were retained and that there would be a place for children to congregate. Their success and determination have been honored by the change of name, from "park" to "playground," in order to reflect the children's use of the space.

The recent restoration has retained the same footprint, as well as the rooms, curbs, and cylinders that had defined the Friedberg park. There is now a ramp in order to be ADA compliant and a second set of broad stairs opposite the first ones. This is a welcoming gesture. The Parks Department has retained the central seating areas, augmenting them with more benches and tables. The space for play equipment, exactly the same dimensions as before, now has a large contemporary model. The fountain is gone. A succession of rings, all of which can be water sprays, offers wet play. Designer Linda Lawton softened the hard concrete surfaces by bringing in more greenery and by adding a more decorative ground surface. This reinterpretation has not detracted from the impression that this is a refuge from the street and a safe place for people to gather.

Manhattan Square Playground
Rochester, New York, 2005 restoration
Landscape Architect: Ken Smith Landscape Architect
Sculptors: Bill and Mary Buchen

Rochester has faced similar concerns in restoring an earlier, largely abandoned older redevelopment project. Landscape architect Lawrence Halprin

(1916–) designed this one in the early 1970s. Like Friedberg and Pei's Brooklyn project, Manhattan Square was a collage of hard surfaces spawned by an urban renewal plan. Halprin had hoped to ignite spontaneous uses from this park's visitors by giving them choices such as ice skating, sitting on the side of a fountain, or playing on a large wooden playground.[29] Whereas Friedberg and Pei inserted their work into a streetscape near high-rises, Halprin designed a 5-acre project for which high-rises were expected to come later. Office towers were never built and the expected mix of users, such as office workers and downtown shoppers, never arrived. With only limited use, this multifaceted project has not been maintained properly for the past two decades.

Similar to many of his other schemes, Halprin placed a multilevel fountain at the heart of his project. In this case, it occupies the edge of a corner site. Different levels of concrete platforms, which support waterfalls and cascades, were burrowed into the ground. The fountain is partially covered by an aluminum space frame, the only one that Halprin designed. Within this landscape of angles and interior open rooms, Halprin carved space for his playground. The playground, given a spacious 12,000 square feet, had up-to-the-minute wooden climbing structures of the 1970s that had been designed in Halprin's office. Set in sand and accompanied by ramps, slides, and hills, this playground was sturdy and inviting. Placing the equipment on sand was a way to accommodate falls and additional play. It was an inexpensive strategy that is not used enough today. The look of permanence did not prevent the playground from being dismantled in the 1980s.

Landscape architect Ken Smith, who is working on Santa Fe Railyard Park and who created the Reading Garden at P.S. 19, has been challenged to upgrade all of these spaces. Smith has argued forcefully and convincingly that the entire square, comprised almost completely of concrete, would be

Fig. 4.15 Ken Smith, section of proposed intervention at Manhattan Square (2004), Rochester, New York. Courtesy of Ken Smith Landscape Architect.

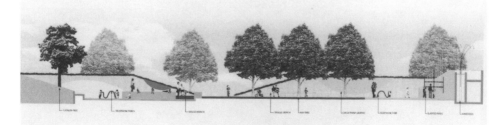

too expensive to destroy. Demolition would eat up most of the budget. He argues, too, that many aspects of the design are worth saving, including an ice skating rink that eventually can function for that purpose in the winter and as a wading pool in the summer.

The client, the city of Rochester, elected to phase the restoration in three cycles. They decided that the playground would be the centerpiece of phase one. Their strategic decision was based on the fact that a playground would bring the greatest number of people into the area in the fastest manner. It would make the biggest difference with the relatively smallest outlay.

Laboring with Bill and Mary Buchen, who worked at Underhill Park in Queens, Smith and his team have reinterpreted Halprin's play area. Their goal was to make it more dependent on experiences than on motor skills. They inserted new equipment and activities, including periscopes and water sprays, into the old plan (fig. 4.15). Smith has divided the area so that older and younger children are separated. A space between the two zones is an area where parents can observe either side. Smith kept all of Halprin's concrete walls, softening them with bright graphics. He replaced many of the steps with gentle slopes, covered with resilient rubber surfacing. The Buchens have added their own musical additions that include "telephone tubes," parabolic benches, wind reeds, and hand chimes.

CHAPTER 5

Variants

Three new kinds of playgrounds need to be acknowledged: civic monuments; unexpected play zones; and specific antidotes for tricky problems. In the early twenty-first century, it is rare but not impossible to locate urban organizations that champion playgrounds as local secular shrines. Playgrounds with ambiguous identities are particular to this time and more common. Quite often, their use rather than their form determines their role as a play space. There are an increasing number of sites where play was not included in the program, often quite purposely, but that have successfully engaged young children and teens. These, lacking the tag of "playground," have managed to escape the control of most safety overseers; they have avoided the eye of overzealous certified inspectors. Young people are challenged by the unexpected ways in which they can explore these venues. The sites have become formidable symbols of rejuvenating cities because of concentrated use by children. Playgrounds also have materialized in order to resolve singular problems: how to fill spatial voids; how to involve underserved communities; and how to give meaning to spaces by invoking collective memory.

Greater Dwight Neighborhood Playground and Community Stage
New Haven, Connecticut, 2004 (design)
Artist: Tom Luckey

This New Haven playground is meant to function as a monument. The Greater Dwight Community Development Corporation (GDCDC), working with Yale University's Urban Design Workshop (YUDW), had been planning a day care center for this low-income area adjacent to the Yale campus. The first site was a well-trafficked corner. Then a larger piece of land, just a bit further down the same street, became available and GDCDC acquired that for the new building. Still retaining the corner property and securing an easement between it and the projected day care facility, the community/ university partnership decided that the original site would be an ideal one for a sizable playground. They wanted this highly visible lot to become both an interesting play space and a marker for this section of town. They were seeking something that would identify the Dwight neighborhood to anyone coming through. YUDW director Alan Plattus has said that they sought a bold recognizable icon, akin to the Watts towers in Los Angeles.[1]

Plattus, long familiar with Tom Luckey's work and his successful climbers for children, brought him into the planning of this site. Luckey was trained as an architect who early in his career shifted to furniture design and sculpture. He has been building for kids since 1985, after his own projects had become exceedingly fantastical. Luckey has designed many one-of-a-kind play pieces, most of which are in children's museum interiors. His projects are multilevel climbers that are held together by cables. In addition to their imaginative designs and beautiful finishes, these pieces lack any clear directive path. They are armatures for play without being too literal or dogmatic. Kids can access the structures in several ways and follow diverse climbing routes. Luckey views his own work, which he fabricates himself, less as a playground and more as a piece of art that is available for climbing. Experimenting with materials, including glass and laminated plywood that has been molded into varied thicknesses and shapes, he has demonstrated

Fig. 5.1 Tom Luckey, playground for the Greater Dwight Community Redevelopment Corporation (2003), New Haven, Connecticut. Courtesy of the Yale Urban Design Workshop (Alan Plattus, Director) and Tom Luckey.

that it is possible to create unique pieces that are safe and stimulating to children. The cost, generally $250,000 or less, is not low, but the works provide excellent value when compared to commercial alternatives.

The New Haven project is giving Luckey a chance to bring his work outdoors and to be used by an expansive number of participants (fig. 5.1). Luckey envisions a multiple-level structure for the New Haven project, which is still in the design phase. It could rise to 25 or 30 feet. He is thinking of using laminated fiberglass or possibly concrete components. Luckey also hopes to split this imposing piece, dedicating the back half to the day care participants and their play experiences. The front, which will be open to the community, will have a number of stages for both climbing and performing. Luckey calls it a celebration stage, a site that will be available for informal concerts and for more planned ones. The end results should create a new type of urban square, one that engages the neighborhood while kids, climbing in the background, remain the backdrop to other activities.

Acacia Park
Colorado Springs, Colorado, 1990s (restoration)
Landscape Design: Colorado Springs Parks, Recreation, and Cultural Services Department

Acacia Park shows that local designers have taken to heart the lessons that Walter Hood taught at Lafayette Square by incorporating a playground into an urban collage. Part of the city's first plan in the 1870s and then the domain of drug dealers and the homeless by the late 1990s, this 3.5-acre park exhibits the open access that Hood advocates. There are no fences or barriers along the perimeter. The corner closest to the business district is the site of a lively computerized fountain that has an hourly rising of a twirling kinetic figure. It, combined with an adjacent piece of playground equipment, are the "hooks" that entice kids and their families to enter the park (fig. 5.2). Once lured in, visitors find extensive greenery, an early-twentieth-century bandshell, shuffleboard courts, picnic tables, and rest rooms. The mixture has made the park a destination for families from all over the city.

Two features distinguish this facility. Both break stereotypes and are full of surprise: the siting of the play equipment and the presence of a police substation. In the late 1990s, the Parks, Recreation, and Cultural Services Department (PRCSD) replaced an older play structure with a more up-to-date model. The local McDonald's franchises paid for both versions. It is to their credit that their largesse is identified only by a small plaque, thereby

Fig. 5.2 Colorado Spring Parks, Recreation, and Cultural Services Department, Acacia Park playground (late 1990s), Colorado Springs, Colorado. Photograph by Robert S. Solomon, 2004.

limiting the commercialization of the playground. The PRCSD design team decided that the new equipment should be placed below grade in order not to interfere with sight lines into the park, toward the bandshell, or outwardly to the surrounding commercial district. The in-house designers lowered the structure and surrounded it with its own concrete wall. Counterintuitively, this enclosure does not detach the playground from the earth but seems to site it further into the land. The designers created an environment that is an intimate space. Access is via ramps or stairs. Both means of descent enhance the play space by providing for additional areas for play or resting. The steps augment the bench seating that is close to the equipment. Local art groups have added mosaics designs to the wall, thereby making it another type of community marker.

The playground does not detract from the park but gives it a new level for exploration. This is especially important because the fountain sits on flat land. In close proximity to the water show, kids in bathing suits like to migrate between the two areas on hot summer afternoons. Augmented with good lighting and the fountain that performs until 10 P.M., the playground draws visitors into the evening. Neither the playground nor the fountain would be as popular independently as they are as a duo.

The police substation demonstrates that legal authorities can have a benign and beneficial presence. The police, rarely needed, set a tone for the whole park. Supervised by a smart, caring woman, the police component takes on a friendly face. Kids using the park know that someone is in charge. They also know that they can pop in, say "hi," and receive a toy or sticker. Park users are varied. Students from a nearby high school come often, knowing that they have to be on good behavior. Senior citizens, who live in housing across the street, feel comfortable with the mix of young and old. Business and government workers, often wearing suits, frequently bring lunch and dine not too far from the homeless population. The latter has not been driven out, but they no longer dominate the scene.

Jamison Square
Portland, Oregon, 2002
Landscape Architect: Peter Walker and Partners

The term "unexpected playscape" seems a bit odd (and "accidental playground" would be far worse!), yet there are play areas that have come about serendipitously. The resulting projects provide spaces where kids can explore, interact, and be a little wild. In this type of arrangement, parents have to be diligent about their children's safety. Caregiver and child must negotiate what is and is not appropriate behavior for each participant, making the adult the mediator between what is possible and what is permissible. This situation is a positive one: It gives the child a less predictable environment than a sanitized playground; at the same time, the caregiver usually feels the need to remain in close enough contact to feel that an experience has been shared by both generations.

Jamison Square in Portland, Oregon, designed by Peter Walker and Partners, is one example of this new breed (fig. 5.3). Its appeal is in the eye-catching water feature that is at the heart of this large piazza. The plaza has become a huge hit, albeit not exactly the way the patron, the Portland Parks and Recreation Department, may have intended. Jamison Square is one of several urban parks planned for this developing residential and office neighborhood,[2] formerly a warehouse and rail yard area, that is now known as the Pearl District.[3] The sophisticated community, which never imagined kids here, had requested a plaza where local residents and day-time workers could engage quietly with each other without interruptions from excessive noise or vehicular traffic.[4] After extensive discussions with residents, Walker concluded that a playful fountain seemed right. Walker designed one that is

Fig. 5.3 Peter Walker and Partners, Jamison Square (2002), Portland, Oregon. Author's photograph, 2002.

low, broad, and stepped. Light-colored granite blocks are the primary material. A programmable computer operates the fountain. Sometimes it spills
a rushing waterfall into a full pool of water. Other times, there is just a
trickle of drops and a small puddle.

Kids and their guardians have commandeered Jamison Square since its
opening in June 2002, The children who come to Jamison Square arrive from

increasingly further distances as the fame of the place spreads. In Portland, where many neighborhoods with commodious single-family homes are a short drive from downtown, parents often forgo apartment living. This does not preclude their taking advantage of this more urban setting. Kids, who usually arrive in bathing suits and with a packed lunch, can play imaginatively. They are chaperoned by caregivers at a close distance who have an unobstructed view of anyone in the water. It is common for adults to place blankets just beyond the water's reach and to plan on spending the day.

Large crowds come to Jamison Square because the experience for kids is more invigorating than a traditional pool and more variable than most playgrounds. The fountain's endlessly wide-ranging force and levels of water are particularly attractive to young children. One mother, sitting nearby on the granite fountain steps, commented that her six-year-old was intimidated by swimming pools because he had not yet learned to swim. This fountain gave him endless opportunities for splashing, playing, and interacting with peers.

Portland contains precedents for a fountain morphing into a community space. Walker readily acknowledges and, in fact, attempts to honor one of them.[5] Two of Portland's landmarks are the nearby Lovejoy Fountain (1966) and the Portland Civic Auditorium's Forecourt Fountain (1970, renamed in memory of Ira Keller in 1978) (fig. 5.4). Landscape architect Lawrence Halprin designed them both. The Forecourt, in particular, has a series of concrete pools, and high walls that appear menacing. Early photographs, taken shortly after opening, show just how quickly the Forecourt Fountain had taken on a role as a local swimming hole and recreation space. Halprin's office seems to have been cognizant of this possibility, and accordingly created significant drops in level within each pool. Turning each ledge into an invisible parapet, Halprin made it almost impossible for anyone to fall from the water. It was intended to be safe while appearing risky.[6]

For young kids, Jamison Square offers some of the same pleasures as its forbearers: the adventure of being somewhere that doesn't look like a playground and might actually be a forbidden zone for play, yet at the same time provides water in unending variations. Pearl District residents, including those who work from home, do not see this situation as positively and have complained bitterly about noise ever since the kids arrived. They have not been placated by the way the character of the park changes, as Yerba Buena Gardens does, as the day goes on. Joggers and local residents walking dogs have a lovely common space in which to sit before starting work; kids give it a playground atmosphere in the afternoon; neighbors reclaim it at night.

Local dissatisfaction with noise has fanned anger toward construction of

Fig. 5.4 Lawrence Halprin & Associates, Forecourt Fountain
(1970), Portland, Oregon. Author's photograph, 2002.

another nearby park. Landscape architect Herbert Dreiseitl and sculptor
Maya Lin were working together on the park, North Park Square. The un-
happiness of each artist with the other is a complicated tale and one not necessarily related to any outside forces. Eventually, Lin pulled her work from
the project. The fact that she called her piece "Playground" did not help it
to be accepted by the local residents, even though Lin meant the term "play-

ground" as a metaphorical, ironic one.[7] Lin wanted her piece to be explored visually rather than physically, and had she continued with the project, that intention might have become more apparent. She is reported to have worked with a manufacturer of rubber cushioning, the same material that is used so extensively on playground surfaces, to employ a version of that substance as her building material. Notwithstanding the project's demise, it is commendable that a high-profile artist has tried to refashion a playground material into a more sculptural substance. Another artist, taking a similar approach, eventually might come up with fresh ideas that could be translated into an actual play endeavor.

Esther Short Park
Vancouver, Washington, 2000
Landscape Architect: Murase Associates

There is a happier agreement between residents and the work of landscape architects in nearby Vancouver, Washington. There, too, an unexpected playscape has become more popular than nearby traditional playground equipment. Water, again, is an important factor in the success. Long seen as a "bedroom community of Portland," Vancouver city leaders sought ways in which to promote their urban area, giving it both a center and an identity. The $2 million restoration of Esther Short Park in 2000 was part of that plan.[8] Portland landscape architects Murase Associates worked with architects Zimmer Gunsul Frasca Partnership (ZGF) to restore and enhance the 5-acre site.

Murase's master plan called for a central plaza, a gazebo, and a large piece of commercial play equipment. The most successful, and somewhat unexpected, play element in the arrangement has been a meandering watercourse (fig. 5.5). It sits on one edge of the site, where the park meets the nearby street. The fountain, comprising small terraced waterfalls, is edged by columnar basalt slabs that offer opportunities for climbing. The flat surfaces of these rocks make them quite safe; their slanted sides make them appear dangerous. This rock perimeter gives parents a place where they can watch and be both close and detached while observing their small fry make their way along a water channel. Kids tend to travel from a densely packed "canyon" to an open misting section. More popular than the standard play equipment, the fountain draws very young and older children. Kids appear to be self-segregating: younger ones like to run through the water-soaked flat surfaces; older ones like to climb on the rocks. Older children guide the smaller ones in navigating the rocks. By becoming a new type of play hub,

Fig. 5.5 Murase Associates, Esther Short Park (2000), Vancouver, Washington.
Photograph by Robert S. Solomon, 2002.

this water feature serves as a transitional space between urban street and bucolic park. Once an eyesore and hangout for an unruly crowd, this park is now—as announced by the presence of children along the street edge— a welcoming family place. Present use has had a positive affect on reviving the business district.

Simple signage has helped remove the city from liability. The sign identifies this as the "Esther Short Water Feature" and warns that rocks can be slippery; running or "horseplay" is prohibited, and use is at any individual's own risk. There are a few other warnings. These alert the users that children must be supervised and that the water is not for drinking. The presence of these few signs appears to have removed legal culpabilities and allowed kids to have a memorable experience to which they can return often.

Mill Race Park Amphitheater
Columbus, Indiana, 1992
Architect: Stanley Saitowitz Office/Natoma Architects, Inc.

Stanley Saitowitz, who practices architecture in San Francisco and teaches at University of California at Berkeley, designed small buildings for the

85-acre, multipurpose Mill Race Park in Columbus, Indiana. Michael Van Valkenburgh, the designer of Teardrop Park, was the landscape architect for this project. In this town, known for its progressive architecture, Van Valkenburgh had to refashion a large flood plain that had become a shantytown and integrate this park into the life of the nearby downtown. Van Valkenburgh placed a large commercial piece of play equipment at the north end of the park. Curving slides and extensive posts and decks scream at the visitor with their bright jarring colors of yellow and brown. It does attract many children.[9]

It is Saitowitz's contribution that gives this park a particular distinction and that offers another unintentional, but successful, play area. Saitowitz was commissioned to design utilitarian buildings that would provide support services for users of the park. These tiny gems, which can be seen as garden follies, include a boathouse and rest rooms. Their industrial materials— steel, concrete, and glass—belie the fact that each of these is a quiet place in its own right. It is Saitowitz's amphitheater, set on the south side of the park and across a vast lawn from the traditional playground, that provides the unanticipated play element (fig. 5.6). Here, the architect has augmented the recreational and play value of this park by allowing for varied use of his structure. Unlike his other buildings for this site, which are diminutive and close to the ground, Saitowitz devised a large raised structure. Either side of the high stage is flanked by stairs that descend to lower ground and to the storage facilities that are hidden underneath the rear. Saitowitz's use of materials, including highly refined red painted steel and concrete, are similar to those of his smaller park structures.

Children have found inventive ways to use the amphitheater. They love the thrill of running up one of the short access ramps, across the stage, and down a ramp on the opposing side. Kids who have even more stamina head to the stairs that go behind the building. These children can be seen, often with panting parents trying to keep up with them, running down one flight of stairs, across the grass, and up the other set of stairs. Kids adore twirling, singing, and bowing when they find their way back to the stage. Imaginative play is highly visible. For other parents, those willing to sit on the sidelines, the steps of the amphitheater provide adequate space for resting and observing. These concrete steps, set into a berm, also offer further chances for play. So does the hillside, which is just fine for rolling down.

By providing a lively play experience, this permanent building increases the possibility that families will gravitate to the area—which, in fact, has happened. Families come in the late afternoons and early evening, often bringing dinner with them. Part of the success is that the possibilities for

Fig. 5.6 Stanley Saitowitz, amphitheater at Mill Race Park (1993),
Columbus, Indiana. Author's photograph, 2003.

play are legion; the amphitheater is as much of a draw for kids as the traditional playground. There are no restrictions on the type of play that can
occur. Saitowitz, an architect who has respect for children's innate maturity
and who believes that they are very accomplished in self-assessing risk, may
have come up with a model for parent-child interaction. At the traditional
equipment, parents record their offspring on video, push swings, or just ob-

serve. At the amphitheater, parents really play with their kids or quietly survey all that is taking place. The pace is less frenetic than the playground and the payoffs may be so much greater.

Spring Creek Towers Playground
Brooklyn, New York, 2003
Landscape Architect: Lee Weintraub Landscape Architecture
and Community Design

Landscape architect Lee Weintraub has used a playground to give meaning to anonymous space, indicating that he has absorbed the lessons of van Eyck. Whereas van Eyck worked with small and even tiny parcels of land, Weintraub has had to find a way to impose individuality on vast emptiness. An academic and an individual practitioner, Weintraub has had success in redefining the exterior areas of the Starrett City housing complex in south Brooklyn. He has used a strategy that gives a vibrant setting to bland off-the-shelf equipment. He also supplements the equipment with a unique piece of his own design.[10]

Anyone who has driven on the Belt Parkway from Brooklyn to Kennedy Airport in Queens has passed Starrett City, renamed Spring Creek Towers in the fall of 2002. It can't be avoided: there are forty-six buildings on more than 150 acres. These medium-rise buildings, between eleven and twenty stories high, house more than twenty thousand people in more than fifty-eight hundred units in an area that borders Brownsville, East New York, and Canarsie. The buildings (Herman Jessor, late 1970s) are not architecturally significant. Starrett, built to provide affordable housing for middle-income families, was helped by subsidies from New York State. In the original landscape design, the firm Zion & Breen (whose Paley Park in Manhattan remains one of New York City's treasures) had tried to modulate the vast openness around which the buildings were constructed. Their solution was a series of grassy mounds that gave character to the otherwise flat topography. Over the ensuing decades, however, these low hills began to deteriorate, and some were even covered by parking garages.

The name change at Starrett signaled complete privatization of the property. The consortium that bought these apartments needed to improve many aspects, so that they could rent them at the market value. They hired Weintraub to give a cohesiveness to the entire area; he saw this as a mandate to improve public space. Weintraub, who grew up in some of the poorest areas of New York, has had extensive experience with community development in the outer boroughs and is director of the program in urban landscape architecture at the City College of New York. In addition to reconfiguring and narrowing Pennsylvania Avenue, the major thoroughfare that divides Starrett City, Weintraub created a series of outdoor rooms. Unable to convince the owner to consider infill housing, which he believed would have sparked livelier use and greater human contact, Weintraub sought a way to invest the assigned spaces with a visual energy that had been lacking.

Two areas, on opposite sides of Spring Creek Towers, were designated for playgrounds. Weintraub chose structures and surfacing that are stock items. What sets these apart is "a kit of parts" for the surfacing under the standard equipment. Taking one of the resilient materials that is demanded by all guidelines, Weintraub has tinkered with a rubberized material and created something new. He has cut it into squares of different sizes and colors that he randomly assembled into a grid pattern. This is ideal for maintenance because a small damaged area can be replaced immediately. On-site crews are free to select whatever color they choose from the proverbial "kit." Their random selection makes for a zany exercise.

Even more significantly, this dramatic surfacing has an effect on the overall space (fig. 5.7). The jarring colors tend to pop out and electrify their surroundings, visually filling the openness. This is true both at ground level

Fig. 5.7 Lee Weintraub, Spring Creek Towers (2002), Brooklyn, New York. Plan of surface grid for a playground. Courtesy of Lee Weintraub Landscape Architecture Community Design.

and at a height of several stories. People looking down from a high floor see more than a piece of equipment; they see pulsating optical illusion. Weintraub gladly acknowledges the role of op artists, such as Bridget Riley, on his sensibility for what he call his "ground paintings." He further defines the space and gives it personality by incorporating a basketball court with a striped surface and a lawn with ribbons of roses. The addition of a small "scarecrow" pavilion increases the possibility that teens will gravitate to the site. Weintraub designed this steel structure, which rises to 20 feet, to pay tribute to the *Wizard of Oz*. He interjects humor at the same time that he provides both a stage for music and a space for small gatherings. The tower adds a distinctive vertical marker to indicate further that this is an area for camaraderie and relaxation.

Tadpole Playground
Boston, Massachusetts, 2002
Landscape Architect: Copley Wolff Design Group
Painter: Mark Cooper

A worthwhile variation on community participation has come out of Boston. The role of the community, contributing as designer and/or builder, lately has come into focus. Similar activism goes back to the 1950s, when people advocated for a community constructing its own unique play facility. Even today, community-built playgrounds remain popular and generate unified town or neighborhood spirit. Monetary savings are sizable but not enormous, usually about 20 percent. Both small and large playground companies (and at least one that claims that it produces unique creations) make it easy to purchase component parts that can be assembled by a local, volunteer workforce.

A bigger question is whether there are alternative ways to marry good deeds with better design. The challenge is to retain community interest in new ways. Is it possible to engage potential users without ceding the designer's integrity and professional gifts? It is a problem that pervades planning playgrounds and planning cities. For a very different context, one critic noted that it "is one thing to have an open planning process in which the public's views are solicited, and it is quite another to put complex planning decisions up to the highest vote."[11] Tadpole Park shows how a thoughtful landscape architect can bring a visual artist into the community design process and arrive at an original alternative to what is often a tired but well-meaning formula of community design.

Jane Shoplick, of the Boston landscape and planning firm Copley Wolff Design Group (CWDG), designed Tadpole Park for Boston Common.[12] She was cognizant of two competing histories here. The Public Garden and the adjacent Boston Common are well known to tourists and residents. They are central to this city's heart and to its view of its own history. The purposes of these two areas, a total of 75 acres, are a bit different. The Common supports a variety of events and active recreation; the Garden is more passive, best known for the swan boats that traverse its large pond. The Common has colonial roots, having been set aside as public land in the early seventeenth century; the Garden was born after the Back Bay was filled in, during the late nineteenth century.

Shoplick chose to relate her playground to the nearby Frog Pond, the same Common site that CWDG had renovated in 1996. Frog Pond was a mid-nineteenth-century fountain and concrete basin that had been in disrepair. CWDG restored its original purpose and included a reflecting pool. The firm created a children's spray fountain and wading pool for the summer; they embedded refrigeration coils to generate ice for a skating rink in the winter.

For the nearby but not adjacent playground, Shoplick created a number of meandering paths to connect both sites. To make the relationship even stronger, Shoplick decided on a frog theme for the new playground, and chose the name Tadpole Playground. By strengthening the link to Frog Pond, Shoplick has created a zone of continuous activities for children, with a special nod to younger children at the playground and to older ones at the pond. The playground site, a mere 90-square-foot patch of land, previously had been a neglected play area. Shoplick felt that it was not possible to salvage its wooden structure from the 1970s. She replaced it with large standard-issue equipment.

Shoplick found a way to support a local artist and to incorporate the ideas of Boston school children into her design (fig. 5.8). In the process, she has helped to refine how a community can contribute to a public playground without diminishing the role of professionals. Shoplick arranged for visual artist Mark Cooper, who specializes in collage, to do a series of workshops with children in Dorchester, a low-income area of the city. Working with seventy-five to one hundred kids in a summer program for nine- to twelve-year-olds, Copper encouraged his students to think fancifully about a playground and what they hoped to see there that related to frogs. Small groups of kids made designs to give concrete form to their ideas. The students de-

Fig. 5.8 Jane Shoplick of Copley Wolff Design Group, Tadpole Playground (2002), Boston, Massachusetts. Mark Cooper, in collaboration with the Citizen's School at the Wilson School in Dorchester, Massachusetts, produced the resin panels at right. Photograph by Robert S. Solomon, 2004.

cided which designs would represent their efforts. Cooper then transferred and incorporated these designs into ten resin panels, each 3 feet long and each of a different color.

Shoplick has placed these panels within the playground by embedding them into the low concrete wall that helps to define the exterior of Tadpole Playground. Her goal was not only to have children express their visions but also to encourage the kids to bring their parents to the park. She and Cooper reasoned that the public role of this space would be enhanced by attracting people who would come specifically to admire what their children had produced. Shoplick and Cooper further connected the young artists to their finished product on the Common by sending the drawings back to their own Wilson School, where they are framed and very visible.

At the playground, the resin panels have good company. Shoplick invited sculptor David Phillips to provide six bronze frogs that would carry out the theme and provide additional whimsy for the site. These, in addition to handsome ceramics by Lilli Ann and Marvin Rosenberg at the entrance, further announce that this is a place for play and art. Cooper's work holds its own while at the same time alluding to the creativity of local kids.

Waterfront Park
Louisville, Kentucky, 2003
Landscape Architect: Hargreaves Associates, with Joanne Hiromura

A recent addition to Louisville shows that emphasizing contextual meaning can bolster local community interest and possibly be another alternative for community-building exercises. Established as a city/county/state entity in 1987, the Louisville Waterfront Development Corporation (WDC) had to grapple with an unsightly area that encompassed layers of transportation and industrial history along the Ohio River. Early on, the WDC and landscape architects Hargreaves Associates of Cambridge, Massachusetts, determined that part of what would become an enormous urban park had to be dedicated to children's play. Hargreaves's master plan, executed in stages, called for reclaiming an abandoned industrial shoreline of 125 acres. The firm created a recreation corridor between two bridges that link the city to Indiana. An expansive Great Lawn and part of a Festival Plaza extend under a nearby expressway, forming continuous flow between the downtown and the waterfront.

The first phase of waterfront changes included a children's play area, nestled within the shaped and sliced land that the landscape architects had created out of formerly flat terrain. It has had success as both a recreation and a teaching device. Some schools have elected to have their annual "field day" at that spot. Others come for more rigorous mental exercises, relying heavily on a WDC curriculum guide about the economic and environmental history of the waterfront. A well-conceived endeavor, this guide compels students to observe and to use math skills to measure aspects of the first redevelopment phase. Students are asked, for example, to determine the slope of such items as the roof of a large play piece, the slope of an aluminum slide, and even the angle of the backs of their weary chaperones.

A larger play area, which opened in July 2003 as part of Phase II, provides more active engagement among users. Called the Adventure Playground, the new development includes an elaborate water feature, with enormous cannons and squirt guns. These appeal to preteens and older kids. David Karem, executive director of the WDC, was largely responsible for the conception of the new playground. Working with playground designer and consultant Joanne Hiromura (Play Site Architecture), Karem and Hargreaves arrived at a contextual underpinning for the water features. The sloped terracing for the rushing water is meant to reflect the nearby Falls of the Ohio.

Fig. 5.9 Hargreaves Associates, Louisville Adventure Playground (2003), Louisville, Kentucky. These fish, designed by Dave Taylor, are part of the water feature designed by Joann Hiromura of Play Site Architecture. Courtesy of Louisville Waterfront Development Corporation.

The water guns have been augmented with metal fish sculptures installed on 10-foot-high stainless steel posts; each fish, 3- to 6-feet long, spouts water too (fig. 5.9). These high water sprays, dubbed "Flying Fish," factually represent seven indigenous fish of the Ohio River, including Longnose gar, Shovelnose sturgeon, and Grass carp. Dave Taylor, a New York state sculptor who specializes in animals, designed the fish. He has provided an assortment of engaging creatures that can rival the appeal of commercial water parks. Providing free access to these in a welcoming setting should help to increase further the variety of users who come here.

**Bright Horizons Family Solutions at GlaxoSmithKline
Durham, North Carolina, 1999
Landscape Architect: Robin C. Moore**

A flood seems an illogical generator of a playground or even a key to tying a play space to its land. Driftwood from a flood has, indeed, become one of the hallmarks of a playground that Robin Moore revamped with the aid of some of his students at North Carolina State University. The final product combines driftwood and a variety of natural elements with three pieces of traditional playground equipment. Once again, the client is a Bright Horizons Family Solutions day-care center. This site is in Durham, North Carolina, for the multinational pharmaceutical giant, GlaxoSmithKline (GSK).[13] The director of this childcare facility knew of Moore from his writings and from workshops that he had conducted nearby.

Moore and his students, through the Natural Learning Initiative (NLI), consulted on the reorganization of this play yard for one year. They then built it during the 1998/1999 academic year, a digression from the research focus of the NLI. Moore and students demonstrated how creativity can be served by mixing plantings and other natural materials with existing structures. Retaining the few pieces of equipment left from the prior schoolyard, Moore's team began by dividing a large space into age-segregated outdoor rooms. They then spread out the existing equipment among these new areas. These pieces have been augmented with two designed and built by Moore's students: a low climber and a water trough that has several elevated levels that demonstrate the effects of gravity on liquid. The vegetation is edible, so that teachers do not have to monitor excessively what goes into mouths.

The driftwood, securely anchored to the ground, appears in two of the new play zones (fig. 5.10). Two students brought it back from the North Carolina coast. The textures and shapes are very attractive to young eyes and hands. Each piece is just low enough to provide a safe climber for toddlers. Teachers report the glow on tots' faces when they can pull themselves over the top. Tires appear here, not for swinging, but as textured containers for plants. Little ones can use these, too, to help pull themselves into a vertical position.

The facility's director and teachers report that use of the standardized equipment has decreased considerably with the revamping. The natural materials offer the variety and stimulation that the kids need. Even more noteworthy, kids appear to behave better and have fewer accidents. In this day of soaring costs, the price to revitalize the GSK playground was approximately $85,000. Although this is not a trivial amount, in the world of play equipment it is a reasonable sum for a comprehensive job. Approximately one-third of that cost was devoted to site preparation.[14]

BHFS had a difficult time, at first, convincing parents that this is a viable playground. When it was first constructed, one parent told the teachers that the daycare center had put into the play yard everything that should have remained on the exterior. Having Moore nearby has been an asset, because he has been able to address parental concerns. Through his insights and their own observations, parents have begun to appreciate what has been accomplished.

Fig. 5.10 Robin Moore and students, Bright Horizons Family Solutions at GlaxoSmithKlein, Research Triangle, Durham, North
Carolina. Author's photograph, 2003.

Fig. 5.11 Oakland (California) Department of Parks and Recreation, Chinese Junk playground (1960s). Photograph by Robert S. Solomon, 2004.

Chinese Junk Playground
Oakland, California, 2005 restoration
Supporters: Wa Sung Community Service Club and
Oakland Department of Parks and Recreation

Oakland has a unique playground that has generated pride and collective memory for generations. It is also a decaying structure for which there is no clear solution. This is the wooden Junk, a traditional boat, that sits on sand near Lincoln Square in Chinatown (fig. 5.11). The Chinese benevolent society, Wa Sung Community Service Club, and Oakland Department of Parks and Recreation were the original sponsors of this project in the 1960s. They now are working together on a restoration plan. A westernized replica of a Chinese sailing ship, the playground appears to be a carefully considered version. The model was a junk that made the trip from Taiwan to San Francisco in 1960. The profile, massing, and heavy wooden beams indicate immediately what the playground intends to represent. The central part of the play ship is intact although there is splintering throughout and many secondary pieces have broken off. The colorful red and green paint is still visible but fading. A low wall surrounds the junk and offers just the right height for observers to sit. Most likely built by the Oakland Parks and Recreation Department and dedicated in 1969, the junk bridged literal and abstract representation. It was always clear what it was, but the ship never dictated how it should be used. The allusion of a wharf, for example, suggests varied opportunities for climbing. The shaky entry plank has been both inviting and a bit menacing.

Evocative of life in China, this boat has become a marker for the elders of the Chinese community in Oakland. Even younger folks, some of whom never lived in the neighborhood, come to use it and bring a new generation of participants. For the local community, no longer strictly Chinese but now peppered with Asians of other ethnicities, the junk still conveys meaning. Families with Wa Sung members have special remembrances, especially the Easter Sunday pancake breakfasts that the club has prepared for three decades. During that well-loved event, families tend to gravitate to the boat. Kids use it and parents sit nearby.

The question is how to restore the structure, make it ADA accessible and safety compliant, and still retain its character. Subtle questions arise, indicating that this is not necessarily a clear-cut decision. Should it be perfectly restored or abstractly recreated? Should wood, which would again be hard to maintain, be the primary material? How much of the original is needed to communicate cultural values that are important to this community? Should the play junk be incorporated into a larger composition for more varied age groups? These and many other questions have to be answered before any action is taken. Here a playground is a microcosm of issues that confront cities that strive to honor the past. Contrast the junk playground with some standard equipment, on a distinctly different but adjacent play lot. The equipment has decorative Chinese motifs. This recent arrival should be a warning that restoration of the junk has to amount to more than the application of spiffy decoration.

In late 2003, when some of the issues were discussed at a meeting of Oakland leaders, the local Chinese community came out forcefully for the retention and upgrading of this aspect of their local history. Wu Sang members, as part of the fiftieth anniversary of their association, have secured partial funding from state grants and have garnered enthusiastic help from the local city council and the parks department. They have also successfully petitioned the Oakland government to rename the site the Wa Sung Community Service Play Area.

CHAPTER 6

Remedies

Different types of artist, including architects, landscape architects, and sculptors, are demonstrating that the best American playgrounds are not inconsequential objects. They are devising tactics that abandon traditional equipment or they use manufactured playgrounds in innovative settings. They are working around stringent safety guidelines by incorporating sensory exploration, innovative didactic experiences, and contextual references into their schemes. Play spaces, which appear at first to be afterthoughts, are also providing stimulating environments for kids and challenging control problems for their caregivers.

During the past decade, many urban planners and previously unidentified patrons have begun to reassess how playgrounds can be a magnet for families and a stabilizing force in a community. The resulting contemporary spaces have uses that go beyond play. They are a particular type of urban space, one that harbors possibilities for many human connections. Play has become abstracted and so have the spaces where it occurs. The resulting public areas, with play as the center of their mission, integrate a variety of activities and a range of generations. In many ways, this is a retreat, albeit a positive one, to ideas that were prevalent in the 1950s. Those earlier notions, which attempted to integrate the playground into a broader context, are finally coming to fruition.

On the negative side, playgrounds persist as devalued generators of change. Excellent playgrounds are still rare in the United States. Most remain not only disconnected from good design and consideration as works of art but also unappreciated as potential community resources. It doesn't help the situation that playgrounds are costly because of legal liability and the ever-present threat of lawsuits. Strategies have yet to be tapped for nontraditional playground sites, for the use of nonprofit design/build initiatives, or for a recently emerging type of designer who specializes in architectural play spaces for young children. Each of these deficits could be remedied by sensible, often readily available solutions. Armed with an awareness of the status quo and a determination to contest it, consumers should be able to guide communities toward better play environments for today's young people.

LAWS

Lawsuits remain an overpowering threat for anything that resembles a playground. Take the case of a piece of sculpture that was on display at the cutting-edge P.S. 1 Contemporary Art Center in Long Island City, New York. In 1999, this institution showed a piece titled *Female Valerio* by the acclaimed German sculptor Carsten Höller. It was part of the show "Children of Berlin: Cultural Developments 1989–1999." Höller built something that looked and functioned like a slide, although it was never intended to be placed in a real playground. Tom Finkelpearl, then the programming director at P.S. 1, had Höller's sculpture fabricated by a legitimate playground manufacturer.[1] He made sure that the sculpture met all of the current American safety guidelines. During the exhibition, Finkelpearl placed guards at the top and bottom of the slide to make sure that the piece was employed correctly, and he posted explicit directions for its use. He even made a point of taking a ride himself each day, thereby checking that all parts were in order and no museum-goer could be hurt. And still, someone who rode the slide one day, and who left the museum without reporting an accident, called P.S. 1 the next day to complain of an injury he had suffered while sliding. Anything that looks like a piece of playground equipment seems to be a lightning rod for people with dollar signs in their eyes.

The Louisville, Kentucky, skateboard facility called the Extreme Park (2002), exists in defiance of litigious intervention, and as a product of enlightened legislation. Lacking guards, fences, or admission fees, and open twenty-four hours a day, this skateboard facility is one of the liveliest public spaces in the United States. It has flourished for several reasons, not the least being existence of state legislation that releases municipalities from responsibility. Kentucky and several other states have passed recreational immunity statutes that ensure public entities that they will not be held responsible for any accident if they do not charge admission.[2] This type of legislation, which allows a suit only if there has been gross negligence, might serve as a model for playgrounds. It's particularly relevant because kids head to skateboard parks after growing weary of dull playgrounds. Ten- to fourteen-year-olds, once included in the planning of playgrounds, are no longer expected to show up. The eight- or nine-year-old set is usually bored with equipment advertised as appropriate for ages five to twelve. Unable to find excitement, nine- and ten-year-olds have begun to prefer skateboarding facilities to playgrounds.

The Mayors' Institute on City Design (MICD), the program that has brought together urban design professionals and politicians several times a year since 1986, might provide a useful model for stimulating discourse about playgrounds as public space. The MICD had a direct role in creation of the Louisville facility.[3] Architect Stanley Saitowitz and Mayor David Armstrong of Louisville struck up a cordial conversation during a dinner at one MICD.[4] The next day, Saitowitz presented a lecture on his work. Armstrong, very impressed with what he saw, told the architect that he thought there might be a way to hire him for a significant task in his Kentucky city. Saitowitz, who had designed an emotionally charged Holocaust memorial for Boston, thought he might be asked to design some sort of commemorative piece. Three weeks later, Armstrong called and offered him the commission for the skateboard park. Armstrong has noted that, appropriate to the project, Saitowitz was willing to take a chance on a project unlike any he had done previously.[5]

The passionate client and daring architect were a good match. Armstrong had the vision to recognize a skateboard facility as a spot where young people would congregate and as an instrument to develop further the revitalization of a slowly improving downtown. He was aided by the fact that ESPN had already come to Louisville to host trials for its Extreme Sports, thereby assuring that a skate park would continue to receive national attention. Safety was also on Armstrong's side. Appearing to be nodes of unsafe (and unsavory) behavior, skateboarding turns out to among the safest of all recreation arenas and a sport that draws on a mixture of ages, races, and socioeconomic strata. The fine skateboard safety record, analogous to evidence from the history of the Adventure Playground, is similarly counterintuitive. Dr. Flaura K. Winston, a pediatric researcher and expert on trauma at Children's Hospital of Philadelphia, has noted that skateboarding in an appropriate park is "twice as safe as basketball and football."[6] The U.S. Consumer Product Safety Commission, not an organization known for being flexible about playgrounds, has indicated that on a per-participant basis, bicycling and soccer incur more injuries."[7]

Armstrong's choice of Saitowitz was inspired. This architect, a master of a high-tech aesthetic, has a sharp interest in the areas where the edges of architecture, landscape architecture, and urban design blur and overlap. He had demonstrated that at Mill Race Park in Columbus, Indiana. Saitowtiz's earlier design for a new streetscape, Promenade Ribbon for San Francisco's Embarcadero, had become a de facto skateboard park, something that angered the city officials but did not necessarily rile Saitowitz and his collaborators Vito Acconci and Barbara Stauffacher Solomon. Saitowitz was more disturbed by the fact that the city had added unsightly brackets to keep the skaters away.[8] For Louisville, Saitowitz took charge of overall composition and organized the 40,000-square-foot space into clearly defined areas. Zach Wormhoudt, a professional skater and landscape consultant, collaborated on the technical details.

Local enthusiasts made a contribution. Approximately one hundred local skaters offered their ideas during a workshop in which they built clay models to resemble what they hoped to see materialize. Two-thirds of the advisory council members for the project were skaters. Their suggestions, based on extensive personal experience, were critical for the architect's understanding of the sport. The collaboration between the users and the designers facilitated Saitowitz's plan without diluting his skill.

The Louisville skateboard park adds two components that playground designers could extrapolate: good craftsmanship and well-conceived integration with the site. The concrete has a refined and smooth finish; its tight bonding material allows water to drain quickly. There are spaces for in-line skaters and a central space for skateboarders and bikers. The 11-foot bowl, embedded into the ground, is the steepest in the United States. The full pipe is the only one in this country (fig. 6.1). Wedged between a parking lot for dairy trucks and a feed producer's silo, the park has an appropriately industrial backdrop. An elegant, slanted metal railing separates skaters from viewers. This barrier is low and open. All spectators can see what is happening; there is no obstructed view of the action. A graceful ramp to the street means that even the handicapped (or perhaps the injured) can enjoy watching. A grassed embankment, adjacent to a highway overpass, provides seating for those who want to rest or just come by and observe.

A comparison with a more typical skateboard park, such as New York's facility in Hudson River Park, reveals huge distinctions. New York's park, which sits in the middle of an otherwise unimpaired esplanade, cuts up the surrounding walkway that parallels the Hudson River. The materials appear to be cheap plywood. A few YooHoo soda banners add to the tackiness. High chainlink fencing and Jersey barriers make it clear that this spot is only for skaters. Viewers are accommodated on flimsy bleachers that offer only limited views. This skatepark seems to be an afterthought. Louisville's facility, on the other hand, blends into its urban surroundings and extracts

Fig. 6.1 Stanley Saitowitz office, Natoma Architects, Inc. Extreme Park (2002), Louisville, Kentucky. Author's photograph, 2003.

new uses and users from its well-planned and permanent presence. It is grand, not humble, yet there is a more modest sense of reclaiming abandoned land.

This Louisville facility has had a positive impact on the economic recovery of the downtown. With its bright lighting and night-and-day action, the park constantly draws people. The setting belies the fact that the gallery and restaurant zone of East Market Street is a few blocks away. Former Mayor Armstrong reports that the skate facility has more visitors per year than the successful, nearby minor league baseball stadium.[9] Armstrong, who now teaches at the University of Louisville, still receives appreciative notes from enthusiastic users. A message from a thirty-five-year-old skater in Dallas said that he would make Louisville his family's vacation destination only because of the skatepark. Quite a few messages have come from fathers excited to bring their teenage kids to the site.[10] It is common to see animated parents skating with their children. Families often make this the destination of their vacation, which draws them into the downtown. When skater Tony Hawk's tour came through, ten thousand fans came out to greet him. A new Courtyard by Marriott hotel notes that occupancy is up, with skaters flying in from all over the country. When that hotel's van is not shuttling guests to the airport, the management puts it into service to take skaters to the park about a mile away. Adjacent to the park, an old house has opened not as a bed and breakfast but as a "sleep chamber," where it is possible to secure a bunk for $17 a night.

This park is creating community in a way that does not seem to depart from the goals that van Eyck enunciated. Kids of different races and ethnicities mingle effortlessly. Many people who finish work late at night, especially those in the medical profession such as residents and interns, are frequent visitors at strange hours. A Christian missionary from Nashville skates whenever he is in town to visit his wife's family. One gentleman, sitting on a portable lawn chair while he reads and watches his thirteen-year-old grandson, tells how he moved from another part of Louisville to this neighborhood. Now his grandson can skate to the park in less than two minutes.

Gregory Stock, the UCLA medical specialist who has written about risk, sees a different type of accomplishment. He notes that historically kids played in the woods or local creeks where there was no one to sue if a youngster got hurt. In the current climate, where adults seek ways to pin blame on someone or something for any negative occurrence, the skateboard park removes that possibility through legislation. Stock believes that the resulting site replicates a naturally occurring situation whereby kids and their actions are just another part of the landscape.[11] He notes that the fabricated, constructed environment of the skateboard park answers the need for a new type of wilderness. Sinuous concrete is our new virgin land. Since young women are the one demographic component that is lacking from skateboarding, mothers might consider ditching Barbie and buying a board to increase their daughters' sense of mastery over their environment.

Successful skating and more generalized playing spaces are similar. Both require urban spaces in which to thrive; both should endow play with a sense of risk; both provide places to socialize without a set agenda; both need to be free and accessible if they are going to have repeat users and promote fellowship; both offer areas for passive reflection or watching as well as for strenuous activity. Playground manufacturers have not ignored the similarities and have sensed a trend. The threat is that their new product line, skateboard facilities that can go almost anywhere, could become as dull as playgrounds.

AFFORDABILITY

Cost remains one of the biggest hurdles for any group considering a playground project. One successful alternative, albeit one for mild climates only, can be seen at Sonoma State University Children's School in northern California. Citing the schools of Reggio Emilia as one of her sources, school di-

Fig. 6.2 Sonoma State University Children's School, Rohnert Park, California.
Photograph by Lia Thompson-Clark, 2002.

rector Lia Thompson-Clark consistently has sought out natural environments that can be substitutes for permanent equipment. At the Children's School, kids use bales of hay for play. This practice is not unique but is a fine example of providing a play space that is variable, safe, and exceptionally inexpensive (fig. 6.2). Hay offers many opportunities for the exploration of science and the discussion of the environment, especially during the composting of the playground after each rainy season. Thompson-Clark augments her equipment with a small embankment slide and large empty wooden spools that used to hold telephone and cable wire. The local phone company usually donates these wood objects.

Another alternative is for a nonprofit institution to employ a university-based design/build program. This merges a training curriculum with an imperative to find unusual conclusions.[12] One of the best-known and most enduring programs is at the University of Washington. There, at the Howard S. Wright Design/Build Studio (WDBS) under the direction of Steve Badanes, students have a terrific track record in creating play areas for the community. Much of the funding for these projects has come from local businesses, foundations, and the Seattle Department of Neighborhoods. Badanes, who began his own design/build firm, Jersey Devil, more than thirty years ago, has orchestrated outdoor projects for WDBS.

The WDBS studio tackled two projects, one in 1995 followed by another in 1997, for the University of Washington Health Sciences Center. These are two courtyards for the Experimental Education Unit (EEU). A unique facility, the EEU provides childcare, operates a research center, and helps train future teachers. The emphasis is on special needs, including neurological, developmental, and behavioral problems. The day-care program has an integrated population, 50 percent of whom are not disabled.

The WDBS's first project at the EEU was a playground for children four to six years old. It was completed in four weeks for $6,000. In a courtyard that had been previously empty, the university students hung an elaborate structure from beams that support the existing roof. This extensive play piece is perfect for versatility and allowing for gross motor activity in addition to more focused motions. WDBS's subsequent project for another courtyard, also at the same site, is intended for infants and toddlers. Without any roof structure here, the University of Washington students had to devise something to protect kids from sun and rain. They came up with a fabric awning pulled taut over a metal frame. They also built several unique play pieces. One of the most engaging is a septic tank covered with ferroconcrete. To soften the surface, a spongy rubber material covers the hard surface and provides color. Entry is through a series of sewer culverts. Again, the results are imaginative and inexpensive (fig. 6.3).

The T. T. Minor School in Seattle makes another WDBS studio project more visible and accessible to the general public. Even before the school contacted Badanes, they were in a fortunate situation. The Seattle Parks Department had closed the street behind the school in order to merge the schoolyard with an adjacent park. The combined areas function as a public space from 6:00 P.M. until the closing at 11:30 P.M.—an idea that is not only practical but also a return to an inventive approach that had been prominent in the early twentieth century.[13] Immediately, there was a chance for this space to be integrated into the community—something that has in fact happened.

In 2001, the Minor School asked Badanes and his students to build new sheds for tools and toys. Badanes said they could provide much more. He and the students built the needed storage, incorporating it into a trellis that defines one wall of the schoolyard. The trellis also serves as a distinguished entry into the park area. The following year, the WDBS students returned to work on a stage that had long been planned for a wall of the school that faces the macadam basketball courts. The challenge was to come up with something that would meet the needs of kids at school, at the same time providing areas that would be useful to local neighbors in the after-school

Fig. 6.3 Howard S. Wright Design/Build Studio, Experimental
Education Unit's toddler zone (1997), at University of Washington, Seattle. Author's photograph, 2003.

hours. The university students and Badanes devised a versatile stage that encourages rope jumping, hip-hop dancing, performances, and is available for graduations. The students took particular care to keep the design- and building-cost low, even finding a decking material that is made from recycled tampon applicators. The resulting area provides a space where parents can relax in the evenings (fig. 6.4).

The WDBS responded to the fact that the Minor School has highly regarded marching-band and choir programs. These, in conjunction with a rigorous curriculum, have helped to instill confidence in the children and to teach discipline in an underperforming school. During the construction phase, WDBS studio members worked days, nights, and weekends on their project. They often took time to talk to students about the design and the construction methods. These acts of kindness become powerful tools for learning, informally teaching kids about design, construction, and the joy of completing a single project. The enthusiastic university designers did not miss out on fun, and frequently jumped rope with the Minor kids.

Another test of Badanes's ability to energize his students comes each year in Vermont. Every summer, Badanes co-teaches (with Bill Bialosky and Jim Adamson) a community design workshop at the nonprofit Yestermorrow Design/Build School in Warren, Vermont. Architecture students, both under-

Fig. 6.4 Howard S. Wright Design/Build Studio, stage at T. T. Minor School (2002), Seattle. Photograph by Robert S. Solomon, 2003.

graduate and graduates, come for the two-week stint. The course is open, too, to people with less professional skills who have a deep interest in a proposed endeavor. In 2003, the project was a playground for a mobile-home park, Verd Mont Trailer Park, in nearby Waitsfield. Although the mobile homes are privately owned, many by people who have long worked for nearby Sugarbush Mountain ski area, the land is owned by the nonprofit Vermont Land Trust. This qualified Verd Mont for inclusion in the Yestermorrow community workshop.

The Verd Mont residents became the client. Their site, a long patch of well-tended grass that sits alongside a road, is at the bottom of a small incline. The mobile-home owners wanted to replace aging playground equipment while retaining its flimsy slide as a memento of the past. They also wanted to be able to use the new playground as a gathering spot for adults, because this lawn is the only public space for the twenty-nine resident families. The new playground therefore had to be as flexible as possible.

The Verd Mont residents raised most of the money for their project by sponsoring benefit events and by making personal contributions. Some local businesses offered small grants and discounted materials. The final budget, which was the cost of materials, was $1,500. Within the two-week period of the course, Badanes and his students met several times with the client to hear their concerns and made a formal presentation to them of their first plan. In the space of the next twelve days, the students designed the playground, built it at the Yestermorrow workshop, dismantled it, installed it at Verd Mont, and finished it *in situ*. The results are extraordinary.

The circular plan is one thing that sets this playground apart from the linearity of most others. The shape began to take form at the beginning of the course, when a Yestermorrow apprentice spotted an advertisement in a Vermont newspaper. A woman in a rural area about two and a half hours from Yestermorrow School was offering a satellite dish with a 12-foot diameter. It was free to anyone who would come and remove it from her property. After much discussion, the students agreed that it could be useful for their project. Some of them went to dismantle and pick up the dish; others remained at Yestermorrow working on a design. When the dish arrived, students stripped and painted it. The round skeletal metal frame, with mesh screening, became the generator of a circular plan; it is now the roof that tops off the structure.

By the end of the second work day, the students had a tentative plan and presented it to the client. They were able to confirm that all safety guidelines had been met. The next few days resulted in revisions and modifications, none of which departed from the centralized plan. In order to increase playability, the students intended to berm up nearby earth into three islands. As the design evolved, it began to illustrate how a vertical separation of children would work (fig. 6.5). Younger ones would be able to use the lower space; older ones would gravitate to the higher areas. The lower level became a pebble pit, bounded on all sides by wide, flat seats that could be used by parents. These would be suitable for watching kids or for meetings with neighbors. Access to the upper level is via nets, a climbing wall, or a ladder. Descent can be via a fireman pole, or the slide salvaged from the old playground. The end product, both a play space and community hub, was fully functional less than two weeks after its inception.

In most cases, Badanes's projects have not suffered from overzealous safety inspection. There was one sad loss, the *Dragon Play Sculpture* for the Denise Louie Head Start program in Seattle (fig. 6.6). Badanes, who executed this with Joan Heaton, Dave Robertson, and Linda Beaumont, still thinks of it as one of the best things he has done.[14] The school commissioned the project in 1995, after hearing about Badanes from one of his former students. The budget was $15,000. The imagery was whimsical, the materials varied. This gawky 60-foot-long dragon, made of a wood frame with composition roofing for scales and a plastic and metal ridge back, provided high and low areas for climbing, sitting, and a quieter protected place under the belly for resting and shelter from the rain. The feet, made of ferrocement, were brightened by tile mosaics. The dragon certainly fit within the tradition of a playground as a piece of distinctive, accessible sculpture. Badanes expanded the play site by placing tires vertically into an adjacent sand area, thereby creating other play opportunities.

No major injuries occurred while the dragon remained at the Head Start school. It did, however, stir fear in the mind of a new principal, who arrived a few years after completion. According to Badanes, she sought a way to get rid of his creation.[15] Her opportunity came when the Head Start program made the switch from part-time facility to all-day fully licensed childcare institution in 1999. At that point, state health inspectors came in, decided the dragon did not meet their standards, and cordoned it off for removal. The children lost a special type of playing space and the possibility of engaging with art that was fantastical. When a moving company wanted $5,000 to transport the dragon to another site, the Denise Louie Center kicked in $1,500, Badanes contributed $1,000, and a local benefactor made up the difference. This donation enabled the playground to be reinstalled in a field in Arlington, Washington. School groups now come by bus to use the dragon, but it has lost its role as the marker of a small community.

Fig. 6.5 Community Design/Build Workshop at Yestermorrow School, in situ completion of Verd Mont playground (2003), Waitsfield, Vermont. Photograph by Kate Stephenson. Courtesy of Yestermorrow Design/Build School.

There is another aspect of this story, one that has the same conclusion but a slightly different, somewhat upbeat twist. When the Denise Louie Center first indicated that the dragon had to go, Badanes had his attorney invoke the federal Visual Artists Right Act (1990). This law prevents the destruction of any work of art that is considered to have "recognized stature." Calling forth that act caused all involved to take a conciliatory stand and try to find a place to which the dragon could be removed. It was a Pyrrhic victory, but Badanes was able to have his *Dragon* declared a legitimate work of art. This was good news in that it meant that the playground would be rescued; it was even better news that a playground had again been considered a work of sculpture.

SITES

The time has come to consider fresh, untried areas for playgrounds. In some regions, planning is underway and a completed project exists in one case. If funding comes through, the grounds of the Clinton Presidential Library Center in Little Rock, Arkansas, will have a playground (Glen Allen of Hargreaves Associates with Joanne Hiromura). The Chicago Park District and the University of Chicago are co-sponsoring an extensive, free children's

Fig. 6.6 Steve Badanes, with Joan Heaton Dave Robertson, and Linda Beaumont. *Dragon Play Sculpture*, for the Denise Louie Head Start Center, Seattle (1995). Photograph by Jared Polesky.

garden (Herb Schaal of EDAW with Wolff Clements and Associates, and the Children's Environmental Research Group). The location is the Midway Plaisance adjacent to the university's home on the city's south side. New Jersey Transit has installed a Mary and Bill Buchen piece at a bus stop adjacent to the Liberty Science Center: *Parabolic Bench* provides seating along with pair of parabolic steel disks that children can activate by clapping or producing other sounds. A long pathway runs between this piece and another of the Buchens' works, *Saturn Seat*. The "ring" of this Saturn serves as a bench, but the sculpture—which includes a star map and, topmost, a sundial gnomon—also invites climbing. These Buchen pieces aren't yet a full-fledged playground but are a step in exploring unrecognized sites. The same could be said about a sculpture that Mary Miss is designing for the state museum in Raleigh, North Carolina. She is beginning a plan that might allow children to crawl through pipes before they emerge in the middle of a retention pond.

Ken Smith recently made a proposal for the Museum of Modern Art that could have implications for future playgrounds. His plan, one of several alternatives for the roof at the reopened MoMA in Manhattan, offers endless adaptability for future play. Smith had to come up with something that would not require water and would weigh very little. His design, which shows that this can be done inexpensively and swiftly adapted to a site, relies on scaffolding pipe, which is available in bright green. Smith proposed laying a grid; at each intersection he would place a spinning plastic daisy. Taking his inspiration from the paintings in the collection of the museum, Smith thought of this as a colorfield of flowers. He is delighted to think of it being adapted by a school or other places that attracts kids. As Smith notes, the current price of plastic daisies is $2.49![16]

The use of rooftops, long a staple for urban schools, is worth considering in other contexts. Roofs on facilities that already attract families could become contemporary playgrounds. Locations could include department stores, supermarkets, movie theaters, and parking garages. This might be less startling than it seems. In the 1940s, shopping mall developer Victor Gruen already had begun to use rooftops for parking, dining, and day care.[17] Sculptor Mary Miss recently has looked at a totally new site, the end of building. She is developing a sculpture for Ohio State University using sliding panels of blackboard slate and mirror aluminum that will be attached to the windowless outside wall of a chemistry building. Miss acknowledges that a forlorn exterior wall could become a site for other artists, or even manufacturers, to consider.[18]

Airports, certainly the background for many childhood behavioral melt-

Fig. 6.7 Acconci Studio, *Flying Floors* (1995–1998), U.S. Airways (Terminal B/C) at Philadelphia International Airport. Courtesy of Acconci Studio.

downs, are ripe for providing amenities for youngsters.[19] With increased security delays and additional connecting time between the flights of financially bankrupt airlines, airports have been slow to provide recreational and learning environments. Individual airlines have missed a rich opportunity to develop loyalty among parents. The airline would not be fostering community as much as invigorating a commonly dead space. There is presently at least one airport design that is not intended for play but provides another model that could be transformed for kids. In the late 1990s, Vito Acconci and Acconci Studio designed an end wall (*Flying Floors*) for the ticketing area of Terminal B/C at Philadelphia International Airport (fig. 6.7).[20] Acconci treated this part of the main floor and the mezzanine, accessed by escalator, as an intermingling of top and bottom spaces and the fusion of several planes. His description is perfect:

> At the end of the ticketing pavilion, the floors come loose. It's as if, now that there's nowhere else to go, the floors take off in flight. The ground floors release plantings from under the ground, as if a jungle was there all the time, waiting to spring out; as the floors fly, they form seats for people within the plantings, and up in the air, and under the floor. The end of the ticketing pavilion is turned into an indoor park.[21]

Fig. 6.8 Acconci Studio, Island on the Mur River (2003), Graz, Austria. It is illustrated on an Austrian postage stamp. Courtesy of Robert Punkenhofer.

Surely, Acconci's ideas could be adjusted for real play, not just the appearance of it. The results could rival van Eyck's success as far as making use of leftover or underappreciated spaces.

With a thirst for urban projects, it is appropriate that Acconci Studio recently has completed a thriving artificial island in the Mur River in Graz, Austria, that brings a playground into an area that previously had been ignored by the public (fig.6.8). The committee Graz 2003 commissioned this island as the centerpiece for this city's designation as the 2003 European Union Cultural Capital. Robert Punkenhofer, an Austrian lawyer who had spent his early years in Graz and who now heads Art & Idea, a consulting service for museums, was the moving force behind the island and its playground. Punkenhofer wanted Graz to commission a work that would help to integrate the river into the daily life of his former hometown. He hoped to honor the Mur, which is no longer polluted, and to use it to link the more and the less economically prosperous sides of the river. He also looked longingly to a playground as an ideal space for parents and children to gather. Punkenhofer's emotions, no doubt, were colored by the fact that as a divorced father he was thinking constantly about his young son who was not always in his custody. Punkenhofer, keenly aware of the art world because of his own professional life, personally chose Acconci and urged the city to hire him.[22]

Acconci and Acconci Studio had to interpret a program with three parts: cafe, amphitheater, playground.[23] They concluded that a 5,000-square-foot steel and glass island could be an oval egg, sliced horizontally. The artists then separated the two pieces, one becoming the open-air performance space seating three hundred and the other the enclosed cafe. Rather than placing them side by side, Acconci Studio envisioned a single structure that twists, so that the elevated amphitheater's floor becomes the domed roof of the indoor cafe. They wanted the island spaces to convey the same flux as the pulsating river.

Acconci Studio positioned the playground in the space created by the linking and overlapping of the two other functional zones. The location is essential because so much of what Acconci and his team are trying to convey is the unpredictability of human interaction. They celebrate that volatility, evidenced in the play of children and in the actions of adults in unusual spaces. Acconci Studio has taken van Eyck's "in-between space" and made it both literal and visible. Adapting equipment made by a German company, Acconci Studio has created a complex climbing system based on a rope grid. A partially opaque plastic tunnel transverses it. Acconci and his studio wanted a play space for kids to explore, areas where they could be children and not miniature adults. They recognized that play could add fun and drama to the other areas. For that reason, the children can be viewed from the cafe and from the amphitheater. Kids, too, can view what happens in the more adult spaces.

The twisting and morphing of space has created an analogous mix of people, without any distinctions between generations who enjoy this urban island. Participants don't just pass by or through; they wait patiently to come in and to spend time there. When Acconci visits, local residents come up to him and express thanks. They say they are seeing the river in a new way. The Austrian federal authorities have been pleased too, and have issued a postage stamp to commemorate this unique environment.

It was unclear at the start of this project if the island would be permanent. The success has been so great, including many letters from citizens to the municipality asking that it be retained, that its seems hard to imagine it will be pulled down anytime soon. If this innovative design is going to become a lasting monument, and Acconci certainly hopes that it does, the city of Graz will have to support and promote it. This should not be difficult; the island had more than nine hundred thousand visitors in its first ten months of operation. After the historic center, the island is now the major tourist symbol for this old Austrian city.

RESPECT

For most Americans, play and playgrounds are not valued. The American Association for the Child's Right to Play (affiliated with the worldwide International Association for the Child's Right to Play) currently is waging a battle to keep recess within daily school schedules. This will be a worthwhile crusade if recess can be more than running around and can be used for exploration and interaction. It's a difficult battle, one in which teachers are not necessarily an easy ally. In September 2002, teachers in the Princeton (New Jersey) Regional School District walked off the job, an action that further elucidates the low regard that teachers have for play. The strike, which lasted only a few hours, received press notoriety because only one of the differences between teachers and the school board had anything to do with salary. A bigger stumbling block was the teachers' insistence that they should not have to supervise children on the playground. They had disconnected the playground from any pedagogical category or even as a key to seeing how children confront each other. The walk-out has serious ramifications that are compounded by the fact that some school principals have abandoned or altered traditional recess because they fear litigation or insurance problems in case of an injury.[24]

A different type of indifference is evident on the West Coast. Landscape architect Richard Haag, who transformed the former Seattle Gas Works (1906) into a 20-acre park in the 1970s, dedicated the compressor house and its abandoned equipment for play experiences. He deemed this "play barn" a key part of his overall plan. Today, the Play Barn equipment carries a telling message stenciled on its side. It reads: STAY OFF STUCTURES [*sic*]. This could be a simple spelling mistake, but it also could be representative of the city's ambivalence. It may be that the stenciling is a way for the city to remove itself from liability. It seems to say, with a wink, that climbing shouldn't happen here, and at least the visitor has been warned. The message is geared toward protecting the city from lawsuits more than addressing the role of the users.

Reflecting a general lack of interest in play, designers often ignore it when they are given *carte blanche*. Haag, a juror for the Santa Fe Railyard Park competition, has reported that play was absent from most proposals. The same thing was true in another event focused on urban revitalization. This was the 2003 competition for ideas to transform New York's High Line, an elevated, abandoned freight rail system (built 1929–1934) that runs for 1.5 miles along the west side of Manhattan. The competition triggered 720 entries from thirty-six countries. Many of the entrants provided spaces for family recreation, with quite a few specifying amusement parks or swimming pools. Most designers turned a blind eye to a playground. One exception was a Danish entry. Three Copenhagen designers, Johanne Donstead, Christine Fulgsang, and Ellen Rasch, included an Adventure Playground of sand and wood. They appear to have been proud of their country's child-oriented heritage and willing to re-employ it today.

Leadership will be key to helping the playground regain status in urban space. In the mid-1990s, the Carnegie Foundation issued a report that urged a connection between architectural education and student community service.[25] This should be the time for another national foundation, one dedicated to urban policy, to proclaim support for playgrounds and offer ways for easier implementation. On a local level, New York's Design Trust for Public Space, which funds a fellowship program whereby artists can investigate public environments, has assumed that role. The Design Trust already has awarded grants that touch on play and/or the connection between schoolyards and the public realm. One went to Marpiellero Pollak Architects, who used their 2002 fellowship to address "Thresholds of Eib's Pond Park 2," The park, in Staten Island, can be accessed from nearby public housing and a public school. Partner Linda Pollak speaks fervently about how this recovery project, an extension of work she had begun before receiving encouragement from the Design Trust, explores the instability and change of a long-forgotten wetland. She has honored the boundaries that define the site. Centered on an outdoor classroom, Pollak's design has provided a mini science center, a dock for fishing and observing water, and an intergenerational refuge where older folks can sit and younger ones can jump on the moveable dock or the boardwalk. Eib's Park has generated intensive community use for recreation and education on this site. The Design Trust fellowship aided better understanding of the site by paying for a land survey and by supporting advocacy through a brochure that makes the project more visible in the local community.

Art museums, aided by universities, also can provide leadership that will give renewed respectability to playgrounds. The contemporary period is ripe for a series of competitions, not unlike those the Museum of Modern Art sponsored in the 1950s and the Corcoran Museum School in the 1960s. A national or international competition could ignite interest in current issues, make consumers aware of varied approaches, and renew a connection between playgrounds and art. A competition could electrify debate about the role of playgrounds in urban design. A relatively small assignment, this endeavor could be much more successful than the often disparaged and tightly controlled contest for a World Trade Center memorial design (2004) in New York City.

P.S. 1 in New York, an affiliate of MoMA, already has one annual competition in place. It is making a significant contribution. Since 2000, this institution has sponsored a Young Architect's Program that asks designers to transform the P.S. 1 entrance courtyard into an urban retreat for the summer. The 2004 winner, the firm n Architects (Eric Bunge and Mimi Hoang), approached this as leisure space that could appeal to adult and non-adult users. This young firm (formed in 1999) took a cue from the fact that the building was an old school, now accessed through a courtyard surrounded by hard concrete walls. They looked to the sky and the ground as key elements that could transform the space. The result is *Canopy*, created quickly and inexpensively out of bamboo (fig. 6.9). Using a living, breathing material, the architects hoped to demand lively and similarly variable use from museumgoers.

Though they thought first of bamboo poles and cable netting, using the bamboo just for shade, n Architecture soon realized that bamboo, which would change from green to brown during its four-month stint at this art center, would accommodate views of the sky and unite several different surfaces. The architects used bamboo to create sweeping, intricate gestures. They manipulated the material to swoop down and create separate rooms without internal barriers. Final spaces included a rainforest, a fog area, and a lounge, all of which were united by sand on the ground.

An airy material that looks flimsy, bamboo has great strength. It is often used for scaffolding in the construction of skyscrapers in Asia. Bunge and Hoang pushed this material into elaborate patterns that had never been tried before. Their extensive research led them to seek out engineering consultants and the president of the American Bamboo Society. The results were somewhat paradoxical. The architects produced a strong, intricate system that became naturally enticing to kids. Although P.S. 1 guards had to spend time yelling at kids to stop climbing, the architects showed that it was possible to use an unusual material in unexpected ways to create real innovative architecture. Someday this might spawn a similar playground. The budget was $60,000.

A Canadian competition recently has shown further how well the competition process works and how satisfying the results can be. Entitled the 13-Acres International Design Competition, it specifically addressed the needs of a schoolyard that functions as a park during nonschool hours.[26] The site was approximately 13 acres. Landscape architect Susan Herrington, who has

Fig. 6.9 n Architects, *Canopy* at P.S. 1, Queens, New York City. Family Day, an event with no admission fee, attracted hundreds of families. Author's photograph, 25 July 2004.

had so much experience in California and who designed the landscape for the Froebel School, in Grand Rapids, Michigan (2005), organized the event. She states the premise quite well in her introduction to the competition document, noting that it was "motivated by the question, why are we designing schoolyards that could barely entertain a chimpanzee? . . . Currently, schoolyards are typified by expanses of pavement, prefabricated play structures, and chainlink fences." Her laments, applicable to the United States as well as Canada, do not seem much different than those of progressive designers such as Richard Dattner in the 1960s. Even more brazenly, Herrington makes note of how design professionals have been removed from the realm of recreational planning, replaced by an emphasis on community consensus. She bemoans how this may have eliminated "the individual or risk-taking dimensions of creativity stimulated by a design competition."[27] To offset this problem, the 13-acres competition asked participants to consider "schoolyards that are layered sites for diverse play and environmental learning."

The entries were impressive. Winning proposals show how the process elicited concepts that were unlikely to come from designers trying to accommodate an equipment-dominated landscape. First-place winner, Nicholas Gilsoul of Belgium, came up with an elaborate system of sustainable gardens and classroom environments. He relegated the more traditional play to an area where vegetation dominated the plot and stimulated a child's imagination. The second-place winner, Claudia Illanes Barrera of Spain, used gravity and a drainage system to provide three distinct areas for extensive programming.[28] The third prize went to Kamni Gill of Cambridge, Massachusetts, who transformed extant ditches into safe, "secret places" in order to encourage independence and sociability.[29]

PROFESSIONALS

During the past decade, a new type of designer has begun to appear. These are usually young architects, frequently women, who have seen a need for a subspecialty that blends designs for childcare, development of playground design, and knowledge of how kids learn. Their concerns are more specific than those of established interest groups, such as the Committee on Architecture for Education within the American Institute of Architects (AIA). The appearance of new professionals is positive news for potential clients. The offer an alternative to the wiles of playground manufacturers who, armed with computer design programs, try to convince clients that architects and landscape architects are superfluous.

Maria Segal and Jim Miller, who co-direct the Early Childhood Studio at the architectural firm Holabird & Root in Chicago, are typical of this grow-

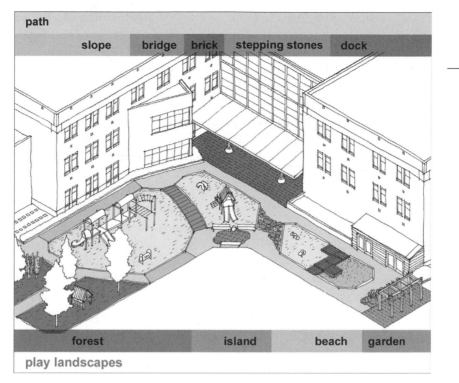

Fig. 6.10 Maria Segal, Holabird & Root LLC, axonometric plan of childcare facility for the Walter and Maxine Christopher Center for Learning and Leadership (2003), Concordia University, River Forest, Illinois. Courtesy of Holabird & Root LLC.

ing breed of new professional. They and their team are using their skills to create interesting interior spaces and varied exterior areas for play. Segal, the lead architect, who has had extensive experience in public housing and work for social service agencies, is conversant with theories of education and development. She and her colleagues cross several disciplines and are equally comfortable at meetings of the National Association for the Education of Young Children and the AIA. She is aware of current trends in curriculum reform and particularly interested in how the Reggio Emilia approach can be adapted to American classrooms and playgrounds. Segal and her team take an inclusive approach, constantly asking themselves how their buildings and recreation areas will support families.

To augment her playground designs, architect Segal draws on a variety of strategies that include natural learning, a series of planned incidents, and a mix of customized and off-the-shelf play equipment. Her plans for the on-site childcare facility for a laboratory school at Concordia University in River

Forest, Illinois, show that she has thought carefully about how a building can create community, retain teachers, and foster independence in children (fig. 6.10). At Concordia, where the childcare center is located within the Walter and Maxine Christopher Center for Learning and Leadership, Segal devoted attention to how each classroom could best take advantage of an interior courtyard. She created a "porch," a large overhang that protects the children from the elements and serves as a transitional zone from interior to exterior. Planned originally to be a place for children to play in the shade or to shake off sandy clothes or dry off wet feet, this area has become important in its own right. Kids gravitate to it as an enclosure, an area for quiet play and a more intimate surrounding than the rest of the bustling yard.

Segal's outdoor design provides a succession of compartmentalized areas, each representing a different abstracted microclimate. She identified these as forest, island, beach, and garden. A path for walking or bicycling snakes among these sites. This arrangement means that the path can become a playground of its own, offering smaller areas and varied textures that include a slope, a bridge, stepping stones, and a dock. Using only minimal equipment, Segal has created a landscape that is appropriate and challenging for small fry. Where necessary, she chose equipment that was not massive but could provide smaller incidents for play: a climber that resembles heartwood stakes; a hollow tube that can be climbed on or over; and some small post-and-deck equipment that is not overwhelming.

OPPORTUNITIES

In the late 1990s, Martha Thorne, associate curator of architecture at the Art Institute of Chicago, asked American architect Steven Izenour to comment on the commission he received to design a McDonald's restaurant (the building, not the playground).[30] The late Izenour, a partner of Robert Venturi and Denise Scott Brown and a coauthor of the seminal *Learning from Las Vegas,* said that this was the job of his dreams. The Venturi firm was, of course, well established as one that respects architecture of the common street, so hiring Izenour made sense. It was clever. By approaching Izenour, McDonald's departed from its cookie cutter approach to design. In this case, someone at McDonald's was paying attention and was interested enough in knowing how their standard edifice would be affected by hiring an architect who was already a fan of their aesthetic.

McDonald's has sadly made few other beneficial contributions to the built environment. Its playgrounds remain abysmal. And yet, playground manufacturers could learn from the way in which McDonald sought out Izenour. For the manufacturers, the intention should not be to find designers who complacently repeat existing designs but rather to encourage work from artists who have never contributed to the mass market. In other words, to hand a dream job to creative individuals. In a small highly unscientific survey, several innovative designers were queried about their willingness to participate in creating designs for playground equipment for the mass market. Mary Miss, Vito Acconci, Stanley Saitowitz, Ken Smith, Eric Bunge, Mimi Hoang, Linda Pollak were asked if they would accept the challenge of creating manufactured playgrounds. Each embraced the idea with verve and excitement. These superb artists—and there are undoubtedly many others who were not questioned who would have the same response—are awaiting just such a perfect opportunity. It would be shameful if American industry did not take advantage of their enthusiasm.

In the late 1960s, when art institutions abandoned interest in playgrounds, the notion of a playground as a work of art was just beginning. The concept did not get a chance to develop fully or extensively. Perhaps it is the time to pick up that crusade and this time do it right. Playgrounds could become an art form that could dignify a community and result in unmitigated respect for children's needs.

One can assume that each of these artists, and their like minded colleagues, would draw on abstraction to define their hypotheses. Many of today's playground pieces have themes such as adventure (pirate ships are still popular) or regal splendor (allusions to castles are everywhere). At the same time, they are directional. The best abstract playgrounds of the past, such as Friedberg's and Dattner's creations of the 1960s, were both abstract and nondictatorial. Users could go anywhere and invent unstructured play situations. Today's playgrounds guide kids in how to perform and leave little room for fantasy or spontaneity. Most modern artists bring a different sensibility toward abstraction to their task. They incorporate abstraction into how a piece is perceived and use abstraction to accommodate free play. This approach elicits a variety of activities from young users.

There is a flip side to this suggestion, and it, too, is valid. The corollary to high design would be something that developmental psychologist Roger Hart calls "no design."[31] Hart, who has been the educational expert for more than fifteen children's gardens, hopes to see a rebirth of Adventure Playgrounds. At the very least, he envisions new sites where kids can experience a multi-age environment, get dirty, experiment with common and even slightly unsafe materials, and create their own play worlds. Hart notes that, contrary to the stereotypical Japanese character, the progressive Setagaya district in Tokyo has established several Adventure Playgrounds. Children can play on slopes, splash with water, and experiment with fire. Parents and children are thrilled with the results.[32] Fortified with information about this type of success, Americans might be more receptive to the Adventure Playground concept.

Americans should widen their perspectives, taking a look at some of the ways playgrounds are commanding space in other foreign countries. Not all recent developments have been positive, even though the overall scene is livelier than the picture in the United States. England is a paradox. The vast London playground in memory of Princess Diana (Land Use Consultants, 2000) is ringed by impenetrable fencing and guarded by an electronic surveillance system that has created an armed fortress. Not far away, several modified Adventure Playgrounds remain—there are a total of eighty in London!—and continue to contribute to the growth of local kids. In Iceland, young landscape architect Emil Gudmundson is designing a Reykjavik schoolyard (Klebergskoli) with berms, driftwood, and a skateboard deck that "imitates the forms of the old Icelandic farmhouse." He wants it to engage and integrate all the school's kids, ages six to fifteen. He hopes to provide wind protection for anyone else who comes to this site during the twenty-four hours a day that it is open. In Rotterdam, the scholar/architect Liane Lefavire, who has written so eloquently about van Eyck's playgrounds, has initiated a long-term playground project with Dollab architects. They take a wide-ranging view that emphasizes the significance of a network of playgrounds rather than a single one. Lefavre demands that their work meet her "PIP principle," meaning that it is "polycentric, interstitial, and participatory."[33] In Germany, landscape architect Peter Latz has built a playground within the old blast furnaces of Duisburg. In Spain, international road signs alert motorists that a rest stop will have a playground. The highway icon for these playgrounds is a see-saw, an immediately recognizable image for play. American college students who worked on a playground in a poor area of Montevideo, Uruguay, have had admiration for these same devices that they never really experienced in their own childhood. These volunteers hand-sawed and sanded logs into a see-saw. Working with scrap wood and metal, the students wanted their creation to be useful to all members of the surrounding community, including the adults (fig.6.11).[34]

Savvy Americans, self-trained to distinguish between legitimate threats and absurd ones, have to become more vociferous. In 2001, the *Denver Post* reported that the local aquarium (opened in 1999) had closed down a successful playground composed of granite slabs. California artist Masayuki Nagase had designed it in 1999, with natural boulders to simulate the Colorado River. The management's action was defensive; having seen some minor injuries, they felt they could not wait for a more serious injury to

Fig. 6.11 Members of the Princeton University team from the Center for Jewish Life who worked on a playground in Montevideo, Uruguay. Photography by Emily Chiswick-Patterson, 2004.

occur. The Denver reporter was left to conclude that the event illustrated the "growing wimpiness of modern playgrounds."[35] That same ambivalence was reflected in the fact that there were no loud protests against the removal. It is up to the general public to know when to scream and cry "foul."

CONCLUSION

The time is ripe for reform and renewal. Each year, more and more well-intentioned nonprofit organizations donate equipment and construction time to underserved areas. These projects are usually community, build partnerships that rely heavily on corporations to encourage their employees to participate. The benefactors and the recipients deserve more challenging and appealing apparatuses as well as access to less-programmed conceptions of play. With high enthusiasm for improving children's environments, people might be ready to learn that planning a play space involves more than selecting a piece of equipment.[36]

The best argument for expanding the concept of a playground and improving equipment is that playgrounds have the potential to enliven neighborhoods. They can bring people together and create community cohesiveness. The playground does have limitations and those, too, should be acknowledged. This is a time, for example, when the entire American population is being bombarded with information about obesity. It is misleading to look to the playground as a panacea for that national epidemic. Yet the playground could become a vital public space that will bring individuals outdoors, occupied, and away from their refrigerators. With more challenging design, playgrounds could give kids a genuine sense of accomplishment and become a tool for instilling unmitigated self-confidence. By bolstering self-image, playgrounds could be the backdoor tool that could lead to healthier and leaner kids.

Playground design is currently in a state analogous to modern architecture in America in the late 1950s. Bereft of the European idealism that had nurtured its conception in the 1920s and 1930s, American modernist buildings were often stylistic replications of themselves, lacking intellectual and design rigor. Modernism was often just another "style," somewhat like the historicism against which it had originally rebelled. Modern architecture activated reformers, including Aldo van Eyck and Louis Kahn. Let's hope that a similar period of reevaluation will come soon from industrial designers, who will reassess and improve on mass-produced playgrounds.

New alliances have to bring together the manufacturers, the artists, and the consumers. There has to be recognition that play can happen with, without, and alongside equipment. The task will not be easy. Commodification of items for children, from relatively modest toys and Halloween gear to highly expensive playgrounds, make it easier to pitch known, well-packaged products than to improvise or adapt. One parent recently noted that "Disney is pretty much in charge of what kids imagine these days."[37] This attitude is hard to buck, further underscoring why it is imperative for manufacturers to consider reform.

Initiating change will be aided by a small backlash that has begun to emerge against overly safe and terminally boring equipment. Janny Scott's article in 2000, "When Child's Play is Too Simple: Experts Criticize Safety-Conscious Recreation as Boring," began a small groundswell.[38] The national press has begun to take notice, and other media have picked up on the theme. The Associated Press syndicated an item in 2003 about dull, overly safe playgrounds, and MSNBC highlighted the story on their Web site. Young architects, just out of graduate school, are not likely to be cowed by certified safety inspectors. Rather than bemoaning their existence, some professionals are saying: "Where do I sign up?" and "How can I become the safety professional? Walter Hood's book, *Urban Diaries*, which is a handbook for a "ground up" approach, is already out of print following its 1997 publication. Young designers are warming to its message.

During the next decade, as theories about the need for childhood risk taking become more widespread and better known, those who commission playgrounds may bring a novel sensibility to what they expect. We hope that they will be aided by legislation that will make it easier for them to be enlightened patrons. State legislators, armed with precise and accurate information about bland playground design, might be ready to consider laws that would make municipalities and nonprofit entities less vulnerable to law suits. This might be the moment to inagurate competitions, enlist help from nonprofit university programs, and incorporate artists into the design process. We might be activating a tremendously exciting period for art and industry. We might, at last, be expanding the definition of a playground. Playgrounds, which used to contribute to the greater good, might once again take on a noble social function. There could be huge benefits for children, adults, and the cities in which they live.

NOTES

Introduction (pages 1–3)

1. Jane P. Perry, *Outdoor Play: Teaching Strategies with Young Children* (New York and London: Teachers College Press, 2001); and Jim Greenman, *Caring Spaces, Learning Places: Children's Environments that Work* (Redmond, Wash: Exchange Press, 1988).
2. Deborah Solomon, "Questions for Bruce Mau," *New York Times Magazine*, 26 September 2004; and Bruce Mau with Jennifer Leonard and the Institute without Boundaries, *Massive Change* (London and New York: Phaidon Press, 2004).

Chapter 1. History: Pre-1960 (pages 7–42)

1. Galen Cranz, *The Politics of Park Design: A History of Urban Parks in America* [1982] (repr. Cambridge, Mass., and London: The MIT Press, 1989). Cranz notes that the early-nineteenth-century parks, intended to bring urban dwellers close to nature, were modeled on seventeenth- and eighteenth-century pleasure gardens of Europe. Her discussion of the first American playgrounds, placed in the context of urban parks, is particularly noteworthy and is used here to provide an overview of the playground movement.
2. For further information on early-twentieth-century views of childhood, see Dominick Cavallo, *Muscles and Morals: Organized Playgrounds and Urban Reform, 1880–1920* (Philadelphia: University of Pennsylvania Press, 1981).
3. H. S. Curtis, *The Play Movement and its Significance* (Washington, D.C.: McGrath and National Recreation and Park Association, 1917/1977), quoted in Stephen J. Smith, *Risk and Our Pedagogical Relation to Children: On the Playground and Beyond* (Albany: State University of New York Press, 1998), 39.
4. Rachel Iannacone, conversation with author, New York City, 19 June 2003. Iannacone has graciously shared her views and research contained in her 2005 Ph.D. dissertation at the University of Pennsylvania, "Open Space for the Under Class: New York City's Small Parks 1885–1920."
5. Garrett Eckbo, Daniel U. Kiley, and James C. Rose, "Landscape Design in the Urban Environment," *Architectural Record* 85 (May 1939), reprinted in *Modern Landscape Architecture: A Critical Review*, ed. Marc Treib (Cambridge, Mass., and London: The MIT Press, 1993), 78–87.
6. "Noguchi: The Bollingen Journey Photographs and Drawings 1949–1956," at the Isamu Noguchi Museum temporary quarters, 13 February–13 October 2003. Introductory remarks were written by curator Bonnie Rychlak.

7. Alex Kerr, "Isamu Noguchi's Playground," in *Play Mountain* (Tokyo: Watari Museum of Contemporary Art, 1996), 132.

8. Michael Gotkin, "The Politics of Play: The Adventure Playground in Central Park," in *Preserving Modern Landscape Architecture: Papers from the Wave Hill–National Parks Service Conference,* ed. Charles Birnbaum (Washington, D.C., and Cambridge, Mass.: Spacemaker Press, 1999), 62.

9. "Design Decade: Playground Equipment," *Architectural Forum* 73 (October 1940): 245.

10. Amy Lyford, "Noguchi, Sculptural Abstraction, and the Politics of Japanese American Internment," *Art Bulletin* 85 (March 2003): 137–51, at 141–42.

11. Letter from John J. Downing, Director of Recreation, New York City Parks Department, to Noguchi, 29 December 1947, file "Playground 1940–1947, 1953–1967, 1975," at the Isamu Noguchi Foundation.

12. "Movie Story," *Architectural Forum* 80 (October 1947): 13–14.

13. Clare C. Cooper provides an excellent summary in "Adventure Playgrounds," *Landscape Architecture* 61 (October 1970): 18–29, 88–91. This is the source of much of the factual information used here. According to Cooper, Sørensen originated the Adventure Playground idea in the early 1930s but had to wait until 1943 to see it come to fruition.

14. Lady Allen's autobiography is interesting for her range of friends, clients, and experiences. She was a founder of the Institute of Landscape Architects in 1929 and had been particularly active, beginning in 1940, in setting up government-sponsored nursery centers for preschool children. In one passage she relates how, when president of the Nursery School Association, she had been unable to secure playthings due to war shortages, but about a year after the bombing of London had begun, she and colleague saw that much of the debris had been left in Hyde Park and the "piles of burnt and half-burnt doors and window frames, paneling and flooring" could become useful materials for children. At that point, she worked on having these converted into simple toys. Marjory Allen and Mary Nicholson, *Memoirs of an Uneducated Lady: Lady Allen of Hurtwood* (London: Thames and Hudson, 1975), 153–60.

15. Lady Allen of Hurtwood, Foreword to Arvid Bengtsson, *Adventure Playgrounds* [1972] (reprint, London: Crosby Lockwood Staples, 1973), 8.

16. *Recreation Magazine* 40 (October 1946): 346–51.

17. Francis Strauven, *Aldo van Eyck: The Shape of Relativity* (Amsterdam: Architectura & Natura, 1988; translation of 1994 edition), 101, identifies Amsterdam town planner Jacoka Mulder as the person who suggested extensive use of public playgrounds in the city.

18. Two recent, excellent studies devoted to van Eyck's playgrounds are Liane Lefaivre and Alexander Tzonis, *Aldo van Eyck: Humanist Rebel, Inbetweening in a Postwar World* (Rotterdam: 010 Publishers, 1999); and Liane Lefaivre and Ingeborg de Roode, eds., *Aldo van Eyck: The Playgrounds and the City* (Rotterdam: NAi Publishers, 2002). Lefaivre and Tzonis present an outstanding discussion

of the intellectual and artistic climate of the postwar period, including the writings of Martin Buber, Jean-Paul Sartre, Henri Lefebvre, Theo van Doesburg, Kurt Schwitters, and Lewis Mumford. They show that van Eyck used the playgrounds to fulfill Martin Buber's directive for human interaction expressed by his well-known phrase, "I and Thou."

19. Strauven, *Aldo van Eyck: The Shape of Relativity,* 26–38.

20. Erik Schmitz, "'Let our children have a playground. They need it very badly,' Letters to the Department of Public Works, 1947–1958," in Lefaivre and de Roode, *Aldo van Eyck: Playgrounds,* 58–65.

21. Aldo van Eyck, "The Child and the City," trans. Ernst Priefert, in *Creative Playgrounds and Recreation Centers,* ed. Alfred Ledermann and Alfred Trachsel (New York: Frederick A. Praeger, 1959), 34–37, at 37. This marks the first English publication of van Eyck's essay, an evolving document on which he had been working since the late 1940s. A more complete, unpublished version (early 1960s) is entitled "The Child, the City and the Artist: An Essay on Architecture." A copy is at the Architectural Archives, University of Pennsylvania. Ledermann and Trachesel's book also deserves notice as one of the first to survey all types of playgrounds after World War II. The demand for the book must have been significant, because a second edition came out in the late 1960s. Many libraries have discarded their copies, making both out-of-print editions readily available for purchase on the Internet.

22. Liane Lefaivre, "Space, Place and Play; or, the Interstitial/Cybernetic/Polycentric Urban Model Underlying Aldo van Eyck's Quasi-unknown But, Nevertheless, Myriad Postwar Amsterdam Playgrounds," in Lefaivre and de Roode, *Aldo van Eyck: Playgrounds,* 24–49.

23. Carol Lawson, "Playgrounds Shaped by Today's Urban Concerns," *New York Times,* 13 July 1989.

24. Lefaivre, "Space, Place and Play," 24; Johan Huizinga, *Homo Ludens: A Study of the Play-Element in Culture* (Boston: Beacon Press, 1955 edition based on 1944 edition).

25. Lee Weintraub, telephone conversation with author, 16 October 2003.
    Van Eyck's interest in the ground plane was manifest in the first exhibition of the COBRA painters at Stedelijk Museum in Amsterdam in 1949. For these abstractionists from Copenhagen, Brussels, and Amsterdam (and thus, the acronym), van Eyck designed rectangular, flat exhibition boxes that sat just a few inches above the floor. Van Eyck, for both the playgrounds and the exhibition, tried to animate previously overlooked surfaces.

26. Francis Strauven, "Wasted Pearls in the Fabric of the City," in Lefaivre and de Roode, *Aldo van Eyck: Playgrounds,* 66–83, at 80.

27. A complete description of the equipment is in Ingeborg de Roode, "The Play Objects: More Durable than Snow," in Lefaivre and de Roode, *Aldo van Eyck: Playgrounds,* 84–101. De Roode notes, in particular, that the "jumping stones" were, in fact, the "play tables" that originally had been in the sandbox. One

drawback should be noted; the sandbox was not always appreciated when sand blew into houses. See Schmitz, "'Let our children have a playground," 59.

28. The one noticeable change has been in the surfacing material below the climbing equipment. Most of these now sit on a springy contemporary material that will soften falls. Today, too, many of the playgrounds are surrounded by low fences.

29. Strauven, "Wasted Pearls," 70. De Roode, notes that "Van Eyck resolutely turned his back on animal shapes, including fairytale ones, on the grounds that they would hamper a child's imagination" ("Play Objects," in Lefaivre and de Roode, *Aldo van Eyck: Playgrounds,* 94).

30. Liane Lefaivre, conversation with author, 25 September 2003, New York. Lefaivre indicated that many of the sites in the heart of the city were on lots where Jews previously had had their houses. The best known of these was Dijkstraat (see fig. 1.8).

31. Van Eyck, "The Child and the City," 37.

32. Lefaivre, "Space, Place and Play," 36.

33. While there was no discussion about changing the nature of playground form, an important debate took place about building living memorials that could include playgrounds. See Andrew M. Shanken, "Planning Memory: Living Memorials in the United States during World War II," *Art Bulletin* 84 (March 2002): 130–48.

34. Holmes Perkins Collection, Architectural Archives at the University of Pennsylvania, Box 3 054.191–054.257.

35. A general impression of park administrators and their concerns comes from author's review of *Recreation Magazine* in the 1940s and 1950s. *Recreation Magazine,* the organ of the National Recreation Association, began as a journal called *The Playground* in 1907. That became *Playground and Recreation Magazine* for a month, before becoming *Recreation* in February 1931. The title, since 1966, has been *Parks and Recreation.*

36. These were paid part-time positions. The number of full-time paid personnel was only about 10 percent of that number. See "A Summary of Community Recreation in 1948," *Recreation Magazine* 43 (June 1949): 100.

37. Ann Hulbert, *Raising America: Experts, Parents, and a Century of Advice about Children* (New York: Alfred A. Knopf, 2003), 226. Hulbert notes that American anxiety about raising children was not new: "Raising children has rated very near to sex—and to success—as an American fixation, especially since the start of the twentieth century and particularly among the middle class."

38. Letter, Audrey Hess to Raymond Rubinow (J. M. Kaplan Fund), 17 June 1961, file "Playground 1940–1947, 1953–67, 1975," at the Isamu Noguchi Foundation. Julius Rosenwald, Hess's grandfather, bequeathed to his family a record of magnanimous and unusual philanthropy. Between 1913 and 1933, his Rosenwald Fund established schools in the South and Southwest. The goal was to improve education for minority students in segregated areas. Rosenwald, who made the conscious decision to use all of the fund's resources in order to effect radi-

cal change, insisted that all money in the fund be spent during his lifetime; when he died, the foundation ceased to exist. Jeffrey Edelstein, graduate student at the Woodrow Wilson School of Princeton University, conversation with the author, 1 May 2003, Princeton, N.J., explained Rosenwald's fiscal model.

39. Aline B. Louchheim (later Aline Saarinen), "U.N. Rejects 'Model' Playground; Moses' Project is Accepted Instead," *New York Times*, 7 October 1951. According to Louchheim, Moses was the person who proposed the idea of a UN playground in 1949.

40. Aline B. Louchheim, "Playground Unit Shown at Museum," *New York Times*, 25 March 1952. Noguchi and Whittlesey were reported to have stressed that this was a concept more than a final design. Philip Johnson, director of MoMA's Architecture Department said that, too. Whittlesey earlier had provided playground proposals for the New York Housing Authority.

41. Dorothy Barclay, "Playgrounds that Are Something More," *New York Times*, 20 April 1952.

42. Museum of Modern Art, quoted in Barclay, ibid.

43. Label for exhibition, 12 March 1952, MoMA Archives.

44. Editorial, signed "T.B.H.," "The Rejected Playground," *Art News* 51 (April 1952): 15.

45. "Model for a Children's Playground," *Architectural Record* 115 (January 1954): 157.

46. "The Record Reports," *Architectural Record* 112 (October 1952): 22, 366. The UN playground was most likely the "complete playground" by Noguchi that was displayed by Creative Playthings at the 1953 National Recreation Congress in Philadelphia. See "New Dimension Put in Play Equipment," *New York Times*, 3 October 1953.

47. Donald Hoffman, telephone conversation with author, 11 July 2003. Hoffman was kind enough to provide a copy of the Play Sculptures catalog from the late 1950s.

48. Theresa Caplan, *Frank Caplan: Champion of Child's Play* (New York: Vantage Press, 1999), 37–41. In this biography of her husband, Caplan traces the beginnings of the company to 1944 when, known as Creative Toymakers, they made hand-crafted wood animals and figures. That corporation went bankrupt and Frank Caplan restructured the business, in 1945, as a retail store called Creative Playthings. According to his wife, she was the owner of record because of her husband's poor credit history. Theresa Caplan notes that Barenholtz later claimed to have founded the company.

49. "Experts to Advise on Toy Selections," *New York Times*, 24 January 1946. It is unclear how Caplan, who came from humble beginnings and had worked earlier with the Youth Service Division of the WPA and then some social-service agencies, had made contact with MoMass..

50. Mary Roche, "New Ideas and Inventions," *New York Times*, 19 January 1949.

51. Amy Ogata, "Object Lessons: Educational Toys and Postwar American Culture," presented at the annual meeting of the College Art Association in New York City, February 2003. Ogata, who currently is writing a book on this topic, has kindly shared her thoughts and expertise on this subject.

52. The Eameses designed a "mechanical horse" in 1944 and Tyng had come up with her "Tyng Toy" in the late 1940s. Tyng's creation allowed for several variations, including a rolling horse, airplane, and wagon. Creative Playthings designed their own abstract "rocking object" in the early 1950s. Anne Tyng, in a conversation with the author on 9 June 2004, in Ewing, New Jersey, indicated that Creative Playthings had discussed with her the possibility of manufacturing the Tyng Toy but that their terms were exploitive and therefore not acceptable to her.

53. "Creative Playthings: An Object Lesson with an Academic Approach," *Interiors* 113 (February 1954): 88–93.

54. "For Your Information," *Interiors* 112 (February 1953): 10.

55. Letter, Caplan to Hess, 2 June 1953, "Playgrounds 1940–1947, 1953–67, 1975," Isamu Noguchi Foundation.

56. Letter, Caplan to Noguchi, 2 June 1953, "Playgrounds 1940–1947, 1953–67, 1975," Isamu Noguchi Foundation.

57. Caplan, *Frank Caplan,* 69–74

58. J. M. Richards, "Art in Use," *Architectural Review* 116 (August 1954): 121–23. A portion of a Møller-Nielsen piece is on the cover, with the note on the title page: "On the cover, children playing in the interstices of a sculpture by Egon Mæller-Nielsen draw attention to the new relationship between art and citizen which is implicit in the ideas of play-sculpture." John E. Burchard, "Try Imagination; Don't Forget Diversion," *Architectural Record* (January 1954): 147–49, chose a Møller-Nielsen piece as one of the illustrations to accompany an article urging designers to incorporate fantasy and surprise into recreational structures.

59. Letter, Caplan to Henry Moore, 11 August 1953, quoted in Caplan, *Frank Caplan,* 77–78.

60. Peter Eisenman, telephone conversation with author, 2 September 2003. Eisenman, who still has fond memories of Barenholtz as his first patron and as a passionate collector of mechanical toys and banks, believes that Barenholtz may have found his architect through the Princeton School of Architecture, where Eisenman was already a faculty member.

61. Scrapbooks at MoMA show that there was wide publicity, including announcements in papers in Toledo, Tulsa, and Portland, Oregon. The first announcement of the competition was in August 1953.

62. "Museum Competitions," 2 August 1953, and "Child Play Devices Sought in Contest," 3 August 1953, *New York Times.*

63. Entry form for "Play Sculpture Competition," closing 15 January 1954, MoMA Archives. In addition to the three primary winners, there were three honorable mentions and four citations.

64. "Child Play Devices Sought in Contest," *New York Times,* 3 August 1953. Caplan claimed that the genesis of the competition was the demise of Noguchi's UN project, whose design had inspired parents to inquire about something different than a traditional playground. He felt that a competition would be one way to meet the new demand. The Creative Playthings name began to be identified

as a sponsor of Noguchi's UN commission, a highly unlikely connection because Caplan and Noguchi did not have formal contact before Audrey Hess introduced them in 1953.

65. "Museum Competitions," 2 August 1953, and "Child Play Devices Sought in Contest," 3 August 1953, *New York Times.*

66. "Play Sculpture," *Arts and Architecture* 71 (August 1954): 12–13, at 12.

67. "New Products," *Architectural Forum* 94 (October 1953): 246.

68. Greta Daniel, assistant curator of design at MoMA, was the competition director. The other jurors were Caplan; Victor D'Amico, director of MoMA's Department of Education; Edith Mitchell, Delaware State Director of Art; Penelope Pinson of *Parents' Magazine;* and George Butler of the National Recreation Association. This was a slightly different lineup than the jury that had been advertised when the competition was announced. That listing included Rene D'Harnoncourt, director of the museum, and different representatives from *Parents' Magazine* and the National Recreation Association. The show ran from 29 June to 22 August 1954.

69. Sanka Knox, "New Play Pieces for Young Shown," *New York Times,* 30 June 1954; Aline Saarinen, "Playground: Function and Art," *New York Times,* 4 July 1954.

70. Memo, Pat May to Dorothy Dudley, 14 July 1954, MoMA Archives.

71. Knox, "New Play Pieces for Young Shown." The winner's name was reported incorrectly as Corazio.

72. MoMA press release no. 64, MoMA Archives.

73. "Play Sculpture," *Arts and Architecture* 71 (August 1954): 13.

74. MoMA press release for the *Courier-News* of Plainfield (New Jersey), noted that he was a GI, working in the office of George Nelson. MoMA. Archives.

75. Saarinen, "Playground: Function and Art."

76. "Art in Use," *Architectural Review* 116 (August 1954): 121. Creative Playthings was not mentioned.

77. "The Metropolis Observed: Public Eye," *Metropolis* 22 (August–September 2003). 38–40, 78.

78. "Up, Down and Over: Philadelphia Children Get Exciting Set of Playgrounds," *Life* 37, pt. 2 (13 September 1954): 118.

79. "Creative Playthings," *Interiors* 113 (February 1954): 92.

80. "Neighborhood Playground," *Progressive Architecture* 36 (December 1955): 102–103.

81. Louis I. Kahn indicated in 1954 that he hoped he would be able to land a playground commission, something his colleague Robert Geddes had just secured. See *Louis Kahn to Anne Tyng: The Rome Letters 1953–1955* (New York: Rizzoli, 1997); see letter 17 June 1954. Geddes has said that the Philadelphia playground was his first major commission.

82. Ledermann and Trachsel, *Creative Playgrounds and Recreation Centers,* 101.

83. "Sculptors Shape Tots' New World," *New York Times,* 21 August 1954; Cornelia Oberlander, "Parks, Playgrounds and Landscape Architecture," *Community Planning Review* 6 (March 1956): 4–12. Oberlander writes that when she received

this commission, only swings and slides were available from commercial manufacturers. She then goes on to say that for the Bigler playground, it was necessary "to create a whole new line of equipment" that depended on "team-work— cooperation from sculptors, playground manufacturers and public officials." It is unclear what her role, if any, was with Creative Playthings. Oberlander also noted that the innovative 1947 exhibit "Better Philadelphia" had spurred interest in neighborhood development.

84. "Sculptors Shape Tots' New World," *New York Times,* 21 August 1954. Within a few years, the material for this became cast stone. James E. Coogan, "New Haven Tries a New Emphasis on Playgrounds," *The American City* (September 1956): 120, has photo of a playground that shows that Creative Plaything's *Spiral Slide* and *Fantastic Village* were already in place there.

85. Caplan, *Frank Caplan,* 75. Staying at the American Hotel, dining at Dikker and Thije, and visiting the Montessori training school on Koninginneweg, the Caplans had many opportunities to see van Eyck's work. *Interiors* magazine, which ran an article on Creative Playthings in February 1954, confirmed Caplan's debt to van Eyck. "Creative Playthings: An Object Lesson with an Academic Approach," *Interiors* 113 (February 1954): 88. The magazine appropriated an image of van Eyck's stepping stones, photographed at the Zaanhof playground in 1950, and used these to illustrate its lengthy article on the Americans. Although Creative Playthings did not put the stepping stones into production, their heritage was obvious.

86. For a discussion of the abundance of Dutch photo books, see Anja Novak, "Innocence Reborn: Child Photography in the Netherlands from 1945 to 1960," in Lefaivre and de Roode, *Aldo van Eyck: Playgrounds,* 103–107.

87. "Sculptured Playground Slide at Lower Cost," *Progressive Architecture* 36 (April 1955): 110–11.

88. "Modern Play Equipment Is Designed to Exercise Both Muscles and Minds," *New York Times,* 28 December 1959.

89. Charles Price, "He's Tough on Kids," *Saturday Evening Post* (2 February 1957): 37–39, 92, 94.

90. Andy Kozar, University Professor at the University of Tennessee, who has written extensively on McKenzie and is preparing a book on Joe Brown, was very considerate to share his research in a conversation, 7 April 2003, Knoxville, Tennessee.

91. Elizabeth Menzies, "The Creative Factor: Joe Brown Designs Mobile Play Equipment That Is 'Unpredictable,'" *Princeton Alumni Weekly* (1 October 1954): 10–11. *The Daily Princetonian* followed with a piece that showed Brown and models of his "Spring-Tree, Climb-Mobile and Playmobile Prototypes," 16 November 1954. Also see Brown's own illustrated statement, "Unpredictability—Margin for Inspiration," *Architectural Record* 118 (September 1955): 225–28. Until the 1950s, Princeton's School of Architecture (founded in 1919) shared space with the Department of Art and Archeology.

92. Letter, Robert Nichols to Brown, 9 June 1954, Box 22, folder 29, Brown Collection at Hoskins Library, University of Tennessee (hereafter cited as Brown Collection). Nichols who had worked at Creative Playthings, wrote that they were, a noncommercial group of architects and landscape architects trying "to get a line on interesting developments" and that they "do need a lot of help." Ironically, they rather than Brown appear to have become a commercial success.

93. Brown, "Unpredictability—Margin for Inspiration," 226.

94. Menzies, "The Creative Factor," 10.

95. Press release, Princeton University, 25 August 1967, Box 68, Faculty Files, Princeton University. Brown said that the boxing ring was inspiration for all of his Jiggle pieces.

96. Price, "He's Tough on Kids," 39.

97. Letter, Brown to John Whelan Jr. (Victor Gruen & Associates), 24 March 1956, Box 22, Folder 7, Brown Collection.

98. Price, "He's Tough on Kids," 92.

99. The Brown Collection, Box 22, file 1, has an article showing the whale featured in a corporate magazine, *Bakelite Review* (January 1957).

100. Letter, Edwin S. Burdell (President of Cooper Union for Advancement of Science & Art) to Brown, 12 August 1953, Box 22, Folder 5, Brown Collection. Burdell informed him about the competition.

101. Brown Collection, Box 22, Folder 10.

102. Brown does not mention them directly, but it is apparent that he was referring to Creative Playthings when he notes that one manufacturer had moved its plant to Princeton. He claimed that this created a situation that "for a while had some people thinking that we were in some way connected." Letter, Brown, to Dorothy Holley of the William Healy School in Chicago, 8 June 1965, Box 22, Folder 13, Brown Collection.

103. Letter, Garrett to Brown, 14 December 1956, Box 22, Folder 7, Brown Collection.

104. Letter, John Whelan to Brown, 20 March 1956, Box 22, Folder 7, Brown Collection.

105. Letter, Walter Gropius to Brown, 19 March 1960, Box 22, Folder 12, Brown Collection.

106. Letter, Brown, to Robert Marsteller, 20 June 1959, Box 22, Folder 12, Brown Collection.

107. Letter, Brown, to Elizabeth Halsey, 26 January 1957, Box 22, Folder 10, Brown Collection.

108. Letter, Brown, to Lillian Mays, 1 July 1957, Box 22, Folder 10, Brown Collection.

109. Brown even began licensing arrangements with large corporations such as Schwinn Bicycle and Monsanto during the 1960s, but nothing was produced.

110. The first edition of Ledermann and Trachsel's book was meant to be a global survey. Most of the examples were European, with just a handful of American representatives.

111. "Russian Children to Romp on Latest American Playground Gear," *New York*

Times, 3 April 1959. The accompanying photograph seems to be all of the Creative Playthings catalog, including *Fantastic Village, Tunnel Maze, Stalagmite Cave,* and a spiral slide probably based on Noguchi's prototype. This article previews the display that would take place in July.

112. For a plan of the Moscow fair, see "The U. S. in Moscow," *Time Magazine* (3 August 1959): 14. The exhibition is the cover story.

113. Dorothy Barclay, "Room for the Play of Fancy," *New York Times,* 19 July 1959.

Chapter 2. History: 1960–1995 (pages 43–91)

1. Tom Jambor, "Definitions of Play: Reflections and Directions," closing key note address, International Play Association World Conference, Espoo, Finland, 16 August 1996.

2. Robert B. Reich, *The Future of Success* (New York: Vintage Books, 2000, updated 2002), 17. The terms "custom" and "customized" can be very tricky in the playground world. The term "customized" is used here to indicate a variation that is one of a kind.

3. Jim Greenman, *Caring Spaces, Learning Places: Children's Environments that Work* (Redmond, Wash.: Exchange Press, 1988), 196. Greenman recognizes this confusion in the 1980s.

4. Every attempt has been made in this and subsequent chapters not to identify any current manufacturer. The intent is to look at the industry, not at individual producers.

5. The site changed slightly as plans developed. It began as 101st to 105th streets in the space between the West Side Highway and Riverside Park. It later became Riverside Park between 102d and 106th streets, and eventually narrowed down to 102d to 103d streets or 103d to 104th streets.

6. "Shouts of Children Echo Again in Revived Uptown Playground: Once-Deserted Area in Riverside Park Gets a Clean-Up and Police Guard in City–Neighborhood Effort," *New York Times,* 8 August 1960.

7. "The Record Reports," *Architectural Record* 112 (October 1952), 22 indicates that donors hoped that the UN playground would be built on another site.

8. Letter, Audrey Hess to Noguchi, 21 October 1960, "Riverside Park—Playground 1960–1961," Isamu Noguchi Foundation.

9. Letter, Hess to Caplan, 22 June 1961, "Riverside Park—Playground 1960–1961," Isamu Noguchi Foundation. Hess writes: "In the meantime, Isamu Noguchi is very anxious to begin working. . . . I told him that you had offered to find an architect and Isamu would like very much to meet whoever you have in mind." She then goes on to write that even before there is a program, it is "indeed essential, that Isamu Noguchi and an architect visit the park site together to study the topography and determine how the terrain lends itself to general divisions of areas." The need for an architect, at first voluntary, became mandatory in 1965. At that time, the Department of Parks and Corporation Counsel of New

York determined that a registered architect had to sign the drawings. Noguchi could participate but only as an associate. Letter, John A. Mulcahy (acting parks commissioner) to Kahn, 14 June 1965, "Riverside Park—Playground 1965," Isamu Noguchi Foundation.

Note, too, a memorandum of questions for Mr. Lessing Rosenwald dated 5 October 1961, which states that Kahn was "the top architect in the United States today and all other architects go to him for advice and opinions." This reflects a possible meeting between organizers of the playground and Audrey Hess's uncle, a brother of Mrs. Levy. He is not known to have participated in any other way in this project. See file "Riverside Park—Playground 1960–1961," Isamu Noguchi Foundation.

10. Box 115, "Kahn—Noguchi Playground," Louis I. Kahn Collection, University of Pennsylvania and Pennsylvania Historical and Museum Commission (hereafter cited as Kahn Collection). The Kahn Collection has correspondence that shows Caplan was made aware of important meetings. Letter, Juliet F. Brudney (Executive Director, Blomingdale Conservation Project), to Noguchi, 28 June 1961, Isamu Noguchi Foundation. She suggests that she, Noguchi, and Caplan have lunch together in order to discuss plans before talking to the Parks Commissioner in September.

11. The MoMA exhibition took place 6 June–16 July 1961.

12. Noguchi, "The Road I Have Walked," part of a lecture he gave when he received the Kyoto Award in 1986, quoted in *Play Mountain* (Tokyo: Watari Museum of Contemporary Art, 1996), 100.

13. Letter, Noguchi to Kahn, 27 August 1961, Box 33, "Adele R. Levy Memorial Playground Noguchi Correspondence," Kahn Collection.

14. Van Eyck and Kahn had frequent opportunities to interact. One of the least known is that van Eyck taught a landscape architecture course, "The Child and the City," at the University of Pennsylvania during the spring semester of 1960, where Kahn was on the permanent architecture faculty.

15. Kahn's TJCC site plan for 1957 introduced a day camp of four small, independent pavilions. He orchestrated them in a complex centrifugal pattern and would have liked to enclose them within an exterior border of hedges. Even more immediate to the New York project, Kahn had presented a master plan, in March 1960, for the Salk Institute for Biological Studies in La Jolla, California. There, Kahn had proposed a cluster of pavilions (a "forum") to house recreation areas that accommodated play, gardens, and a "wilderness" zone.

16. Jay Jacobs, "Projects for Playgrounds," *Art in America* 55 (November/December 1967), 40. Jacobs mentions a 1965 exhibition of "toys-by-artists" and an early 1960s exhibition of "Sculptors Toys" at the Royal Marks Gallery. Tyng gave one of her toys to Kahn's daughter Sue Ann. See Anne Tyng, *Louis Kahn to Anne Tyng: The Rome Letters 1953–1955* (New York: Rizzoli, 1997), 39.

17. "Mrs. David M. Levy Dead at 67; Civic and Social Services Leader; Philanthropist Aided Youth, Education and Refugee Work—Collected Art," *New York*

Times, 13 March 1960. Mrs. Levy had been a member of the executive committee of the Museum of Modern Art. Thomas Hess, in his capacity as editor of *Art
News,* wrote a moving tribute to Levy, his wife's aunt, in an editorial in the April
1960 issue.

18. Karal Ann Marling, *As Seen on TV: The Visual Culture of Everyday Life in the 1950s*
(Cambridge: Harvard University Press, 1994), 47.

19. "Dr. David M. Levy, 84, A Psychiatrist, Dies," *New York Times,* 4 March 1977.
Dr. Levy was cited in Margaret Talbot, "The Bad Mother," *The New Yorker* (9 and
16 August 2004), 62–75 at 68. Dr. Levy, who was one of several honorary
chairmen, does not appear to have taken an active role in the workings of the
playground memorial committee.

20. Eleven organizations, including the Frederick Douglass Housing Project (West
104th Street), the Children's Aid Society, the West Side Day Nursery, and residents of nearby apartment houses held meetings on 15 June and 22 June 1961;
Box 115, "Kahn-Noguchi Playground," Kahn Collection.

21. Audrey Hess, notes taken at meeting of 6 November 1961; Box 115, "Kahn-
Noguchi Playground," Kahn Collection.

22. Letter, Newbold Morris to Helen Harris (United Neighborhood Houses of New
York), 20 February 1962, Isamu Noguchi Foundation.

23. A summary, at least from the point of view of proponents of the playground, can
be found in a report dated 9 September 1963, "Neighborhood Committee for
Riverside Park Development," Box 115, "Kahn-Noguchi Playground," Kahn Collection. Funds were handled by the United Neighborhood Houses of New York.

24. "Riverside Group Scores Park Plan," *New York Times,* 2 October 1963.

25. Isamu Noguchi, *A Sculptor's World* (New York and Evanston: Harper & Row,
1968), 178.

26. Unsigned memo, 7 February 1963, Box 115, "Kahn-Noguchi Playground," Kahn
Collection.

27. Aline B. Louchheim (later Aline Saarinen), "UN Rejects 'Model' Playground;
Moses' Project is Accepted Instead," *New York Times,* 7 October 1951.

28. Murray Illson, "Playground Design Exhibition Given Cool Reception by Mor-
ris," *New York Times,* 17 February 1964. The exhibition, which took place at the
Architectural League, was sponsored by the Park Association of New York City.
Andrew Shanken has been kind enough to share a copy of the catalog.

29. Joseph Lelyveld, "Model Play Area for Park Shown," *New York Times,* 5 February
1964.

30. "Parks Are for Park Purposes," *New York Times,* 8 February 1964.

31. Letter, Noguchi to Kahn, 3 December 1964, Box 33, "Adele R. Levy Memorial
Playground Noguchi Correspondence," Kahn Collection.

32. Quoted in "Remarks: Louis I. Kahn," in *Perspecta* 9/10 (1965); 330. These remarks were based on a lecture Kahn had given at Yale in October 1964.

33. "Briton Criticizes U.S. Playgrounds," *New York Times,* 16 May 1965. Philadelphia and New York were on her tour.

34. Transcript of conversation between Kahn and Linn, 14 May 1965, Box 58, "Linn, Karl," Kahn Collection.

35. When Levy died, Wagner had said, "Perhaps no man or woman in our lifetime has given more of their time and energy to the great humanitarian causes of the day than this fine and noble woman. Her loss will be particularly felt by the thousands of less fortunate people whom she was willing to help toward a better life. Mrs. Wagner and I counted Mrs. Levy among our closest personal friends and we are deeply saddened by her death." "Rites for Mrs. Levy Set," *New York Times*, 14 March 1960.

36. "City Moves to Build a Disputed Center," *New York Times*, 28 December 1965.

37. Ralph Blumenthal, "Fight over Park Nearing Climax," *New York Times*, 13 February 1966; Letter, Hess to Julius Edelstein of Mayor's Office, 25 October 1965, Box 115, "Adele R. Levy Memorial Playground," Kahn Collection. Hess claims that Lindsay had declared, during the election, that he was against the park.

38. Ralph Blumenthal, "Mayor Now Backs Levy Playground," *New York Times*, 19 February 1966.

39. Edith Evans Asbury, "Park Chief Plan to Slash Red Tape," *New York Times*, 1 May 1966.

40. Letter, Hess to Kahn, 27 January 1966, Box 80, "Adele R. Levy Playground Contract—Correspondence," Kahn Collection.

41. Noguchi, "The Road I Have Walked," 100.

42. Richard Dattner, *Design for Play* (New York: Van Nostrand Reinhold Company, 1969), 66.

43. Edith Evans Asbury, "Group Abandons Levy Memorial," *New York Times*, 7 October 1966. Even today, architects still take notice of the Kahn-Noguchi project even though it is not the best-known work of either artist. Landscape architect Nicholas Quennell still teaches it in his classes at Columbia. William Sharples and Christopher Sharples, architects of SHoP (Sharples Holden Pasquarelli) remember his discussion and remain impressed by the totality, abstraction, and adaptability of the design. William Sharples and Christopher Sharples, conversation with author, 29 April 2003, New York City. Another architect, Billie Tsien (Todd Williams, Billie Tsien) found the design "magical" when she became familiar with it while designing a Noguchi exhibition in the 1990s. Billie Tsien, conversation with author, 17 August 2004, New York City.

44. Charles Mee Jr., "Putting the Play in Playgrounds," *New York Times*, 6 November 1966.

45. Jacobs, "Projects for Playgrounds," 45.

46. Richard Dattner, conversation with author, 7 February 2002, New York City.

47. Dattner, *Design for Play*, 34.

48. Seymour Gold, *Urban Recreation Planning* (Philadelphia: Lea and Febiger, 1972), quoted in the introduction to Paul Wilkinson, ed., *Innovation in Play Environments* (New York: St. Martin's Press, 1980), 16. Also Gold, "Non-Use of Neighborhood Parks," in *Transactions of the American Institute of Planners* (November 1972): 369–78.

49. Dattner, *Design for Play*, 15–40.

50. M. Paul Friedberg with Ellen Perry Berkeley, *Play and Interplay: A Manifesto for New Design in Urban Recreational Environment* (New York: Macmillan Company, 1970), 35–36.

51. Marisa Angell Brown, "The Spaces in Between: Theatrical Space and the Architecture of Social Housing in Postwar New York," a paper delivered at the annual meeting of the Society of Architectural Historians, Providence, Rhode Island, 17 April 2004. Brown makes a strong connection between playground commissions and the desire to reduce juvenile crime.

52. Friedberg, *Play and Interplay*, 42.

53. Mee, "Putting the Play in Playgrounds."

54. M. Paul Friedberg, *Playgrounds for City Children*, Bulletin 27-A of the Association for Childhood Education International (1969), 6–11.

55. Friedberg, *Play and Interplay*, 36–43.

56. Mee, "Putting the Play in Playgrounds."

57. Brown, "The Spaces in Between."

58. Friedberg, *Play and Interplay*, 175.

59. The best analysis of Dattner's playground is Michael Gotkin, "The Politics of Play: The Adventure Playground in Central Park" in *Preserving Modern Landscape Architecture: Papers from the Wave Hill–National Parks Service Conference*, ed. Charles Birnbaum (Washington, D.C., and Cambridge, Mass.: Spacemaker Press, 1999), 60–77.

60. Hoving wrote the introduction to Friedberg's *Play and Interplay*. No longer the Commissioner of Parks but by then director of the Metropolitan Museum of Art, Hoving was apparently not tainted by the Kahn-Noguchi debacle. His reputation as someone opposed to the progressive ideas of the Kahn-Noguchi proposal seems to have been cleared by 1967, when Jay Jacobs lauded Hoving's efforts to bring innovation to parks. See Jacobs, "Projects for Playgrounds," 39. There is a curious letter in the Joe Brown Collection (Box 22, file 13) that shows that the New York City Parks and Recreation Department invited Brown to meet then-mayor Lindsay on 31 August 1965. An unidentified hand scrawled at the top notes "Tom Hoving '53 Metropolitan," presumably a reference to Hoving's class at Princeton and his connection with the Metropolitan Museum.

   Morris Lapidus, the architect in the 1950s for the Fontainebleau and Eden Roc hotels in Miami Beach, also had a relationship to Hoving that involved playgrounds. Lapidus claimed that Hoving commissioned him to design the Bedford Stuyvesant Community Pool, a vast structure that had an extensive playground on the roof of the locker rooms. It appears to have been built in the early 1970s and owes a great deal to Kahn and Noguchi's work. The project was published in *Architectural Record* 155 (June 1974): 98–99. Lapidus maintained that Hoving asked for "a park built of concrete without a single blade of grass or single tree." See Morris Lapidus, *Too Much is Never Enough* (New York: Rizzoli International Publications, 1996), 9–10, although Lapidus's account is marred by faulty dates.

61. Richard Dattner, conversation with author, 7 February 2002, New York City.

62. Dattner, *Design for Play*, 66.

63. Gotkin, "The Politics of Play," 67–68.

64. Richard Dattner, conversation with author, 7 February 2002, New York City.

65. Dattner, *Design for Play*, 51.

66. Simon Nicholson, "How Not to Cheat Children: The Theory of Loose Parts," *Landscape Architecture* 62 (October 1971): 30–34.

67. "Design Notebook: Cherishing Landscapes as Living Art," *New York Times*, 30 November 1995.

68. Many letters of support for these playgrounds can be found at offices of Landmark West!, the New York City preservation group.

69. Letter, Martha Mendelsohn to Karen Putnam (Central Park Conservancy), 21 July 1996. Files of Landmark West!

70. Letter, Lissa Goldberg to Henry Stern (Parks Commissioner), 3 June 1999. Files of Landmark West!

71. Billie Tsien, conversation with author, 17 August 2004, New York City.

72. The Michael Bloomberg family paid for the restoration in 1997.

73. Dattner, conversation with author, 25 September 2003, New York City. The name of Dattner's company was 2001 International.

74. Alfred Ledermann and Alfred Trachsel, *Creative Playgrounds and Recreation Centers* [1959] (2d revd. ed., New York: Frederick A. Praeger, 1968), 156–57; Alison Dalton, "M. Paul Friedberg's Early Playground Designs in New York City," in Birnbaum, ed., *Preserving Modern Landscape Architecture*, 57–59.

75. Friedberg continues to design for one of the large manufacturers.

76. "Design for Children," *Architectural Forum* 117 (November 1962): 84–92. The Emdrup Adventure Playground is included.

77. Rudolph's apartments were published in "A New Urban Pattern," *Architectural Forum* 116 (March 1962): 99–101.

78. "Child-Size Domes," *Architectural Forum* 116 (April 1962): 40–41.

79. For an excellent discussion of earthworks, including a precursor by Claes Oldenburg in Central Park in 1967, see Suzann Boettger, *Earthworks: Art and the Landscape of the Sixties* (Berkeley: University of California Press, 2002).

80. Gotkin, "The Politics of Play," 70; *Architectural Record* 42 (August 1967).

81. Rita Reif, "Showroom? It's More Like a Playroom," *New York Times*, 11 December 1967. There is no indication that Lax's pieces, using a weatherized United States Plywood material, were ever installed in a New York City park.

82. Jacobs, "Projects for Playgrounds," 39.

83. Lisa Hammel, "Everything Was Quiet in the Plastic City Until . . . ," *The New York Times*, 11 November 1966. Jacobs had referred to this playground, indicating that it was in Riverside Park; Hammel's article indicates that the exhibition was in the lobby of the Pepsi-Cola building. Parks Commissioner Thomas Hoving, who had attended the opening reception, indicated he wanted to move the equipment, at least for a short time, to a Brooklyn vest-pocket park.

84. Ruth Inglis, "Architecture: The Fun Palace," *Art in America* (January/February 1966): 69–72.

85. MoMA press release, 18 May 1967, MoMA Archives. The playground is no longer extant. When Audrey Hess died in 1974, the *New York Times* obituary headline of 26 August read: "Audrey Hess, Led Unit for Families: Head of Citizens Committee for Children Dies at 50." She had been president from 1970 to 1972.

86. Ledermann and Trachsel, *Creative Playgrounds*, 62, notes that all three had been built at Cypress Hills.

87. Information on Cypress Hills comes from MoMA press release, 18 May 1967, MoMA Archives; Ledermann and Trachsel, *Creative Playgrounds*, 62–63; and Jacobs, "Projects for Playgrounds," 51. The New York Community Trust and Louis S. Auchincloss paid the cost of design; the housing authority and the Vincent Astor Foundation covered cost of construction. The MoMA press release mentions that a second project would be a play space for teens at Ravenswood Houses.

88. Charles Forberg, conversation with author, 7 July 2004, Mt. Kisco, New York. Forberg, who had studied at Black Mountain College and then at the Harvard Graduate School of Design, worked for Barnes from 1955 to 1958. He then started his own firm, where he designed exhibitions, including many for the United States Information Agency. Cypress Hills was his only work for a public housing site.

89. MoMA press release, 18 May 1967, MoMA Archives.

90. Report of National Recreation Congress, *Recreation Magazine* 40 (April 1946).

91. Charles Forberg, conversation with author, 7 July 2004, Mt. Kisco, New York.

92. Jacobs, "Projects for Playgrounds," 50.

93. Michael Gotkin has pointed out the modernist setting, designed by landscape architect Hideo Sasaki. Gotkin, "The Politics of Play," 63.

94. Rita Reif, "Realism Returning to Playground Equipment," *New York Times*, 4 July 1963.

95. Ledermann and Trachsel, *Creative Playgrounds*, 164.

96. Mark N. Finston, "Playgrounds Becoming Too Safe for Children," *Newark Star-Ledger*, 12 April 1966.

97. See correspondence, Brown Collection, Box 22, Folders 13 and 14.

98. Philadelphia enacted "percent for art" legislation in 1959.

99. Friedberg, *Playgrounds for City Children*, 48. Friedberg was among those who believed that artists and children had to compromise too much to accommodate each other.

100. Cummins Engine Foundation pays all architectural fees for public projects if the public agency chooses an architect "from a list of first-rank American architects."

101. William D. Chambers, general counsel of Irwin Management Company, Inc., conversation with author, 1 April 2003, Columbus, Indiana. Chambers was

kind enough to provide much of the background information on Columbus and its mall. The original names of the project were the Courthouse Center, to denote the mall, and the Commons, to indicate the part the Miller family had deeded to the city as public space.

102. Cesar Pelli, telephone conversation with author, 16 April 2003.

103. "Piazza, American Style: Courthouse Center and the Commons," *Progressive Architecture* 57 (June 1976): 64–69.

104. M. Paul Friedberg, *Handcrafted Playgrounds: Designs You Can Build Yourself* (New York: Vintage Books, 1975).

105. Jeremy Joan Hewes, *Build Your Own Playground!* (Boston: Houghton Mifflin Company, 1975), 7. Hewes notes (57) that Beckwith had worked with the de Young Museum in San Francisco to organize workshops and a community-built "framework" for a playground on the museum grounds.

106. For a complete record of the Yard, see Robin C. Moore and Herbert H. Wong, *Natural Learning: The Life History of an Environmental Schoolyard* (Berkeley: MIG Communications, 1997). Susan Henderson has generously shared her extensive, excellent research on Weimar schools.

107. Robin C. Moore, "Generating Relevant Urban Childhood Places: Learning from the 'Yard,'" in *Innovation in Play Environments,* ed. Paul F. Wilkinson (New York: St. Martin's Press, 1980), 45–75.

108. Moore and Wong, *Natural Learning,* 202.

109. Ibid., 198.

110. Rita Kimball (principal of Washington Elementary School), telephone conversation with author, 8 September 2003. Nearby, and emerging from a slightly different thrust, restauranteur Alice Waters founded the Edible Schoolyard in 1997. See Peggy Orenstein, "Food Fighter," *The New York Times Magazine* (7 March 2004).

111. Denise Brown (Assistant Recreation Co-Coordinator), telephone conversation with author, 4 April 2003.

112. Clare C. Cooper, "Adventure Playgrounds," *Landscape Architecture* 61 (October 1970): 20, indicates that there had been two earlier, temporary Adventure Playgrounds in or near Berkeley in the late 1960s. See Arvid Bengtsson, *Adventure Playgrounds* [1972] (reprint, London: Crosby Lockwood Staples, 1973), 149, for discussion of the first American Adventure Playground, a temporary experiment sponsored by *McCall's* magazine in Minneapolis in 1950.

113. Hewes, *Build Your Own Playground,* 65.

114. Bengtsson, *Adventure Playgrounds,* 149.

115. Marjory Allen and Mary Nicholson, *Memoirs of an Uneducated Lady: Lady Allen of Hurtwood* (London: Thames & Hudson, 1975), 243.

116. Cooper, "Adventure Playgrounds," 27.

117. For data on increasing number of lawyers, see Robert D. Putnam, *Bowling Alone: The Collapse and Revival of American Community* (New York: Simon & Schuster, 2000), 144–47.

118. "'Berkeley Marina Playground," a fact sheet in the files of Berkeley Recreation Department (n.d.), indicates that supporters first approached the city about the playground in December 1978.

119. The undated fact sheet "Berkeley Marina Playground" (ibid.) appears to be a report that reflects the first year of operation. Primary funding came from the Bank of America Foundation. The site was created on a landfill.

120. Berkeley Recreation Department files. The same advertisement also advises which bus would reach the site.

121. Ilya Tovbis, a worker on the playground during the summer of 2002, has generously recounted his experiences, in e-mail to author, 23 January 2003.

122. Clare M. Reckert, "Education Boom Spurs Take-Overs," New York Times, 12 March 1967.

123. "Briton Criticizes U.S. Playgrounds," New York Times, 16 May 1965.

124. Edward Hudson, "Soaring Premiums for Risk Coverage Troubling Suburbs," New York Times, 20 March 1977.

125. Andrea Jolles, "Play Areas No Fun for Co-op Boards," New York Times, 5 October 1980.

126. Nancy Blodgett, "Premium Hikes Stun Municipalities," ABA Journal, 1 July 1986. The following years were marked by similar hostility between cities and the insurance companies. In 1994, a suit was settled between twenty states and thirty-two insurance companies. The states maintained that the insurance companies had conspired "to restrict the availability of liability coverage to municipalities in the 1980s." Kirk Johnson, "Big Lawsuit is Settled by 32 Insurers: Municipalities Reach $36 Million Agreement," New York Times, 7 October 1994.

127. Johnson, "Big Lawsuit."

128. "New Playground Equipment Approved," St. Louis Post-Dispatch, 9 March 1989.

129. John D. Morris, "Consumer Product Safety Unit Gears Up," New York Times, 19 June 1973.

130. The CPSC addressed equipment for five- to twelve-year-olds in its first handbooks; this was remedied in 1991 when the new version included equipment for two- to five-year-olds. Frances Wallach, "Playground Safety: What Did We Do Wrong?" Parks & Recreation 27 (April 1992): 52–57, 83 at 57.

131. Lizabeth Cohen, A Consumers' Republic: The Politics of Mass Consumption in Postwar America (New York: Alfred A. Knopf, 2003), 357–63.

132. Marianna Riley, "Playground Safety Thrust is Seesaw's Downer: Park Staples Vanish Under New Guidelines," St. Louis Post-Dispatch, 27 December 1993.

133. Douglas Martin, "That Upside-Down High Will Be Only a Memory; Monkey Bars Fall to Safety Pressures," New York Times, 11 April 1996.

134. Patricia Leigh Brown, "In City Parks, A Childhood Joy is Now a Rarity," New York Times, 11 May 1995.

135. Carol Lawson, "Playgrounds Shaped by Today's Urban Concerns," New York Times, 13 July 1989.

136. Quoted in Brown, "In City Parks."
137. It's hard to prove this accusation, no matter how intriguing it is; Colgate has seen its detergent sales decrease at the same time that Proctor and Gamble has reported improvements. Both companies declined to return repeated telephone calls.
138. James L. Sipes, "Playground Safety: Issues of Risk, Liability and Fun," *Landscape Architecture* 90 (February 2000): 38, 40–42, at 42.
139. Peter Geraghty (San Jose Redevelopment Agency project manager) telephone conversation with author, 26 February 2002.
140. Eric Schlosser, *Fast Food Nation: The Dark Side of the All-American Meal* (Boston and New York: Houghton Mifflin Company, 2001), 47. At this writing, it is unclear if McDonald's is supporting its playgrounds program as strongly as it did in the past. McDonald's will not release any information without first clearing its use.
141. Andrew Shanken, conversation with author, 22 September 2003, Princeton, New Jersey.
142. Arlene Brett, Robin C. Moore, and Eugene F. Provenzo Jr., *The Complete Playground Book* (Syracuse: Syracuse University Press, 1993), 148.
143. Jennie Lindon, *Too Safe for Their Own Good? Helping Children Learn about Risk and Lifestyles* (London: National Early Years Network, 1999), 11.
144. Ibid.
145. Jim Greenman, *Caring Spaces, Learning Places,* 77.
146. Jim Greenman, telephone conversation with author, 16 April 2003.
147. Jim Greenman, *Caring Spaces, Learning Places,* 175.
148. Letter, Richard Haag to author, 7 July 2003.
149. Cecilia Perez and Roger A. Hart, "Beyond Playgrounds: Planning for Children's Acces to the Environment," in Wilkinson, *Innovation in Play Environments,* 252–271.
150. Sharon Stine, *Landscapes for Learning* (New York : John Wiley & Son, Inc., 1997), 28–29.
151. Jennie Lindon, *Too Safe for Their Own Good,* 5.
152. Gregory Stock, telephone conversation with author, 21 July 2003.
153. To compound bureaucratic possibilities, the National Program for Playground Safety at the University of Northern Iowa has it own four-day "Safety School." Participants, who pay $445 for the session and an additional $100 to take a two-hour exam on the last day, can become "certified." Since this is different from the "certified playground safety inspectors" who are minted by the National Recreation and Park Association, it is unclear what the Iowa program is selling.
154. Stacey Suecoff, J. Avner, K. Chou, E. Crain, "A Comparison of New York City Playground Hazards in High- and Low-Income Areas," *Archives of Pediatric and Adolescent Medicine* 154 (April 1999): 363–66.
155. O. Alton Barron (Assistant Clinical Professor of Orthopedic Surgery, Columbia

University College of Physicians and Surgeons), conversation with author, 8 June 2004, New York City.

156. Paul F. Wilkinson and Robert S. Lockhart, "Safety in Children's Formal Play Environments," in *Innovation in Play Environments*, ed. Paul F. Wilkinson (New York: St. Martin's Press, 1980), 85–96, at 95. Current reports from "Personal Injury Verdict Reviews" indicate that recent suits for playground injuries have been against municipalities in Wisconsin and California and a YMCA in Tennessee. In each case, the plaintiff maintained that a child's playground was caused by inadequate supervision. Few sue the manufacturers, any more.

157. Jim Greenman, *Caring Spaces, Learning Places*, 77.

158. Chris Young, "Play: Equipment and Surfacing," *Landscape Design Extra* 63 (February 1996).

159. David Ropeik and Nigel Holmes, "Never Bitten, Twice Shy: The Real Dangers of Summer," *New York Times*, 9 August 2003.

160. Jeffrey Steingarten, *It Must've Been Something I Ate* (New York, Vintage Books, 2003), 110–112.

161. Michael Specter, "Miracle in a Bottle," *The New Yorker* (2 February 2004). Americans have a tough time evaluating risk when it really does exist. Note, for example, the way they have bought into the unregulated health pill and potion industry.

162. Frank Furedi, *Paranoid Parenting* (Chicago: Chicago Review Press, 2002; published in a different form in the United Kingdom, 2001).

163 Barry Glassner, *The Culture of Fear* (New York: Basic Books, 1999), 72. Glassner's chapter "Youth at Risk" is the most relevant for this discussion.

164. Jane C. Loeffler, *The Architecture of Diplomacy* (New York: Princeton Architectural Press, 1998); and Catesby Leigh, "Coming Soon to Baghdad: Embassy in a Box," *The Wall Street Journal*, 2 June 2004.

165. Deborah Lupton, ed., *Risk and Sociocultural Theory: New Directions and Perspectives* (Cambridge: Cambridge University Press, 1999). One essay in this volume is particularly relevant: Stevi Jackson and Sue Scott, "Risk Anxiety and the Social Construction of Childhood," 86–107.

166. Furedi, *Paranoid Parenting*, 46.

167. Will Blythe, review of Tom Perrotta's novel *Little Children*, in the *New York Times Book Review* (14 March 2004): "To listen to these parents, it would seem that children are the ultimate in moral accouterments. You'd think that no previous generation had ever had them quite the right way."

168. For those seeking an overview of educational theories, see Carol Garhart Mooney, *An Introduction to Dewey, Montessori, Erickson, Piaget and Vygotsky* (St. Paul: Redleaf Press, 2000); and a very well conceived pamphlet written by Marianne Valentine, *The Reggio Emilia Approach to Early Years Education*, published by Scottish Consultative Council on the Curriculum in 1999.

169. Kathy Hirsh-Pasek and Roberta Michnick Golinkoff, *Einstein Never Used Flash Cards: How Our Children Really Learn—And Why They Need to Play More and Memorize Less* (Emmaus, Pa.: Rodale, 2003), 230.

170. Roger Hart (Co-Director of Children's Environments Research Group at City University of New York), conversation with author, 18 June 2004, New York City.

171. Roger Hart, e-mail correspondence with author, 27 July 2004; Gerald W. Bracey, *On the Death of Childhood and the Destruction of Public Schools* (Portsmouth, N.H.: Heinemann, 2003), 1. Doris Fromberg, in her introduction to Jane Perry's *Outdoor Play: Teaching Strategies with Young Children* (New York: Teachers College Press, 2001), describes the current academic situation as "an era of fundamentalist political forces that advocate for an academic-transmission curriculum, a narrow conception of teacher-proof curricular scripts and linear paper-and-electronic-workbook materials, high-stakes standardized testing of isolated skills, and a limited image of education as based in an indoor classroom."

172. Deborah Meier, *In Schools We Trust* (Boston: Beacon Press, 2002), 15 and 14–18.

173. Ibid. 6. In addition to this book, see Deborah Meier, *Will Standards Save Public Education?* ed. Joshua Cohen and Joel Rogers (Boston: Beacon Press, 2000).

174. Statement issued by the workshop on "Children in Human Settlements," held in June 1976 at the United Nations' Habitat Human Settlements Conference in Vancouver, Canada. Quoted in Wilkinson, *Innovations in Play Environments,* 3.

175. William Glasser in an interview with *U.S. News & World Report,* 23 May 1977.

176. Theodore Sizer, "A Sense of Place," in Meier, *Will Standards Save Public Education?*

Chapter 3. Patrons (pages 95–125)

1. Jim Ryugo (Interim Director, Parks and Recreation Department, City of Oakland, California), telephone conversation with author, 14 October 2002.

2. Brian Drypolcher (Program Manager, southwest region, TPL), telephone conversation with author, 18 February 2003. TPL sponsored eighteen months of meetings with local citizens. The competition was worldwide, but each team had to have at least one New Mexican on its list of participants. Much of the information in this section comes from Mary Miss, conversations with author, 4 March 2003, 12 March 2004, and 27 September 2004, New York City; and Ken Smith, conversations with author, 16 October 2002 and 18 March 2004, New York City.

3. Much of the information is this section has been provided by Cheryl Barton, conversation with author, 23 May 2003, San Francisco.

4. Information in this section comes from Anita Hill (Executive Director, Yerba Buena Alliance), conversation with author, 21 May 2003; and Paul Friedberg, conversation with author, 18 January 2002, New York City.

5. Susan Herrington has discussed her philosophy and work in articles that include "The Received View of Play and the Subculture of Infants," *Landscape*

Journal 16 (Fall 1997): 149–60; and "Playgrounds as Community Landscapes," *Built Environment* 25 (November 1999): 25–34.

6. TLC is one of several programs run by Compass, an organization that gets over 40 percent of its annual revenue from local government. According to Compass, 22 percent of San Francisco children live in poverty. Information about TLC comes from Lisa Gelfand, conversations with author, 20 May and 21 August 2003, San Francisco; Susan Herrington, telephone conversation with author, 31 January 2002.

7. Information in this section comes from Vito Acconci, conversations with the author, 25 September 2002 and 11 May 2003, Brooklyn, New York; and Martha Schwartz, telephone conversation with author, 12 March 2003.

8. Gloria Moure, "From Words to Things," in *Vito Acconci: Writings, Works, Projects,* ed. Gloria Moure (Barcelona: Ediciones Poligrafa, 2001), 19.

9. Dean Sobel, "From Thought to Monument," in Dean Sobel, guest curator of *Vito Acconci/Acconci Studio: Acts of Architecture* (Milwaukee: Milwaukee Art Museum, 2001), 15–41, at 30.

10. Vito Acconci, conversation with author, 25 September 2002, Brooklyn, New York.

11. Art for the World, though an independent nonprofit organization, is loosely connected to the United Nations via the World Health Organization, High Commission for Refugees, and the Food and Agriculture Organization.

12. Acconci Studio members for *Klein Bottle* are: Vito Acconci, Dario Nunez, Peter Dorsey, Sergio Prego, Kyle Steinfeld, Michael Day, Anthony Arnold, Jean Humke, and Matthew Wood.

13. Marc Treib, "A Constellation of Pieces," *Landscape Architecture* 92 (March 2002): 59–67, 92, at 67.

14. Galen Cranz, *The Politics of Park Design: A History of Urban Parks in America* [1982] (reprint, Cambridge, Mass., and London: The MIT Press, 1989), 77.

15. New York City recently has revived the practice. Glenn Collins, "'Leaves of Grass,' Anyone? A Reading Room Returns to Bryant Park," *New York Times,* 27 May 2003.

16. Information in this section has been provided by Aditya Advani, telephone conversation with author, 5 June 2003.

17. Information in this section comes from Ken Smith, conversations with author, 28 October 2002 and 2 July 2003; and Cathy Zarbis, conversation with author, 11 June 2003, New York City. The original designation was "Learning Garden." As the project progressed, the principal and the patrons agreed to emphasize reading.

18. Information in this section comes from Jim Greenman, telephone conversation with author, 16 April 2003; and Victoria Baker, conversation with author, 1 April 2003, Columbus, Indiana.

19. "Special School: Nursery for Teaching, Research, Testing," in *Architectural Record* 133 (May 1963): 174–76.

20. Information in this section comes from Leslie Roffman, conversation with au-

thor, 22 August 2003, San Francisco; and Mark Horton, conversation with author, 1 May 2002, San Francisco.

Chapter 4. Strategies (pages 126–158)

1. Information for this section comes from Susan Herrington, telephone conversation with author, 31 January 2002.
2. As of this writing, the project is in jeopardy.
3. Information for this section comes primarily from Walter Hood, conversation with author, 21 May 2003, Oakland, California.
4. The San Francisco exposition, similar to the 1893 Columbian Exposition in Chicago the previous year, contained villages that attempted to replicate foreign settings. The Chicago venue was famous for its representation of Morocco; San Francisco adapted a street from Cairo.
5. *Places* 15 (Winter 2003); much of this issue is devoted to the redevelopment of San Jose. Information for this project also comes from Cheryl Barton, conversation with author, 23 May 2003, San Francisco.
6. Thomas R. Aidala and Rita Skevos, "The San Jose Experience: Vision, Plan, Strategy," *Places* 15 (Winter 2003): 12–19.
7. For an excellent discussion of the frequent disjunction between these goals and their accomplishments, see Tom Finkelpearl, *Dialogues in Public Art*. (Cambridge, Mass., and London: The MIT Press, 2001), 2–51. The inflated conclusion can be seen, of course, in the number of cities that now seek a visible museum as a panacea for ailing downtowns. This "Bilbao effect" reached Philadelphia, for example, in the form of a campaign to move the Barnes Foundation from the suburbs to the center of the city.
8. Harold L. Ickes, "Space for Play," *Recreation* 40 (July 1946): 179–83, 219.
9. Martin Flores, conversation with author, 5 March 2004, San Jose, California. Flores, senior landscape architect for the San Jose Redevelopment Agency, selected Barton after visiting studios of many landscape architects.
10. The New York City Parks and Recreation Department had a different strategy for a similar facility, the Playground for All Children (late 1970s) in Flushing Meadows Park in Queens. This has been restored, keeping some of architect Hisham Askouri's signature details, such as a large space frame superstructure, as cultural history.
11. The ADA guidelines for playground accessibility are complicated. The goal is to give all users access to at least 50 percent of the activities that are raised above the ground. The number of activities and their location determine whether ramps or transfer stations are needed. There is also a proportionate system of determining how the total number of elevated activities affects the number of those required at ground level.
12. Chambers makes the case that the similar intimidation keeps young girls away

from the same type of equipment. Chambers, conversation with author, 2 October 2002, New York City. Additional information comes from Donna Walcavage, conversation with author, 18 October 2002, Brooklyn, New York; and Sonja Johansson, conversation with author, 21 November 2002, Lincoln, Massachusetts.

13. Walcavage, Johansson, and Otterness designed their pieces for Rockefeller Park. Teardrop Park is slightly east of the Otterness installation. The Rockefeller family had been one of the early proponents of development in this part of lower Manhattan. Battery Park City Authority is now known as the Hugh L. Carey Battery Park City Authority.

14. Gary Hack, conversation with author, 4 March 2003, Philadelphia, Pennsylvania. Hack noted too that the team had had extensive designs for unique play equipment. When there was a change of leadership at Battery Park Authority, the designers faced the possibility of increased liability for one-of-a-kind work. At that point, they had no choice but to scrap the first plans and substitute off-the-shelf catalog items, albeit used in more interesting, "customized" ways than at most playgrounds. This shift of liability to the manufacturer enabled the project to proceed. Comparative images of the proposed and built playgrounds can be seen on page 316 of Stephen Carr, Mark Francis, Leanne G. Rivlin, Andrew M. Stone, *Public Space* (Cambridge: Cambridge University Press, 1992). Additional information for this section came from Donna Walcavage, conversation with author, 18 October 2002, Brooklyn, New York; Sonja Johansson, conversation with author, 21 November 2002, Lincoln, Massachusetts; Tom Otterness, conversation with author, 28 October 2002, Brooklyn, New York.

15. CLHS purposely requested only half-courts in order to ensure that the active recreation would remain low-key and to prevent the formation of any competitive leagues.

16. For discussion of the plans for Battery Park City, see David L. A. Gordon, *Battery Park City: Politics and Planning on the New York Waterfront* (Amsterdam: Gordon and Breach Publishers, 1997).

17. Craig Brown wrote about it in the 2 August 2001 edition of the *London Daily Telegraph*. The *Daily News* piece was written by Jonathan Lemire, 30 July 2001.

18. Michael Van Valkenburgh, "Faculty Project: Teardrop Park," *Harvard Design Magazine* 12 (Fall 2000): 92.

19. David W. Dunlap, "A Chip Off the Old Park: A 1.9-Acre Gem is to Open Today Downtown," *New York Times*, 30 September 2004.

20. Ibid.

21. Mikyoung Kim, *Inhabiting Circumference* (Washington, D.C.: Grayson Publishing, 2002), np.

22. Information for this section comes from Donald Carso (former principal) and Irene Coe (current principal) of Moylan School, conversation with author, 25 April 2003 Hartford, Connecticut. See also Paul Bennett, "Playtime in the City," *Landscape Architecture* 89 (September 1999).

23. Paul Zielbauer, "Poverty in a Land of Plenty: Can Hartford Ever Recover?" *New York Times*, 26 August 2002. This front-page article proclaims that this state

capital is "the most destitute 17 square miles in the nation's wealthiest state and a city where 30 percent of its residents live in poverty."

24. Information for this section comes from Walter Hood, conversation with author, 21 May 2003, Oakland, California.

25. Clare Cooper Marcus, "Unexpected Company," *Landscape Architecture* 93 (June 2003).

26. Information for this section comes from Richard Blender, conversation with author, 27 March 2003, Chicago.

27. Information for this section comes from Mary and Bill Buchen, conversation with author, 24 January 2003, New York City.

28. Information in this section comes from Tom Richman, conversation with author, 16 May 2003, San Francisco; and Michael Painter, telephone conversation with author, 26 September 2003. Landscape architect Painter, who designed this concrete tour de force in the late 1970s, completed two other concrete slides at about the same time in San Francisco (in Golden Gate Park and at Hill Top Park in Hunter's Point). He reports that liability concerns have quashed commissions for more recent versions.

29. Originally called South East Loop Park, Halprin's plans are documented at the Halprin Collection at Architectural Archives, University of Pennsylvania. Halprin's office produced a booklet on the history of the project. Halprin's copy, in the Architectural Archive, is source of background material here. Further information comes from Ken Smith, conversation with author, 25 June 2003, New York City. For a recent discussion of preserving Halprin's work, see Patricia Leigh Brown, "For Shaper of Landscapes, A Cliffhanger," *New York Times*, 10 July 2003.

Chapter 5. Variants (pages 159–181)

1. Information for this section comes from conversations with Alan Plattus (director of the Yale Urban Design Workshop), 24 and 30 January 2004, New Haven; and Tom Luckey, telephone conversation with author, 2 February 2003.

2. There are plans for five thousand housing units by 2027; an electric trolley already links this area to other parts of the city. "First Thursdays"—the first Thursday night of each month, when galleries stay open late—-attract many people. It is a program begun by the late William Jamison, a local art dealer for whom the park is named.

3. Mark Hinshaw, "Pearl of Wisdom: The Transformation of Portland's Pearl District Demonstrates Lessons Learned from Other Cities," *Landscape Architecture* 92 (April 2002): 34–40, notes that the area—which he identifies with a Soho-type of transformation from light industry to a nucleus of shopping and trendy living—claims that the name "Pearl" emerged "from the notion of a shining pearl hidden inside an ugly oyster."

4. "Improvement Plans for South Park Square," *Portland Parks & Recreation Newsletter*, July 1999.

5. Randy Gragg, "Going with the Flow," *The Oregonian,* 10 June 2002. Walker specifically refers to Halprin's other, nearby Lovejoy Fountain.

6. Jory Johnson, *Modern Landscape Architecture: Redefining the Garden* (New York: Abbeville Press, 1991), 4. Johnson believes that Angela Danadjieva of Halprin's office was responsible for the design of Forecourt Fountain. Johnson notes that no serious injuries have occured there; there was one fatality that was later considered a suicide. Sadly, the genius of the Forecourt design became even more apparent after a 2004 tragedy at the Fort Worth Water Gardens (Philip Johnson & John Burgee, 1974). At the Texas site, the hardscape and splashing water were actually very dangerous. One of the areas, which was 9 feet deep and contained the recycling pump, was the place where an eight-year-old and three potential rescuers (including two other children) drowned. The depth and suction were a lethal combination.

7. Randy Gragg, "A 'Playground' for the Pearl," *The Oregonian,* 2 February 2003. The Lin sculpture is described as "an undulating 40 by 50 foot, rubber-coated sculpture."

8. Michael Brick, "A Suburb Finds That Outlying Development Is Hurting Its Downtown," *New York Times,* 4 September 2002, C10. Much of the information on downtown Vancouver comes from Dan Jenkins (principal, Murase Associates), conversation with author, 26 July 2002, Portland, Oregon.

9. Information in this section comes from Stanley Saitowitz, conversation with author, 21 May 2003, San Francisco.

10. Information for this section comes from Lee Weintraub, conversation with author, 20 February 2002, Yonkers, New York.

11. Paul Goldberger, *Up from Zero: Politics, Architecture, and the Rebuilding of New York* (New York: Random House, 2004), 148.

12. Information in this section comes from Jane Shoplick, conversation with author, 21 November 2002, Boston.

13. Information about the Bright Horizons facility and Moore's work comes from Robin Moore, conversation with author, 10 April 2003, Raleigh, North Carolina, and Lori Little (director of BHFS at GlaxoSmithKline), conversation with author, 10 April 2003, Durham, North Carolina.

14. Moore estimates that a childcare facility for thirty or forty children could achieve similar success for about $60,000, and that even facilities for many more children could arrive at solutions that would cost less than $100,000.

Chapter 6. Remedies (pages 182–211)

1. Tom Finkelpearl (now director of the Queens Museum), conversation with author, 14 April 2003, Queens, New York.

2. The Kentucky statute is KY 411.190, Kentucky State Recreational Use Statute. Kentucky's statute went into effect in 1966 and was amended in 1998, 2000,

and 2002. In some states, playgrounds and skateboard parks are referred to in the legislation. Most state courts appear to have affirmed the validity of such laws. As early as 1990 (*Davis v. Authority 68104*), the Illinois Supreme Court held that the city's immunity was extended to playgrounds operated by the Chicago Housing Authority.

3. James S. Russell, ed., *The Mayors' Institute: Excellence in City Design* (Washington, D.C.: National Endowment for the Arts / New York: Princeton Architectural Press, 2002).

4. David Armstrong, conversation with author, 3 April 2003, Louisville, Kentucky; and Stanley Saitowitz, conversation with author, 21 May 2003, San Francisco. Armstrong was mayor during 1998 to 2002.

5. David Armstrong, telephone conversation with author, 26 September 2003.

6. Flaura K. Winston, quoted in Eric Nagourney, "Safety: An Edge for Skateboarding," *New York Times,* 22 October 2002. J. William Thompson, "A Good Thrashing: A Landscape Architect's Perspective on Skateparks," *Landscape Architecture* 88 (March 1998): 78–87, 100, at 81, notes that "successful claims against cities for public skateparks are virtually nonexistent." That, too, happened in Louisville. There was a serious accident soon after the park opened when an eleven-year-old, who was not wearing a helmet, fell off his bike and into one of the bowls. The family sued Louisville (a combined city/county entity) for negligence and a judge dismissed the case in June 2004.

7. Dave Merrill, "Skateboarding Grinds Out Urban Revival," *USA Today,* 30 July 2002.

8. Eric Fredericksen, "Architecture That Shreds," *Architecture* (April 2002): 46.

9. David Armstrong, conversation with author, 3 April 2003, Louisville, Kentucky.

10. E-mails are on file in the office of the Louisville Parks Department.

11. Gregory Stock, telephone conversation with author, 21 July 2003; Roger Hart, conversation with author, 18 June 2004, New York City.

12. A good source of information on the variety of programs available is found in Jason Pearson, *University-Community Design Partnerships: Innovations in Practice* (Washington, D.C.: National Endowment for the Arts / New York: Princeton Architectural Press, 2002).

13. Galen Cranz, *The Politics of Park Design: A History of Urban Parks in America* (Cambridge, Mass., and London: The MIT Press, 1989), 81.

14. Steve Badanes, conversation with author, 26 June 2003, Seattle, Washington.

15. Badanes, telephone conversation with author, 15 September 2003.

16. Ken Smith, conversation with author, 25 June 2003, New York City.

17. M. Jeffrey Hardwick, *Mall Maker: Victor Gruen, Architect of an American Dream* (Philadelphia: University of Pennsylvania Press, 2004), 94–102.

18. Mary Miss, conversation with author, 12 March 2004, New York City.

19. Garrett Eckbo, Daniel U. Kiley, and James C. Rose, "Landscape Design in the Rural Environment," *Architectural Record* (August 1939), reprinted in *Modern Landscape Architecture: A Critical Review,* ed. Marc Treib (Cambridge, Mass., and

London: The MIT Press, 1993), 83–87 at 86. In the context of rural recreation, they mentioned the local airport as a place of interest.

20. Members of Acconci Studio for this project were Luis Vera, Celia Imrey, Dario Nunez, Jenny Scrider, Charles Doherty, Saija Singer.

21. Acconci statement in *Vito Acconci: Writings, Works, Projects,* ed. Gloria Moure (Barcelona: Ediciones Poligrafa, 2001), 264.

22. Unless noted otherwise, information about the playground at Graz 2003 comes directly from Vito Acconci, conversation with author, 26 September 2002, Brooklyn, New York; and telephone conversation with Robert Punkenhofer, 28 October 2003.

23. The Mur River runs through several countries, including Hungary and Austria.

24. "No Time for Play," *The Economist* 359 (16 June 2001): 35.

25. Pearson, *University-Community Design,* 12. The report was "Building Community: A New Future for Architecture Education and Practice."

26. The documentation for this competition can be found in Susan Herrington, *Schoolyard Park: 13-Acres International Design Competition* (Vancouver: Centre for Landscape Research, University of British Columbia, 2002). The competition let participants choose between two sites, both in the town of East Clayton, Surrey, in British Columbia. There were 254 completed submissions, representing thirty-three countries. These were judged in May 2001.

27. Herrington, *Schoolyard Park,* 2.

28. Barrera worked with Andre Harris Diez and Loles Herrero Canela.

29. See Herrington, *Schoolyard Park,* 25–34, for complete descriptions of the winning projects.

30. Martha Thorne, conversation with author, 30 March 2003, Chicago, Illinois.

31. Roger Hart, conversation with author, 18 June 2004, New York City.

32. For more information on Japan, see Alfie Kohn, *The Schools Our Children Deserve* (Boston and New York: Houghton Mifflin Company, 2000), 107. Kohn notes that, in spite of an intimidating high school exam, Japanese education is very unstructured and child-activated in elementary school.

33. Lefaivre e-mail to author, 14 October 2004.

34. Rabbi Jim Diamond, conversation with author, 12 October 2004; and Emily Chiswick-Patterson, conversation with author, 13 October 2004, both in Princeton, New Jersey. Diamond and Chiswick-Patterson participated in Princeton's alternative spring break by helping (with students from the University of Southern California) to construct a large playground for the El Cerro neighborhood of Montevideo. Other American universities, working through the Hillel (Jewish student) program in Uruguay, sent representatives during other weeks of spring break.

35. Mark Obmascik, "Aquarium Going Soft on Children: Foam Structure to Replace Rock-Sculpture Playground," *The Denver Post,* 11 March 2001.

36. Sharon Stine, *Landscapes for Learning* (New York: John Wiley & Son, 1997),

writes about this and shows how the distinction between play space and equipment was drawn a decade earlier.

37. Lisa W. Foderaro, "Homemade Costumes Become as Rare as Goblins," *New York Times*, 31 October 2003.

38. *New York Times*, 15 July 2000.

SELECTED BIBLIOGRAPHY

This bibliography combines historic sources on playgrounds with material that offers additional information on contemporary designers and their projects.

Allen, Marjory, and Mary Nicholson. *Memoirs of an Uneducated Lady: Lady Allen of Hurtwood*. London: Thames & Hudson, 1975.

Art & Idea. *Building an Island: Vito Acconci/Acconci Studio*. Ostfildern-Ruit: Hatje Cantz Verlag, 2003.

Boettger, Suzann. *Earthworks: Art and Landscape of the Sixties*. Berkeley: University of California Press, 2002.

Bengtsson, Arvid. *Adventure Playgrounds*. 1972, reprinted London: Crosby Lockwood Staples, 1973.

———. *Environmental Planning for Children's Play*. New York and Washington: Praeger Publishers, 1970.

Birnbaum, Charles, ed. *Preserving Modern Landscape Architecture: Papers from the Wave Hill–National Parks Service Conference*. Washington, D.C., and Cambridge, Mass.: Spacemaker Press, 1999.

Borden, Iain. *Skateboarding, Space and the City: Architecture and the Body*. Oxford and New York: Berg, 2001.

Brown, Patricia Leigh. "He Measures Oakland's Beat, and Parks Bloom in Return." *New York Times*, 20 March 2004.

Caro, Robert A. *The Power Broker: Robert Moses and the Fall of New York*. New York: Alfred A. Knopf, 1974.

Carr, Stephen, Mark Francis, Leanne G. Rivlin, and Andrew M. Stone. *Public Space*. Cambridge: Cambridge University Press, 1992.

Cavallo, Dominick. *Muscles and Morals: Organized Playgrounds and Urban Reform, 1880–1920*. Philadelphia: University of Pennsylvania Press, 1981.

Cooper, Clare C. "Adventure Playgrounds: Europe Leads U.S. in Reuniting its Children with the 'Lost Landscape of Spontaneity.'" *Landscape Architecture* 61 (October 1970): 18–29, 88–91

Cranz, Galen. *The Politics of Park Design: A History of Urban Parks in America*. 1982, reprinted Cambridge, Mass., and London: The MIT Press, 1989.

Dattner, Richard. *Design for Play*. New York: Van Nostrand Reinhold Company, 1969.

———. *Civil Architecture: The New Public Infrastructure*. New York: McGraw-Hill, 1995.

Davern, Jeanne M., ed. *Places for People*. New York: McGraw-Hill Book Company (An Architectural Record Book), 1976.

Finkelpearl, Tom. *Dialogues in Public Art*. Cambridge, Mass., and London: The MIT Press, 2001.

Francis, Mark, and Andreas Reimann. *The California Landscape Garden*. Berkeley: University of California Press, 1999.

Friedberg, M. Paul. *Playgrounds for City Children*. Washington, D.C.: Association for Childhood Education International, 1969.

———. *Handcrafted Playgrounds: Designs You Can Build Yourself*. New York: Vintage Books, 1975.

Friedberg, M. Paul, with Ellen Perry Berkeley. *Play and Interplay: A Manifesto for New Design in Urban Recreational Environment*. New York: The Macmillan Company, 1970.

Frost, Joe L., and Barry L. Klein. *Children's Play and Playgrounds*. Boston: Allyn and Bacon, 1979.

Gardner, Howard. *Frames of Mind: The Theory of Multiple Intelligences*. New York: Basic Books, 1983.

Gastil, Raymond W., and Zoe Ryan, eds. *Open: New Designs for Public Space*. New York: Van Alen Institute, 2004.

Glassner, Barry. *The Culture of Fear*. New York: Basic Books, 1999.

Gordon, David L. A. *Battery Park City: Politics and Planning on the New York Waterfront*. Amsterdam: Gordon and Breach Publishers, 1997.

Graves, Donna. "Constructing Memory: Rosie the Riveter Memorial: Richmond, California." *Places* 15 (Fall 2002): 14–17.

Greenman, Jim. *Caring Spaces, Learning Places: Children's Environments that Work*. Redmond, Wash.: Exchange Press, 1988.

Guggenheimer, Elinor C. Illus. M. Paul Friedberg. *Planning for Parks and Recreation Needs in Urban Areas*. Twayne Publishers with the Center for New York City Affairs and the New School for Social Research: New York, 1969.

Hardwick, M. Jeffrey. *Mall Maker: Victor Gruen, Architect of an American Dream*. Philadelphia: University of Pennsylvania Press, 2004.

Hart, Roger. *Children's Participation: The Theory and Practice of Involving Young Citizens in Community Development and Environmental Care*. London: Earthscan Publications, 1997.

Hayden, Dolores. *The Power of Place: Urban Landscapes as Public History*. Cambridge, Mass., and London: The MIT Press, 1995.

Herrington, Susan. *Schoolyard Park: 13-Acres International Design Competition*. Vancouver: Centre for Landscape Research, University of British Columbia, 2002.

Hewes, Jeremy Joan. *Build Your Own Playground!* Boston: Houghton Mifflin Company, 1975.

Hood, Walter. *Urban Diaries*. Washington, D.C., and Cambridge, Mass.: Spacemaker Press, 1997.

Hulbert, Ann. *Raising America: Experts, Parents, and a Century of Advice about Children*. New York: Alfred A. Knopf, 2003.

Johnson, Marilyn S. *The Second Gold Rush: Oakland and the East Bay in World War II*. Berkeley: University of California Press, 1993, 1996.

Landecker, Heidi, ed. *Martha Schwartz: Transfiguration of the Commonplace*. Washington, D.C., and Cambridge, Mass.: Spacemaker Press, 1997.

Ledermann, Alfred, and Alfred Trachsel. Trans. Ernst Priefert. *Creative Playgrounds and Recreation Centers*. New York: Frederick A. Praeger, 1959, 1968.

Lefaivre, Liane, and Ingeborg de Roode, eds. *Aldo van Eyck: The Playgrounds and the City*. Rotterdam: NAi Publishers, 2002.

Lefaivre, Liane, and Alexander Tzonis. *Aldo van Eyck: Humanist Rebel, Inbetweening in a Postwar World*. Rotterdam: 010 Publishers, 1999.

Lindon, Jennie. *Too Safe for Their Own Good? Helping Children Learn about Risk and Lifestyles*. London: National Early Years Network, 1999.

Lupton, Deborah, ed. *Risk and Sociocultural Theory: New Directions and Perspectives*. Cambridge: Cambridge University Press, 1999.

Lytle, Donald E., ed. *Play and Educational Theory and Practice*. Play and Cultural, Studies, vol. 5, 2003.

Marling, Karal Ann. *As Seen on TV: The Visual Culture of Everyday Life in the 1950s*. Cambridge: Harvard University Press, 1994.

Metz, Tracy. Trans. Peter Mason. *Fun! Leisure and Landscape*. Rotterdam: NAi Publishers, 2002.

Miss, Mary. *Mary Miss*. New York: Princeton Architectural Press, 2004.

Moore, Robin C., and Herbert H. Wong. *Natural Learning: The Life History of an Environmental Schoolyard*. Berkeley: MIG Communications, 1997.

Moure, Gloria, ed. *Vito Acconci: Writings, Works, Projects*. Barcelona: Ediciones Poligrafa, 2001.

Nicholson, Simon. "How Not to Cheat Children: The Theory of Loose Parts." *Landscape Architecture* 62 (October 1971): 30–34.

Pearson, Jason. *University-Community Design Partnerships: Innovations in Practice*. Washington, D.C.: National Endowment for the Arts/New York: Princeton Architectural Press, 2002.

Perry, Jane. P. *Outdoor Play: Teaching Strategies with Young Children*. New York: Teachers College Press, 2001.

Piedmont-Palladino, Susan, and Mark Alden Branch. *Devil's Workshop: twenty-five Years of Jersey Devil Architecture*. New York: Princeton Architectural Press, 1997.

Process Architecture 82 (May 1989). Special issue, "M. Paul Friedberg: Landscape Design."

Ravitch, Diane. *The Language Police: How Pressure Groups Restrict What Students Learn*. New York: Alfred A. Knopf, 2003.

Russell, James S., ed. *The Mayors' Institute: Excellence in City Design*. Washington, D.C.: National Endowment for the Arts/New York: Princeton Architectural Press, 2002.

Saunders, William S., ed. *Richard Haag: Bloedel Reserve and Gas Works Park*. New York: Princeton Architectural Press, 1998.

Schlosser, Eric. *Fast Food Nation: The Dark Side of the All-American Meal*. Boston and New York: Houghton Mifflin Company, 2001.

Scott, Janny. "When Child's Play Is Too Simple: Experts Criticize Safety-Conscious Recreation as Boring." *New York Times,* 15 July 2000.

Sennett, Richard. *The Conscience of the Eye.* New York: Alfred A. Knopf, 1990.

Seymour, Whitney North Jr. *Small Urban Spaces: The Philosophy, Design, Sociology and Politics of Vestpocket Parks, and Other Small Urban Open Spaces.* New York: New York University Press, 1969.

Shanken, Andrew. "Planning Memory: Living Memorials in the United States During World War II." *Art Bulletin* 84 (March 2002): 130–147.

Sobel, Dean, guest curator. *Vito Acconci/Acconci Studio.* Milwaukee: Milwaukee Art Museum, 2001.

Sorvig, Kim. "Railyard Remake in Santa Fe: Supplanting the Usual with the Unusual," *Competitions* 12 (Fall 2002): 18–31.

Treib, Marc, ed. *Modern Landscape Architecture: A Critical Review.* Cambridge, Mass., and London: The MIT Press, 1993.

Valentine, Marianne. *The Reggio Emilia Approach to Early Years Education.* Scottish Consultative Council on the Curriculum, 1999.

Van Valkenburgh, Michael. "Faculty Project: Teardrop Park," *Harvard Design Magazine* 12 (Fall 2000): 92–93.

Vitra Design Museum. *Kid Size: The Material World of Childhood.* Milan: Skira editore, 1997.

Wilkinson, Paul F., ed. *Innovation in Play Environments.* New York: St. Martin's Press, 1980.

Williams, Wane R. *Recreation Places.* New York: Reinhold Publishing Corporation, 1958.

Zapatka, Christian. "Interview with Mary Miss," *Lotus International* 88 (1996): 34–49.

INDEX

Page numbers in boldface indicate illustrations.

Acconci Studio, 111–13, 197–200, 207; *Flying Floors*, 197–198, **197**; *Klein Bottle* Playground, 111–13, **113**; *Land of Boats*, 111–12, **112**; Mur River Island, 198–200, **198**

Acconci, Vito, 111–13, **112**, **113**, 197–200, **197**, **198**

Advani, Aditya, 116–18, **117**

Adventure Playground, 12–14, **12**, 75–77, **76**

Ain, Gregory, 26

Allen, Lady of Hurtwood, 13, 14, 52, 56–58, 75

American Playground Device, **9**

American Society for Testing and Materials, 80

Americans with Disabilities Act, 80–81, 127, 135, 153

Armstrong, Mayor David, 184–86

Art for the World, 112–13, **113**

Art in America, 62, **64**, 65–67

Art News, 25

Atlanta (Georgia), 126–27, **127**

Austria, Graz, 198–200, **198**

Badanes, Steve: *Dragon Play Sculpture*, 193–95, **195**; T. T. Minor School, 189–91, **191**; University of Washington Health Sciences Center, 189–91, **190**; Yestermorrow Design/Build School, 191–93, **194**

Balsley Associates, 36, **36**

Barenholtz, Bernard, 26–27, 29, 68

Barnes, Edward Larabee, 36, 65

Barton, Cheryl: Rosie the Riveter Memorial, 98–101, **100**, ; McEnery Children's Park, 132–35, **134**

Barton, Office of Cheryl, 98–101, **100**, 132–35, **134**

Berkeley (California), 72–75, **74**, **76**, 121–22, **122**

Bettelheim, Bruno, 88–89

Blender, Richard: Fellger Park, 148–50, **150**

Boston (Massachusetts), 173–75, **175**

Bracey, Gerald, 89

Bright Horizons Family Solutions: Cummins Child Development Center, 120–23, **123**; GlaxoSmithKline, 177–79, **179**

Brown, Joe, 36–41, **38**, **40**, 69

Breuer, Marcel, 26

Bruner, Jerome, 88

Buchen, Bill and Mary: Underhill Playground, 150–53, **152**; Manhattan Square Playground, 156–58, **157**

Bunge, Eric, 202–3, **203**, 207

CBS, 26, 77

Caplan, Frank, 26–27, 29, 34, 45

Catalyst, 153–55, **154**

Chambers, Nancy, 135–38

Chicago (Illinois), 20–21, **22**, 78, **110**, 148–50, **150**

Colorado Springs (Colorado), 161–63, **162**

Colorado Springs Parks Recreation and Cultural Services Department: Acacia Park, 161–63, **162**

Columbus (Indiana), 69–72, **70**, **71**, 120–23, **123**, 168–71, **170**

Columbus (Ohio), 196

Consumer Federation of America, 85

Cooper, Mark: Tadpole Playground, 173–75, **175**

Copley Wolff Design Group, 173–75, **175**

Corcoran Museum School, 62, 201

Crawford, Robert, 33, 39

Creative Playthings, 7, 26–30, **28**, 34–37, **34**, 40, 42, 67–68, 77, 81

Creeft, Jose de, 67, **68**
Cunliffe, Mitzi Solomon, 36

Dallas (Texas), 78
Dattner, Richard, 53–62, **58**, **61**, 72, 136,
    204, 207
Davis (California), 128–30, **129**
Denmark, Copenhagen, 12–13
Design Trust for Public Space, 201
Detroit (Michigan), 111, **112**
Diller, Elizabeth, 114
Dreiseitl, Herbert, 166
Dorazio, Virginia Dortch, 31, **31**
Durham/Research Triangle (Durham,
    North Carolina), 177–79, **179**

Eames, Charles, 27
Eames, Charles and Ray, 41–42
Eckbo, Garrett, 10, 22, 34, 41, 116
Eisenman, Peter, 29
Erikson, Erik, 13
Esherick, Joseph: The Harold E. Jones
    Child Study Center, 121, **122**
van Eyck, Aldo, 7, 14–22, **16**, 30, 33–34,
    59, 171; Bertelmanplein, 15–18, **17**, **18**,
    34; Chicago, 20; Dijkstraat, 20–21, **21**;
    Herenmarkt, 19; Jonas Daniel Meyer-
    plein, 19–20, **20**

Finkelpearl, Tom, 183
Forberg, Charles, 65–67, **66**, 115
Friedberg, M. Paul, 53–62, **61**, 72, 207;
    Jacob Riis Houses, 55–57; M. Paul
    Friedberg and Partners, 55–57, **56**,
    101–4, 155–56, **155**; Rooftop at Yerba
    Buena Gardens, 101–4, **103**

Gang, Jeanne, 108–11, **110**
Gardner, Howard, 89
Garguile, Robert J., 32
Gelfand, Lisa, 128; Gelfand Partners
    Architecture, 104–8, **106**; Homeless
    Prenatal Project, 107–8, **109**; Tender-
    loin Childcare Center, 105–7, **106**
Gifu Prefecture (Japan), 113–15, **114**
Gill, Tim, 86
Glassner, Barry, 87–88
Golinkoff, Roberta Michnick, 89

Gordin, Sidney, 32, **32**
Great Britain (London), 13–14, 208
Greenman, Jim, 84, 86, 120
Gropius, Walter, 41
Gruen, Victor, and Associates, 41, 69–72,
    70, **71**

Haag, Richard, 85; Gas Works Park, 200;
    Santa Fe Railyard Park Competition,
    200
Halprin, Lawrence: Forecourt Fountain,
    165–66, **166**; Lovejoy Fountain, 165;
    Manhattan Square, 156–58, **157**
Hargreaves Associates, 176–77, **177**
Hartford (Connecticut), 143–46, **145**
Hart, Roger, 81, 207
Harvard University, 22, 36–37
Hawk, Tony, 186
Hawley, Christine, 114
Herrington, Susan: Infant Garden,
    128–30, **129**; 13-Acres International
    Design Competition, 202, 204; Ten-
    derloin Childcare Center, 105–7, **106**
Herzog & de Meuron, 130
Hess, Audrey, 24, 27, 44–53, 65
Hess, Thomas, 24–25, 48, 52
Hiromura, Joanne (Play Site Architec-
    ture), 176–77, **177**
Hirsh-Pasek, Kathy, 89
Hoang, Mimi, 202–3, **203**, 207
Hoffman, Donald, 26
Holabird & Root: Walter and Maxine
    Christopher Center for Learning and
    Leadership, 204–6, **205**
Hood, Walter: Lafayette Square, 146–48,
    147, 161; George and Judy Marcus
    Garden of Enchantment, 130–32, **131**;
    Urban Diaries, 210
Hood Design, 130–32, 146–48
Horton, Mark: Mark Horton/Architecture,
    123–25, **125**
Hoving, Thomas P. F., 53, 57
Huizinga, Johan, 17
Huxtable, Ada Louise, 62

International Play Equipment Manufac-
    turers Association (IPEMA), 80
Isozaki, Arata, 114
Izenour, Steven, 206

Jacobs, Jay, 44, 65–68
Jimenez, Carlos, 120–23, **123**
Johansson and Walcavage, 135–38, **136**, 138–41, **140**
Johansson, Sonja: Children's Playgarden at Rusk Institute of Rehabilitation Medicine, 135–38, **136**; Nelson A. Rockefeller Park Playground, 138–141, **140**
Johnson, Philip, 30

Kahn, Louis I.: Adele Rosenwald Levy Memorial Playground, 44–53, **51**, **52**, 65; Memorial Playground, Western Home for Children, 46, **47**; Trenton Jewish Community Center, 46
Kerem, David, 176
Kiley, Daniel, 10, 22
Kim, Mikyoung: Mikyoung Kim Design, 143–46, **145**; Moylan School, 143–46, **145**
Kimball, Rita, 74–75

Labatut, Jean, 37
Lax, Michael, 62
Lefaivre, Liane, 14–15, 17, 208
Ledermann, Alfred, and Alfred Trachsel, 36, 67–68
Levy, Adele Rosenwald, 24, 44–53, 65
Levy, David, Dr., 48
Lin, Maya, 166–67
Lindon, Jennie, 84
Lindsay, Mayor John, 52–53
Louisville (Kentucky), 176–77, **177**, 183–87, **186**
Luckey, Tom, 159–61, **160**

Mann, Fredric R., 33
Marcus, George and Judy, 130–32
Marpiellero Pollak Architects, 201
Mayer & Whittlesey, 24
McDonald's Corporation, 82–84, **83**, 206–7
McKenzie, R. Tait, 37
Meier, Deborah, 90
Miller, Jim, 204
Miss, Mary, 207; Ohio State University Sculpture, 196; Santa Fe Railyard Park and Plaza, 96–98, **98**

Moore, Henry, 29
Moore, Robin, 72–75, 120, 143; Glaxo-SmithKline, 177–79, **179**; Environmental Yard, 72–75, **74**
Morris, Newbold, 45, 48–49
Moscow (Sokolniki Park): American National Exhibition, 41–42
Moses, Robert, 10, 15, 25
Møller-Nielsen, Egon, 27, 29, 33–34, **34**, 68
Murase Associates: Esther Short Park, 167–68, **168**
Museum of Modern Art (New York City), 7, 25–26, 29–40, **31**, **32**, 45, 65, 68, 95, 196, 201

n Architects, 202–3, **203**
National Program for Playground Safety, 86
National Recreation and Park Association, 8, 79–80
Natural Learning Initiative, 178, **179**
Netherlands, Amsterdam 7, 12–22
New Haven (Connecticut), 62, **63**, 159–61, **160**
New M. H. de Young Museum, 130–32, **131**
New York City: *Alice in Wonderland*, 67, **68**; Adventure Playground, 58; Battery Park City playgrounds, 138–43; Bedford Stuyvesant Superblock Midblock Playground, 155–56; Children's Play Garden at Rusk Institute of Rehabilitation Medicine, 135–38, **136**; Cypress Hills Playground, 65–67, **66**; Design Trust for Public Space, 201; Adele Rosenwald Levy Memorial Playground, 44–53, **51**, **52**, 65; Museum of Modern Art and Creative Playthings playground competition, **31**, **32**; MoMA roof, 196; Nelson A. Rockefeller Park Playground, 138–41, **140**; P.S. 1 Contemporary Art Center, 183, 202, **203**; P.S. 19, 118–20, **119**; *The Real World*, 138, 140–41, **142**; Jacob Riis Houses, 55–57, **56**; Spring Creek Towers Playground, 171–73, **172**; St. Mark's Children's Playground, 155–56; Teardrop Park, 138, 141–43,

New York City (continued)
143; Underhill Park, 150–53; United
Nations playground, 24–25, **24**, 33,
48, 52
New York City Parks and Recreation Department: St. Mark's Children's Playground, 155–56, **155**; Underhill Park,
150–53, **152**
Nichols, Robert, 36–37
Noguchi, Isamu, 24, 27, 54; *Contoured
Playground*, 11, 24, 48; Adele Rosenwald Levy Memorial Playground,
44–53, **51**, 65; *Play Mountain*, 10–11;
Playscapes, 126–27, **127**; *Spiral Slide*,
10–11, **11**; United Nations Playground,
24–25, **24**, 33, 48, 52

Oakland (California), **83**, 146–48, **147**,
161, 180–81, **180**
Oberlander, Cornelia Hahn, 33–34, **34**
Ogata, Amy, 26–27, 81
Otterness, Tom: *The Real World*, 138,
140–41, **142**

Palo Alto (California), 34–35, **35**
Pelli, Cesar, 41, 69–72, **70**, **71**
Philadelphia (Pennsylvania), 33, **34**, 39,
41, 46, **47**, 69, 197–98, **197**
Piaget, Jean, 13, 55, 88
Plattus, Alan, 159–61, **160**
Playground Associates, 36–37, **36**
Polio, 30
Pollak, Linda, 201, 207
Portland (Oregon), 163–67, **164**, **166**
P.S. 1 Contemporary Art Center, 183,
202, **203**
Public Interest Research Group, 85
Punkenhofer, Robert, 198–99, **198**

Reggio Emilia, 89, 187
Richman, Tom: Brigadoon Park, 153–55,
154
Richmond (California), 98–101, **100**
Robin Hood Foundation, 118, **119**
Rochester (New York), 156–58, **157**
Rohnert Park (California), 116–18,
117, 187–88, **188**
Ropeik, David, 87
Rose, James, 10, 22

Royston, Robert, 34, 116; Mitchell Park,
34–35, **35**
Royston Hanamoto Alley & Abey, 34–35,
35, 116–18, **117**

Saitowitz, Stanley, 207; Extreme Park,
183–87, **186**; Mill Race Park Am-
phitheater, 168–71, **170**
San Francisco (California), 60, **61**, 101–4,
103, **106**, **109**, 123–25, **125**, 130–32, **131**
San Jose (California), 132–35, **134**,
153–55, **154**
Santa Fe (New Mexico): Railyard Park and
Plaza, 96–98, **98**, 200–201
Sasaki, Hideo, 36
Schwartz, Martha, 113–15, **114**
Schwartzenberg, Susan, 98–101
Seattle (Washington), 189–91, 193–95,
190, **191**, **195**, 200,
Segal, Maria, 204–6, **205**
Sejima, Kazuyo, 114
Shoplick, Jane: Tadpole Playground,
173–75
Sizer, Theodore, 91
Smith, Ken: Ken Smith Landscape Archi-
tecture, 96–98, 118–20, 156–58;
Manhattan Square Playground,
156–58, **157**; Museum of Modern Art
roof plan, 196; Reading Garden at P.S.
19, 118–20, **119**; Santa Fe Railyard
Park and Plaza, 96–98
Sonoma State University Children's
School, 187–88, **188**
Specter, Michael, 87
St. Louis (Manchester, Missouri), 79
Steingarten, Jeffrey, 87
Stock, Gregory, 85, 187
Sutton-Smith, Brian, 88

Takahashi, Akiko, 114
Thompson-Clark, Lia, 188, **188**
Trust for Public Land, 96
Tsien, Billie, 60
Tzonis, Alexander, 14
Tyng, Anne, 27

United States Consumer Product Safety
Commission, 79, 85–86
Uruguay, Montevideo, **209**

Vancouver (Washington), 167–68, **168**
Van Valkenburgh, Michael Associates, 138, 141–43, **143**
Vitali, Nino, 27
Vygotsky, Lev, 73, 89, 135

Wa Sung Community Service Club, 180–81, **180**
Walcavage, Donna: Children's Play Garden at Rusk Institute of Rehabilitation Medicine, 135–38, **136**; Nelson A. Rockefeller Park Playground, 138–41, **140**
Walker, Peter, and Partners, 163–67, **164**

Warren (Vermont), 191–93, **194**
Welliver, Neil, 62, **63**
Weintraub, Lee: Lee Weintraub Landscape Architecture and Community Design, 171–73, **172**
Wilkinson, Michael, 148, **150**
Wilkinson Blender Architecture, 148–50, **150**
Winston, Robert, 27, 37
Wong, Herbert, 72–75
Wright, Frank Lloyd, 39

Yale Urban Design Workshop, 159–61, **160**